# MAYFLOWER FAMILIES
## Through
## Five Generations

DESCENDANTS OF THE PILGRIMS
WHO LANDED AT
PLYMOUTH, MASS. DECEMBER 1620

# VOLUME FIVE

**FAMILIES**
**EDWARD WINSLOW** — *Ruth C. McGuyre & Robert S. Wakefield*
**JOHN BILLINGTON** — *Harriet W. Hodge*

Published by
General Society of Mayflower Descendants
1991

First printing, October 1991

Signatures on endpapers were reproduced from these sources:

Edward Winslow: William Bradford, "History of Plymouth
   Plantation" (Boston 1912), 2:157
Josiah Winslow: Bradford's History 2:296
Mary (Billington) Sabin: Bristol Co., Mass., PR (Samuel
   Sabin 1699)
Seth Billington: Plymouth Co. PR #2002 (Isaac$^3$ Billington
   1712)
John Martin: Bristol Co., Mass., PR (John Martin 1720)

Library of Congress Cataloging-in-Publication Data
(Revised for volume 5)

Mayflower families through five generations.

    Edited by L.M. Kellogg and others.
    Includes bibliographical references and indexes.
    Contents: v. 1. Families: Francis Eaton, Samuel
Fuller, William White -- v. 2. Families: James Chilton,
Richard More, Thomas Rogers -- [etc.] -- v. 5. Families:
Edward Winslow--Ruth C. McGuyre & Robert S. Wakefield,
John Billington--Harriet W. Hodge.
    1. Pilgrims (New Plymouth Colony)--Genealogy.
2. Massachusetts--Genealogy.  I. Kellogg, Lucy Mary.
II. General Society of Mayflower Descendants.
F63.M39   929'.2'0973     75-30145
ISBN No. 0-930270-01-0 (v. 2)

ISBN No. 0-930270-04-5 (v. 5)

# HISTORY OF THE PROJECT

The Five Generations Project is officially thirty-two years old this year. The concept of the project was developed by both George E. Bowman in Boston and Herbert Folger in San Francisco in the early 1900s. The format we use was developed from that of the Alden Memorial published in 1867. The project was unanimously approved at the Annual General Board Meeting of the Mayflower Society, New York, September 19, 1959. We were now going to get valuable information on the genealogy of the Mayflower families into the hands of the general public. In 1975 the first Silver Book was published with the genealogies of the first five generations of descendants of the families of Pilgrims Francis Eaton, Samuel Fuller and William White, followed by Volume Two in 1978 with the families of James Chilton, Richard More and Thomas Rogers. Volume Three, in 1980, has the family of George Soule, and in 1990, Volume Four, the family of Edward Fuller.

In the year 1986 the first of the Mayflower Families in Progress pamphlets was published: the family of Pilgrim Peter Brown in four generations, under the Project Chairmanship of Cay Lanham. She directed the publishing of four more Pilgrim families in this format, those of Francis Cooke, William Bradford, Edward Fuller and Richard Warren. It was decided to publish the material we had gathered thus far, to make it available to the Historians of the Society and the general public. Too much valuable information had already been lost and we had waited too long a time for these genealogies.

In 1987, when Mrs. Lanham became Governor General, Executive Committee Member-at-Large Edith Bates Thomas became Director of the Project. Since that time the families of Degory Priest, Stephen Hopkins and Isaac Allerton for four generations and the Edward Winslow, John Billington and Myles Standish families for five generations have been published in the Mayflower Families in Progress format. Mrs. Thomas subsequently directed the publishing of second and third editions of these MFIPs, with added information and documentation, to meet the public need for this material. Our goal is always to use primary source documentation if it can possibly be obtained. In 1990, Mrs. Thomas also supervised publication of the book Mayflower Families, Volume Four: Edward Fuller.

iii

In the last five years we have made a great deal of progress through the work done by the present outstanding workers on this project and by work done for many years by those who are no longer with us: Lewis Neff, George Bowman, Claude Barlow, Lucy Mary Kellogg, Robert M. Sherman, Harlan Thomas, Lee D. van Antwerp, Russell Warner and Milton Terry. We must not forget the most generous donations of our members which have made it possible for us to gather more primary source documentation for this work. In the words of Robert M. Sherman, "The project continues a labor of love."

Edith Bates Thomas

# THE SOCIETY EXPRESSES THANKS

The Mayflower Society is grateful to many people for assistance in preparing this volume for publication. Some names have unfortunately escaped the record, but the contribution of each is appreciated and herewith acknowledged.

## EDWARD WINSLOW

The Mayflower Society wishes to thank Ralph Van Wood, Jr. for his major contribution to this manuscript. The society also thanks Janice Beebe, Frederick R. Boyle, Roberta Bratti, Dorothy C. Chase, Harriet Hodge, Gertrude E. Lanman, Ann Reeves, Robert M. Sherman, Ruth Wilder Sherman, Eugene A. Stratton and Neil D. Thompson for their contributions to this Winslow family.

## JOHN BILLINGTON

The Mayflower Society gratefully acknowledges the contributions of Billington family data from: Claude W. Barlow, David Dumas, Judith Elfring, Wayne C. Hart, E. Virginia Hunt, Roger D. Joslyn, Mary Holland Lancaster, Barbara Lambert Merrick, H.L. Peter Rounds, Ruth Wilder Sherman, Eugene A. Stratton, Milton E. Terry, Mr. and Mrs. Robert G. Thurtle, Earl C. Tourgee, Mr. and Mrs. Robert S. Trim, Jonathan P. Twiss, Robert S. Wakefield and Elizabeth Pearson White. Previewed by: Ann S. Lainhart and Robert S. Wakefield.

Five Generations Committee Chairmen during the course of preparation: Cathryn P. Lanham; Edith Bates Thomas.

INDEX: George Reeves.

TYPING: Harriet W. Hodge.

ART WORK: Charles F. Mathewson

Winslow Portrait: courtesy of the Pilgrim Society, probably painted in London by Robert Walker, and shows the year as 1651 and his age as 57.

OFFICERS OF THE GENERAL SOCIETY

1990-1993

| | |
|---|---|
| GOVERNOR GENERAL | Miss Mildred Ramos |
| ASSISTANT GOVERNOR GENERAL | Hewitt Arthur Conway |
| SECRETARY GENERAL | Mrs. Francis R. (Barbara) Poblocki |
| TREASURER GENERAL | Eugene A. Fortine |
| HISTORIAN GENERAL | Mrs. Paul F. (Caroline) Kardell |
| ELDER GENERAL | The Rev. Sherwood W. Anderson |
| CAPTAIN GENERAL | Robert Allen Greene |
| SURGEON GENERAL | Dr. John A. Blosser |
| COUNSELLOR GENERAL | Walter Howard Mayo III |

MEMBERS-AT-LARGE, EXECUTIVE COMMITTEE

Richard L. Husband      Bruce C. MacGunnigle      Harry L. Walen


FIVE GENERATIONS PROJECT COMMITTEE

1991

Director Mrs. Robert L. Thomas
Mrs. Paul F. Kardell
Mrs. Frank W. Lanham
Mrs. Clayton M. Merrick
Mr. Robert S. Wakefield

## TABLE OF CONTENTS

## TO THE READER

Among the immigrants to Massachusetts between 1620 and 1650 were at least two named Billington, five Winslows, eight Eatons and sixteen Fullers. These figures permit the reader to estimate the chance that his early Massachusetts ancestor, of one of those names, is a member of a family in this book.

The authors have assembled families as correctly and as completely as circumstances permitted. Their work is based largely on carefully researched articles in genealogical journals and family histories, together with probate and land records, and town and church vital statistics. Family tradition, in the absence of confirmatory evidence, has not been accepted as proof of a line. This has regretfully, resulted in the rejection of a few lines which the Society accepted in its early years, but were based on insufficient or erroneous evidence. On the other hand, many new potential lines have been uncovered.

Paucity of records sometimes renders it virtually impossible to follow a family or individual to another town: An entire family disappears, or one or more children are labelled "n.f.r." (no further records found). The authors often offer tentative identifications using the word probably, when evidence is nearly conclusive, and possibly, when evidence is merely suggestive. This is done in the hope that a reader, tracing back his ancestry through such clues, may come upon real proof and so establish the new line.

Spelling was far from consistent even after the Revolution. To a great extent names in this book have been spelled as found in each record. This often provides different spellings of an individual's name at his birth, upon marriage, and in a deed or will. For example, Hayward is found as Heywood and even Howard for the same person; Marcy and Mercy are many time interchangeable. With variant spellings so commonplace, use of "(sic)" is restricted to exceptional examples. To assist the reader, most variant spellings of a name are lumped together in the Index, rather than separately alphabetized.

A reader who finds either an error or additional information regarding any family or individual in this volume down to the birth of sixth generation children, but not beyond, is urgently requested to send such material to:
FIVE GENERATIONS PROJECT, P.O. Box 297, PLYMOUTH MA 02360

GOVERNOR EDWARD WINSLOW
1595-1655

# EDWARD WINSLOW

of the

# MAYFLOWER

*Compiled by*

Ruth C. McGuyre
Robert S. Wakefield, FASG

Ruth Cecelia Ellenwood McGuyre was born in Palo Alto, California, grew up in Ithaca, New York and since 1944 has lived in Wichita, Kansas. She joined the California Society of Mayflower Descendants in 1952, transferred to the Kansas Society in 1954 and now maintains a dual membership. Beginning with attendance at General Congress in 1978 as Acting Assistant General for Kansas, then as Assistant General for Kansas until 1988, she has attended every General Congress meeting. She served the Kansas Society as Historian for three years, and was a member of the General Society Nominating Committee in 1987.

The mother of one daughter, Mrs. McGuyre is a descendant of William Brewster through her mother, Cecelia Freeman Atherton, of Edward Doty through her father, Frank Oakes Ellenwood, and of Richard Warren on two lines through her paternal grandfather and grandmother. A graduate of Cornell University with an A.B. degree, she has engaged in genealogical research since 1948, and especially enjoys presenting programs about the Mayflower Pilgrims and showing the Mayflower House slides to historical and patriotic groups.


Robert S. Wakefield is one of the most respected genea- logists in the country. Born in San Mateo, California, he was employed for many years by the Southern Pacific Transportation Company. He is descended from both Stephen Hopkins and John Howland, and in 1973 joined the California Society of Mayflower Descendants. He holds the prestigious title of Fellow of the American Society of Genealogists. Many of his articles have appeared in leading genealogical publications. Mr. Wakefield has been an active member of the Five Generations Project of the General Society of May- flower Descendants since 1976, when he undertook preparing the Richard More manuscript for publication in Mayflower Families Two. In 1977 he began work on the Peter Brown Family manuscript, now in Mayflower Families in Progress format, and has contributed substantially to many more Pro- ject families since that time. He has been a member of the Five Generations Project Committee for four years. He is a very important member of both the Project and the General Society of Mayflower Descendants.

# EDWARD WINSLOW

Edward Winslow was baptized at Droitwich, co. Worcester, England on 28 Oct. 1595, the son of Edward and Magdalene (Oliver) Winslow and apparently a grandson of Kenelm Winslow.

At the time of his first marriage in Leyden, Holland he was called a printer of London. He is believed to be the principal author of Mourt's Relation (1622) and was the author of Good News From New England, or A Relation of Things Remarkable in That Plantation (1624); Hypocrisie Unmasked (1646); and New England's Salamander (1647).

His first wife died shortly after the Pilgrims landed in Plymouth and his marriage to Susanna White, widow of William White of the Mayflower was the first marriage in Plymouth. Marriages in Plymouth were a civil affair and in 1635 Edward Winslow was jailed for seventeen weeks in Fleet Prison in London when Archbishop Laud had him persecuted for solemnizing marriages as a magistrate.

In the earliest known list of those who signed the Mayflower Compact in 1620, he is listed third, after John Carver and William Bradford. There is some question whether the list reflects the original order of those who signed, but it would be quite logical for Carver, Bradford and Winslow to sign first.

Edward Winslow was one of the company which first explored the shores of Cape Cod, was among those who first landed at Plymouth, and who selected Plymouth as the place of settlement. He was one of the principal leaders of Plymouth Colony, serving as Assistant many times and in 1633 he was elected Governor of the colony, its third governor after Carver and Bradford. (Christopher Martin acted as Governor on the Mayflower, but died shortly after the landing in Plymouth and is not considered to be one of the governors of the colony.) Edward Winslow was also elected Governor in 1636 and 1644.

In September 1623 Edward Winslow returned to England on the Anne to transact business for the colony and returned in March 1624 on the Charity with supplies and three heifers and a bull, the first cattle in Plymouth. In 1630 and 1635 he also made trips to England. In 1644 he was the commissioner for Plymouth to the newly formed Confederation of New England colonies.

In 1646 he went to England for the last time and accepted employment in Oliver Cromwell's government serving in several capacities. On 27 December 1654 Edward Winslow was appointed commissioner, along with Admiral William Penn and General Robert Venables, of the ill-fated expedition to the West Indies to capture the island of Hispaniola from the Spanish. Cromwell apparently expected the island to be settled by New Englanders. After the defeat at Santo Domingo, Edward Winslow died of a fever on the voyage from Hispaniola to Jamaica and was buried at sea.

In a series of articles in the New England Historical and Genealogical Register, John Hunt raised the question of whether the Mayflower Winslows were yeomen or gentlemen and concluded they were gentlemen. Edward was the eldest of five sons and all came to Plymouth: Edward and Gilbert on the Mayflower, John on the Fortune in 1621, Josias on the White Angel in 1631 and Kenelm before 1 January 1632/3.

The only known portrait of a Mayflower passenger is the 1651 portrait of Edward Winslow painted by Robert Walker which is in the Pilgrim Society collection.

Edward Winslow wrote his will 18 December 1654:
"I Edward Winslowe of London, Esquior, being now bound on a voyage to sea in the service of the comon welth do make publish & declare this to be my last will & testamt touching the disposing of my estate. ffirst I doe give will devise & bequeath all my lands & stock in New England & all my possibilities & porcons in future allotmts & divicions to Josias my onely sonne & his heires, hee allowing to my wife a full third parte thereof for her life Also. I give to the poore of the Church of Plymouth in new England Tenn pounds & to the poore of marshfielde where the chiefest of my estate lyes Tenn pounds, Also I give my lynnen wch I carry with me to sea to my daughter Elizabet & The rest of my goods wch I carry with mee I give to my sonn Josias hee giving to each of my brothers a suite of apparell & I make my said son Josias my executor of this my will, and Colonell venables my overseer of my goods in the voyage & my fower frends Dr. Edmond wilson; mr John Arthur, mr James shirley and mr Richard ffloyde, over seers for the rest of my prsonall estate in England
witness my hand & Seale the Eighteenth of December In the yeare of our Lord God one Thousand Six hundred fifty & ffower.
Sealed & subscribed
in the presence of:                      pr me Edw: Winslow (seal)
Jon Hooper
Gerald Usher servant to Hen: Colbron"

_____

   The following poem was written by one of Edward Winslow's
shipmates at the time of his death:

        The Eighth of May, west from 'Spaniola shore,
        God took from us our Grand Commissioner,
        Winslow by Name, a man in chiefest Trust,
        Whose Life was sweet, and conversation just;
        Whose Parts and Wisdome most men did excell:
        An honour to his Place, as all can tell.


References:  BRADFORD'S  HIST  (1952).  STODDARD  pp. 160-3.
             BANKS ENGLISH ANCESTRY pp. 98-9. DEXTER  p.640.
PLYMOUTH  COLONY  ITS  HISTORY  &  PEOPLE  1620-1691, Eugene
Aubrey  Stratton,  Salt  Lake  City,  1986.  NEHGR  38:21-6;
121:25-9;  122:175-8;  124:182-3.    MD  4:1-3 (will & poem);
5:224- 33; 25:151-63; 26:11-23, 68-80, 128-38, 150-61 ("Good
Newes"); 27:49-71 ("Hypocrisie Unmasked").   PLYMOUTH COLONY
RECS 1:5 (Gov. 1633), 36  (Gov. 1636), 2:71 (Gov. & Comm. to
the United Colonies 1644).

EDWARD WINSLOW

FIRST GENERATION

1  EDWARD[1] WINSLOW, b. Droitwich, co. Worcester 18 Oct.
1595; bp. St. Peters, Droitwich 20 Oct 1595; son of Edward
and Magdalene (Oliver) Winslow;[1]  d. at sea in the West
Indies 8 May 1655.[2]  "He fell sick at sea betwixt Domingo
and Jamaica and died the eighth day of May, which was about
the sixty-first year of his life."[2]
    He m. (1) Leyden, Holland shortly after 12 May 1618 (some
say 16 May) ELIZABETH BARKER.[3]  She came on the Mayflower
and d. Plymouth 24 March 1621.[4]
    Edward  m.  (2)  Plymouth  12  May  1621  SUSANNA (____*)
WHITE,[5]  the first marriage in Plymouth Colony. Susanna
d. between 18 Dec. 1654, the date of Edward Winslow's will,
and 2 July 1675, the date of her son Josiah's will, which
fails to mention her.[2,6]  She m. (1) William White of the
Mayflower, who d. Plymouth 21 Feb. 1621.[7]  They had two
sons, Resolved and Peregrine White.[7]  See MAYFLOWER
FAMILIES, Vol. I, p. 96 ff. for an account of this family.
    In a letter dated 30 Oct. 1623 to his uncle Mr. Robert
Jackson in England, Edward Winslow wrote: "My wife hath had
one child by me, but it pleased him that gave it to take it
again unto himselfe; I left her with child at my departure
(whom God Preserve) but hope to be with her before her
delivery."[8]  The third lot in the 1627 division of cattle
includes Edward Winslow, Susanna Winslow, Edward Winslow,
John Winslow, Resolved White and Peregrine White, which
provides proof of children Edward and John.[9]
    In a letter dated 28 Nov. 1640 to John Winthrop, Edward
Winslow wrote: "God being pleased still to exercise me under
his hand by taking away one of my children by death, & some
others in my ffamily exercised with sicknes, together with
some other outward losses in my cattle..."[10]  Governor
Bradford's account of the Mayflower Passengers in 1651
includes: "Mr. Ed: Winslow, his wife dyed the first winter;
and he maried with the widow of mr White, and hath .2.
children living by her marigable, besids sundry that are
dead."[11]
    The will of Edward Winslowe of London, Esquior, dated 18
Dec. 1654 mentioned only son Josias; wife; and daughter
Elizabeth.[2]

    Children (WINSLOW) by second wife, b. Plymouth:[2,8,9,10]

        i    child[2] b. and d. 1623
        ii   EDWARD prob. the child b. 1624; d. aft. 22 May
             1627, unm. Perhaps he or his brother John was
             the child who d. in 1640.
        iii  JOHN b. ca. 1626; d. after 22 May 1627, unm.
    2   iv   JOSIAH b. ca. 1629
    3   v    ELIZABETH b. during 1630s

---

*Note: The often repeated claim that Susanna is the same as
Ann, daughter of Robert Fuller and sister of Samuel and
Edward Fuller of the "Mayflower" is highly unlikely, if not
impossible. That Ann was bp. Redenhall 22 April 1577 [NEHGR
55:411] and would have been 43 years old at the time of
Susanna's marriage to Edward Winslow 12 May 1621 in Plymouth
(when Edward was 25 years old), and at least 53 years old
when daughter Elizabeth was born. In his letter of 30 Oct.
1623 to "Uncle Mr. Robert Jackson," Edward Winslow asked to
be remembered to his father-in-law [NEHGR 109:242-3].
Robert Fuller (father of Samuel and Edward) was buried in
Redenhall 23 May 1614, over 9 years before this letter was
written [NEHGR 55:414]. Robert Fuller's will of 19 May 1614
mentions "daughter Ann Fuller" [NEHGR 55:415-6]. This was
over two years after William White married Ann Fuller in
Leyden 27 Feb. 1612 [MD 7:193-4]. Samuel Fuller's will of
30 July 1633 does not mention a sister Susanna (or Ann)
Winslow. [See MF1:96-8 for further comments on this
subject.]

References:   1. NEHGR   4:297-303;   17:159-62;   21:209-11;
             24:329.   2. MD 4:1-3.   3. MD 8:100.   4. MD
30:3.   5. BRADFORD'S HIST (1952) p. 86.   6. MD 5:82-6(Josiah
Winslow's will).   7. MF1:96ff.   8. NEHGR 109:242-3.   9. PLY-
MOUTH COLONY RECS 12:10.   10. COLLECTIONS OF THE MASSA-
CHUSETTS HISTORICAL SOCIETY, Vol. VI, 4th series, Boston,
1863, pp. 171-2.   11. MD 1:12.


SECOND GENERATION


2 JOSIAH[2] WINSLOW (Edward[1]) b. Plymouth ca. 1629; d. at
Careswell, the Winslow Mansion, Marshfield 18 Dec. 1680 ae
52.[1]
     He m. London, England 1651 or Boston 1657 PENELOPE
PELHAM,[2] bp. Bures, co. Essex, England 1633;[3] d.
Marshfield 7 Dec. 1703 ae 73;[4] daughter of Herbert and
Jemima (Waldegrave) Pelham. Herbert Pelham, in his will
dated 1 Jan. 1672, named dau. Penelope, wife of Josiah
Winslow.[2]
     Josiah Winslow was Governor of Plymouth Colony from 1673
until his death in 1680.[5] He was appointed Major in 1658,
Assistant Governor 1657-72, and Commander-in-Chief of the
United Colonial Forces during King Phlip's War in 1675 to
1676.[5] He was the first native-born governor and first
native-born general in New England.
     The will of Josiah Winslow of Marshfield, dated 2 July
1675, presented 2 March 1680/1, named sister Elyzabeth
Corwin, wife of Captaine Georg Corwin; kinsman John Brook,
"son to my said sister"; brothers Resolved and Peregrine
White; kinsman William White; aunt Mrs. Elyzabeth Pelham;

brother  Edward  Pelham;  Elyzabeth  Gray;  dau.  Elyzabeth
Winslow;  son  Isack;  "cuzen"  Mr.  Peter  Sergiant;  "cuzen"
Nathaniel Winslow; wife Penelope Winslow.[6]

Children (WINSLOW) b. Marshfield:

       i   daughter³ b. 13 March 1658; d. 15 March 1658.[7]
4     ii  ELIZABETH  b. 8 April 1664.[8]
      iii EDWARD  b. 14 May 1667; bur. 11 Dec. 1667.[8]
5     iv  ISAAC  b. ca. 1671; [based on age at death][6]

References:  1. MARSHFIELD  VR p.  390.  2. MA  PIONEERS pp.
           351-2.  3. NEHGR 33:285-91.  4. MARSHFIELD VR
p. 43.  5. NEHGR  4:299-300.  6. MD 5:82-6(Josiah's will).
7. MARSHFIELD VR pp. 3,5.  8. Ibid. p. 6.


    3 ELIZABETH² WINSLOW (Edward¹) b. Plymouth in 1630s; d.
Boston shortly before 23 April 1698, prob. the "Mis. Curwin"
who d. Boston 23 Sept. 1697.[1]
    She m. (1) before 1656, perhaps in England, ROBERT
BROOKS,[2] b. prob. England; d. bef. 22 Sept. 1669;[2]
perhaps son of Robert and Anne (_____) (Derrick) Brooks of
Maidstone, Eng. and Marblehead MA.[3]  The will of John
Brooke, citizen and scrivener of London, dated 28 March
1659, named cousin Robert Brooke and John Brooke, son of the
said Robert Brooke, under age 21.[4]  This may refer to this
family.
    She m. (2) Salem 22 Sept. 1669 GEORGE CORWIN,[5]  b.
Workington, Cumberland, Eng. 10 Dec. 1610;[6]  d. Salem 3
Jan. 1684/5.[5]  He m. (1) in England, Elizabeth (Herbert)
White, by whom he had Abigail, John, Jonathan, Hannah,
Abigail, Hannah and Elizabeth.[5]
    George Corwin (or Curwin) came to New England in 1638,
was a Freeman in 1665, representative for a number of years
and Captain in King Philip's War in 1675-6.[6]  In June 1682
George Corwin deposed he was aged about 70 years, that he
came into this town (Salem) about 44 years ago.[5]
    When the estate of George Corwin was administered April
1685, it was appraised at nearly 6000 pounds. Distribution
was made to the widow; son Jonathan; the children of
deceased son John; dau. Susanna; Josiah Walcott for his
wife; James Russell for his wife and to the widow for the
other children.  Samuel Gardner filed claims for the portion
due his wife.[5]  On 22 March 1685/6 land was assigned to
Josiah Wolcott in right of his wife, and to Mrs. Eliza
Corwin, the Relict of Capt. George Corwin, and guardian to
her dau. Susanna Corwin.[7]
    An agreement was made 25 Dec. 1696 to allow Madam
Elizabeth Corwin to use a certain part of the house
belonging to her late husband. Grantors were Josiah Wolcot
in right of wife Penelope, dau. of Capt. George Corwin and

Edward Lyde in right of former wife Susannah, dau. of Capt.
George Corwin.[8]
    On 23 April 1698 Edward Lyde of Boston, merchant, was
appointed to administer the estate of his mother-in-law
Elizabeth Corwin, late of Boston, widow, deceased.[9]

    Child (BROOKS) perhaps b. England:

        i   JOHN[3] b. ca. 1656; d. Charlestown 25 Dec. 1687 ae
            31, apparently unm.[10]   No probate has been
            found.

    Children (CORWIN*) b. Salem:[11]

6   ii   PENELOPE  b. 7 Aug. 1670
7   iii  SUSANNA   b. 10 Dec. 1672

*No proof found for a son George as stated in SALEM BY
PERLEY 2:37-8 and NEHGR 10:304.

References:   1. BOSTON VR 9:237.   2. MD 1:238-40.  3. MA
              PIONEERS, p. 71.   4. TAG  43:100-2.   5. MA
PIONEERS p. 119.  6. SALEM BY  PERLEY 2:37-8.  7. Essex Co.
Court Rec. 46:20.   8. Essex Co.  Court Rec. 15:102(Madam
Elizabeth Corwin).   9. Suffolk Co.  PR #2447, 8:140
(Elizabeth Corwin).  10. CHARLESTOWN VR 1:139.  11. VR SALEM
1:210.

                    THIRD GENERATION


4  ELIZABETH[3] WINSLOW (Josiah[2], Edward[1]) b. Marshfield 8
April 1664; d. Pembroke 11 July 1735, ae 72.[1]
    She m. Marshfield 4 Sept. 1684 STEPHEN BURTON,[2]   b.
prob. England; d. Bristol 22 July 1693;[3]  son of Stephen
Burton.  He m. (1)  after 9 Feb.  1673 Abigail Brenton, who
was buried Bristol 30 March 1684,[3]  by whom he had
Stephen, Martha and another daughter.[4]
    On 18 May 1681 Stephen Burton of  Boston, merchant, and
wife Abigail sold land at Mt. Hope.[5]
    Stephen Burton was  one of the founders  of Bristol, then
Plymouth Colony, but now RI.  He was Deputy for Bristol  in
1685, 1686 and 1690, Selectman for Bristol in 1689 and 1690,
and was  the first Recorder of Deeds for Bristol Co., MA.[6]
The 11 Feb. 1688/9 list of all families of "New Bristol" included Stephen Burton, wife, 2 children and one servant.[7]
    Stephen Burton  died intestate  and his  heirs  are
indentified in  four deeds,  two each  in Bristol Co. and
Middlesex Co.  On  1 July 1715 Martha Church  of Newport RI,
widow, dau. of Stephen Burton late of Bristol deceased, sold
to Nathaniel Blagrove 1/4 of  a parcel of  land in Bristol.
On 13 May 1715 Thomas Burton,  trader, and Elizabeth Burton,

spinster, both of Duxbury, "two of ye children and heirs of
Stephen Burton, late of Bristol," sold to Nathaniel Blagrove
the other three quarters.[8]   On the 7 June 1728 Martha
Church of Newport RI, widow, sold to Robert Richardson 1/4
of 1/16 of a tract of land in Dunstable, Middlesex Co., MA.
On 6 Aug. 1728 Thomas and Elisabeth Burton Jr., both of
"Duxborough" (Duxbury), sold to Nathaniel Cotton 3/4 of 1/16
part of the same land.[9]

Children (BURTON) b. Bristol:

    i   PENELOPE[4] b. 8 Aug. 1686;[10]  prob. the "dr. of
         Mr. Burtons" bur. March 1687.[11]
   ii   "Mr. Burton's infant" bur. Feb. 1687 (1687/8);[11]
  iii   ELIZABETH  b. after 1687/8;  living unm. 6 Aug.
         1728 Duxbury,[9]  and almost surely the witness
         to a deed dated 28 Dec. 1737.[12]
 8 iv   THOMAS  b. 19 March 1692/3;[10]

References: 1. VR PEMBROKE p. 394.   2. MARSHFIELD VR p. 11.
         3. RI VR Bristol 6:121.  4. MD 10:56-9 5. Bris-
tol Co. LR 6:12(Stephen & Abigail Burton).  6. PLYMOUTH
COLONY RECS 6:165;186(deputy), 207(selectman), 241 (deputy),
242(selectman).   7. EARLY REHOBOTH 1:75-6(1688-9): census
calls him Stephen "Bucklin." 8. Bristol Co. LR 33:260(Thomas
and Elizabeth Burton); 33:261(Martha Church). 9. Middlesex
Co. LR 28:229(Thomas & Elizabeth Burton); 30:183(Martha
Church). 10. RI VR Bristol 6:67.  11. Bristol Church
Records.  12. Plymouth Co. LR 31:186.


5  ISAAC[3] WINSLOW (Josiah[2], Edward[1]) b. Marshfield ca. 1671;
d. there 14 Dec. 1738, age 67.[1]
    He m. Boston 11 July 1700 SARAH WENSLEY,[2]  b. Boston 11
Aug. 1673;[3]   d. Marshfield 15 or 16 Dec.  1753 ae 80;[4]
dau. of John and Elizabeth (Paddy) Wensley.
    Isaac Winslow was Chief Justice of the Inferior Court of
Common Pleas and Judge of Probate for Plymouth County.[5]
Isaac Winslow of Marshfield, by deed, gave to son John
Winslow of Plymouth, part of a farm in Marshfield, the other
part given to his other son Edward; dated 24 Feb. 1724/6;
ack. same day.[6].
    In his will dated 24 May 1736, probated 6 April 1739,
Isaac Winslow of Marshfield named son John Winslow; son
Edward; wife Sarah; dau. Penelope Warren wife to Mr. James
Warren of Plymouth; dau. Elizabeth Marston the wife of Mr.
Benjamin Marston of Salem.[7]
    The will of Sarah Winslow of Marshfield, widow, dated 5
Sept. 1753, proved 4 Feb. 1754, named son John Winslow; son
Edward Winslow; sister Hopestill Oliver; dau. Elizabeth
Marston; grandchildren Ann Warren and Sarah Warren, daus. of

Penelope Warren, her deceased dau.; grandchild James Warren,
Jr., child of her deceased dau. Penelope.[7]

   Children (WINSLOW) b. Marshfield:[8]

       i  JOSIAH[4] b.  27 July  1701; Captain  killed in  an
          engagement  with  Indians  in  Gorgess River at
          Eastward (ME)  1 May 1724, in  the 23rd year of
          his age, apparently unmarried. He had graduated
          from Harvard College in 1721.[9]
    9  ii  JOHN b. 27 May 1703
   10 iii  PENELOPE b. 21 Dec. 1704
   11  iv  ELIZABETH b. 13 Dec. 1707
        v  ANNA b.  29  Jan.  1709/10;  d.  Boston 16 Sept.
           1723.[10]
   12  vi  EDWARD b. 7 June 1714

References: 1. MARSHFIELD VR pp. 47,390; & BOSTON NEWS OBITS
            3:580.  2.  BOSTON VR 28:2.  3. Ibid. 9:130.  4.
MD 9:185.  5. NEHGR 4:301-2.  6. Plymouth Co. LR 20:35(Isaac
Winslow).  7.  MD  24:30-35(wills  of  Isaac  &  Sarah).  8.
MARSHFIELD  VR pp.  26,31.  9.  Ibid. p.  86; &  BOSTON NEWS
OBITS 3:581.  10. MARSHFIELD VR p. 85.


6  PENELOPE CORWIN[3] (Elizabeth[2] Winslow, Edward[1]) b. Salem 7
Aug. 1670; d. there 28 Dec. 1690.[1]
    She m.  Salem 19  Feb.  1684/5*  JOSIAH WALCOTT,[2]  b.
perhaps England ca. 1657; d.  Salem 9 Feb. 1728/9, ae 71.[3]
He m. (2) Boston 1 May  1694 Mary Freke,[4]  by whom he  had
Freke,  Thomas,  Mehitable,  Josiah,  John,  Mary, Sarah and
Freke.[5]
    Josiah Walcott  was a merchant in Salem  and Judge of the
Court of Common Pleas.[6]
    On 17 April 1729 Mary Wolcot, widow,  John Wolcot, Walter
Price  and Joseph  Orne, Jr.  posted bond  to administer the
estate of Josiah Wolcott, late of Salem, deceased.[7]

   Children (WALCOTT) b. Salem:[5]

       i  ELIZABETH[4] b. 30 March 1688; d. 12 July 1702.[1]
      ii  JOSIAH b. 21 Dec. 1690; d. 4 Jan. 1690/1.[1]

*Some sources say  19 Feb. 1686, but VR  SALEM shows 19 Feb.
1684/5.

References:    1. VR SALEM 6:341.  2. Ibid. 3:246.  3. BOSTON
               NEWS OBITS 3:586.  4. BOSTON VR  9:218.  5. VR
SALEM 2:439.   6. SALEM BY  PERLEY 3:192.   7. Essex Co.  PR
#28740(Josiah Wolcott)

7  SUSANNA CORWIN[3] (Elizabeth[2] Winslow, Edward[1]) b. Salem 10
Dec. 1672; d. bef. 22 Oct. 1696.[1]
     She m. Salem 29  Nov. 1694 EDWARD LYDE,[2]  b. Boston ca.
1662,  d. Boston  between 18 Jan.  1722 and 25  May 1724;[3]
son of Edward and Mary (Wheelwright) Lyde.  He m. (2) Boston
22 Oct.  1696 Deborah Byfield,[1]   by whom he  had Deborah,
Mary, Byfield  and Ann.[4]   He m.  (3) Boston  6 June  1709
Katherine (_____) Brinley.[5]
     The will of Rev.  John Wheelwright of Salisbury  dated 25
May 1679 named grandson Edward Lyde, under 21.[6]
     Edward Lyde  posted bond 9  Sept. 1699 to  administer the
estate  of his  late wife  Susanna Lyde, deceased intestate.
The documents  show that  Susanna was  dau. of  Capt. George
Curwin, formerly of Salem.[7]
     Edward Lyde of Boston made his  will 18 Jan. 1722, proved
25 May 1724,  naming wife Katherine; children  Byfield Lyde,
Deborah  Brindle and  Mary  Craddock.  Son Byfield Lyde and
sons-in-law  Francis  Brindley  and  George  Craddock  were
appointed executors.[3]
     Susanna Corwin evidently had no issue.

References: 1. SAVAGE 3:133.  2. VR SALEM 3:246.  3. Suffolk
           Co. PR 5:186; #4909(Edward  Lyde).  4. BOSTON VR
9:241; 24:8,29,49.  5. Ibid. 28:24.  6. Essex Co. PR 3:345-7
(John Wheelwright).  7. Suffolk Co. PR 14:74(Susanna Lyde).
See also SALEM BY PERLEY 2:38,357.


                         FOURTH GENERATION


8  THOMAS BURTON[4] (Elizabeth[3] Winslow, Josiah[2], Edward[1]) b.
Bristol  19  March  1692/3;  d.  Pembroke  22 Oct.  1779, age
87.[1]
     He m. Duxbury 10 May 1722 ALICE WADSWORTH,[2]  b. Duxbury
15 April  1697;[3]  d. Pembroke 9 June 1791, ae 95;[1]  dau.
of Elisha and Elizabeth (Wiswall) Wadsworth; a descendant of
Pilgrim  John  Alden.  The  will  of  Elisha  Wadsworth  of
Duxborough,  dated 12  Jan. 1741,  included payment to Alice
Buston  (sic)  "one  of  the  sisters  of  my dau. Elizabeth
Wadsworth."[4]
     On 7  Nov. 1722 Thomas Burton, Deputy Sheriff of Duxbury,
sold to Nathaniel Byfield "all that one half of a common lot
in  Bristol which came  to me in  Right of my father Stephen
Burton, late of sd. Bristol, deceased."[5]
     Thomas Burton  was a school teacher  in Duxbury but moved
to Pembroke about  1730, where he was  called yeoman.[6]  No
probate  record  for  Thomas  Burton  is  found  in Plymouth
County.

     Children (BURTON) three b. Duxbury, last b. Pembroke, all
recorded Pembroke:[7]

         i   MARTHA[5]  b. 19 June 1723; d. 15 Sept. 1723.[1]
13      ii   PENELOPE   b. 27 Oct. 1724
14     iii   ELEANOR   b. 4 May 1728
15      iv   ELIZABETH  b. 9 May 1737

References: 1. VR PEMBROKE  p. 394.    2. VR DUXBURY  p. 228.
             3.Ibid.  p.   178.    4. Plymouth  Co.  PR  13:424
(Elisha  Wadsworth).    5. Bristol   Co.  LR  14:402(Thomas
Burton)  6. DUXBURY RECS p.241.  7. VR PEMBROKE pp. 55-6.


9  JOHN[4] WINSLOW  (Isaac[3], Josiah[2], Edward[1])  b. Marshfield
27 May 1703; d. Hingham 17 April 1774, aged 72.[1]
     He m.  (1) Marshfield 16 Feb.  1725 MARY  LITTLE,[2]  b.
Marshfield 9 Sept.  1704;[3]  d. there shortly before 4 Dec.
1772;[4]  dau. of Isaac and Mary (Otis) Little, a descendant
of Pilgrim Richard Warren.  Isaac Little of Pembroke, in his
will dated 15 Aug. 1751, named dau. Mary Winslow.[5]
     John m.  (2) BETHIAH (BARKER) JOHNSTON, b.  Pembroke 17
Feb.  1715;[6]  d. there 21 Nov.  1790 in 75th yr.;[7]  dau.
of  Thomas  and  Bethia  (Little)  Barker,  a  descendant of
Pilgrim Richard Warren.   She m.  (1)  Pembroke 31 July 1738
James Johnston of Scotland.[8]
     John Winslow commanded a   company in the Cuba   expedition
of  1740; was a Colonel in  the expedition to Nova Scotia in
1755;  and was  Commander-in-Chief at  Fort William Henry on
Lake George in 1756  during the French and Indian  War.  His
obituary calls him "General."[9]
     John  Winslow  of  Marshfield  sold  all  his  estate  in
Marshfield to  Pelham Winslow of Plymouth  and Isaac Winslow
of Marshfield on 28 June 1773.[10]
     On  6  June  1774  Pelham  Winslow  of Plymouth and Isaac
Winslow of  Marshfield were appointed  administrators of the
estate  of  John  Winslow  of  Marshfield.   In  June  1776,
administration  on  the  estate of  John Winslow "of Hingham,
reduced Captain in Colonel William Shirley's 1st Regiment of
Foot"  was  granted  to  Elisha  Hutchinson, attorney for only
children  Pelham  and  Isaac  Winslow  "now in Mass. or Nova
Scotia," the relict having renounced.[11]

     Children (WINSLOW), all by wife Mary,  first b. Plymouth,
others b. Marshfield:

         i   JOSIAH[5]  b.  5 Sept.  1730;  d. Plymouth 1 March
             1730/1.[12]
16      ii   PELHAM  b. 8 June 1737.[13]
17     iii   ISAAC  B. 27 April 1739.[13]

References:  1. BOSTON NEWS  OBITS 3:580.    2. MARSHFIELD VR
             p. 145  3.  Ibid. p. 30.  4. BOSTON NEWS  OBITS
3:581.   5. Plymouth  Co.  PR  14:530(Isaac  Little).  6. VR

PEMBROKE p. 23.   7. HINGHAM HIST 3:31.   8. VR PEMBROKE
p. 230.    9. NEHGR 4:301.   10. Plymouth Co.  LR  57:175.
11. Plymouth  Co.  PR  23:52(John  Winslow).  12. MD 14:242.
13. MARSHFIELD VR p. 47.


10  PENELOPE[4]  WINSLOW  (Isaac[3], Josiah[2], Edward[1])  b.
Marshfield 21 Dec. 1704; d. Plymouth 25 May 1737 in her 33rd
year.[1]
     She m.  Marshfield 30  Jan. 1723/4  JAMES WARREN,[2]   b.
Plymouth 14 April 1700;[3]  d. there 2 July 1757 in the 58th
year of his age;[3]  son of James and Sarah (Doty) Warren, a
descendant of Pilgrims Edward Doty and Richard Warren.
     The gravestone of James  Warren calls  him "Col."  James
Warren  of  Plymouth,  whose  will  dated  31  May 1757,  was
probated 19 July 1757,  named son James Warren,  Junr. Esqr;
daughter Ann Warren; and daughter Sarah Sever.[4]

     Children (WARREN) b. Plymouth;[5]

18     i   JAMES[5] b. 28 Sept. 1726
      ii   ANN b. 5  July 1728; d. Kingston 16  Oct. 1757 in
              30th yr., unm;[6]  No Plymouth Co. PR.
19   iii   SARAH  b. 23 May 1730
      iv   WINSLOW b.  23  May  1733;  d. Cambridge 9 March
              1747, ae 15.[7]
       v   JOSIAH  b. 2 March 1735/6; d. 22 April 1736.[5]

References:  1. (PLYMOUTH) BURIAL HILL p. 21.  2. MARSHFIELD
             VR p.  144.  3. MD 1:208.  4. Plymouth Co.  PR
#21875;14:298(James Warren).  5. MD 13:201  6. MD 7:222.
7. VR CAMBRIDGE 2:780.


11  ELIZABETH[4]  WINSLOW  (Isaac[3], Josiah[2], Edward[1])  b.
Marshfield 13  Dec. 1707; d. Salem  20 Sept.  1761 in  53rd
yr.[1]
     She m.  Marshfield 20 Nov. 1729 BENJAMIN MARSTON,[2]  b.
Salem  24 Feb.  1696/7;[3]  d.  Manchester 22  May 1754 aged
57y/3m;[4]  son of  Benjamin and Patience  (Rogers) Marston.
He m.  (1) Cambridge  24 June  1725 Mehitable  Gibbs,[5]  by
whom he had no children.
     Benjamin Marston graduated in 1715 from Harvard.  In 1722
he began 23 years service as Sheriff of Essex County.[6]
     The  will  of  Benjamin Marston of Manchester, dated 23
April 1754,  proved 17 July 1754,  named wife Elizabeth; son
Benjamin,  and other  children: Elizabeth,  Patience, Sarah,
John, Lucia and Winslow.[7]

     Children (MARSTON), first 4  b. Salem; next 4 bp. Marble-
head; last 2 b. Manchester:[3,8,9]

20     i   BENJAMIN[5]  b. 22 Sept. 1730
21    ii   ELIZABETH  b. 4 March 1731/2
22   iii   PATIENCE  b. 2 Jan. 1733/4
      iv   SARAH b. 19 March 1735; d. Plymouth 2 April 1772,
           unm.[10] No Plymouth Co. PR.
       v   PENELOPE  bp. 1 July 1739; d.y.
      vi   JOHN bp. 29 May 1740;  d. Salem 25 April 1761, ae
           abt. 21y, unm.[1]
     vii   PENELOPE  bp. 1 Aug. 1741;  d. bef.  father's 23
           April 1754 will.
    viii   LUCY  bp. 9 Sept. 1744; d.y.
23    ix   LUCY  b. 4 Feb. 1748
       x   WINSLOW  b. 3 Oct. 1749;  d. 6  Sept. 1755  ae 6
           yrs.[11]

References:   1. VR  SALEM  6:55.   2. MARSHFIELD VR p. 146.
           3. VR  SALEM 2:57-8  4. VR  MANCHESTER p. 276.
5. VR CAMBRIDGE  p. 257. 6. HARVARD  GRADS 6:93-6.  7. ESSEX
CO. PR  #17842(Benjamin  Marston).   8. VR MARBLEHEAD 1:334.
9. VR MANCHESTER p. 89.  10. PLYMOUTH CH RECS 1:400.  11. VR
SALEM 6:56.  See also:  SALEM BY  PERLEY 2:78-9.  and NEHGR
27:291-307,390-403.

12  EDWARD[4]  WINSLOW  (Isaac[3], Josiah[2], Edward[1])  b.
Marshfield 7 June 1714; d. Halifax, Nova Scotia 8 June 1784,
aged 71 yrs.[1]
    He m. Plymouth 10 April  1741 HANNAH (HOWLAND) DYER,[2]
b. Plymouth 19 Dec. 1712;[3]  d. Fredericton, New Brunswick
23 May 1795;[1]  dau. of Thomas  and Joanna (Cole)  Howland.
She was a descendant of Pilgrim John Howland.  Hannah m. (1)
Plymouth 29 Oct. 1734 William Dyer,[4]  by  whom she had a
dau. Hannah who  d.y., and another  dau. Hannah b.  1737,[5]
who was brought  up as a member of  Edward Winslow's family.
Thomas Howland of Plymouth, gentleman, made his will 1 Oct.
1739, naming wife Joanna and dau. Hannah Dyre, wife of
William Dyre, among others.[6]
    Edward Winslow graduated from  Harvard in 1736.[7]  In
1754 he  bought land  on North  Street in  Plymouth from his
brother-in-law  Consider Howland,  and  had built there the
house which  is now the Mayflower  Society House.[8]  Edward
Winslow was the  first magistrate in the County of Plymouth,
Collector of His Majesty's  Customs, Registrar of the  Court
of Probate and jointly with  his son, Clerk of the Courts of
Common Pleas and General Sessions of the Peace.[1]
    Because of his loyalty to England, he was deprived of his
offices in 1775, but  remained at  Plymouth until  December
1781, when all  his property was  seized for debt.[1]  With
his  wife and daughters,  he went to  New York City where he
took  refuge with  the  British garrison,  joining his son
Edward who was serving there with  the British  army.  Two
years  later, on 13 Aug.  1783,  the  family embarked for

Halifax, Nova Scotia.[1] No probate record for Edward
Winslow is to be found in Nova Scotia.

Children (WINSLOW) b. Plymouth:[9]

    i   JOHN[5] b. 14 May 1741; d. 17 July 1742.[9]
   ii   PENELOPE b. 19 April 1743; d. New Brunswick 23
        Jan. 1810; unm.[11]
  iii   SARAH (SALLY) b. 24 Feb. 1744/5; d. unm.
        Fredericton, NB, betw. 24 March 1823 and 8
        March 1824, the dates her will was written and
        probated.[10] In her will she named grand-
        nephew Henry George Clopper; niece Hannah
        Smith, wife of Henry Smith, Esq.; niece Lucy
        Woodford, wife of Dr. [Wm.] Woodford; and niece
        Penelope Clopper, wife of Garret Clopper.[11]
        The foregoing heirs were children and a
        grandchild of Sarah's half-sister Hannah (Dyer)
        Miller. An appended document with the will,
        signed by Sarah, states that she was living in
        the family of her nephew Edward Winslow Miller
        [husband of Mary Winslow, daughter of her bro-
        ther Edward] and had assigned to him a bond
        worth 250 pounds, half the value of her total
        estate, "for that branch of my family."[10]
24  iv  EDWARD b. 20 Feb. 1746
     v  son b. 11 March 1748; d. within a few hours.[9]

References:   1. WINSLOW PAPERS p. 7.   2. MD 4:112.   3. MD
            14:159.   4. MD 14:75.   5. MD 14:242.   6. MD
27:81-7(Thomas Howland will).   7. HARVARD GRADS 10:100-109.
8. MQ 46:16-17.   9. MD 15:115.   10. EARLY NB PR RECS 1785-
1835, pp. 496-7; and New Brunswick PR 1:297 (Sarah Winslow).   See: BOSTON NEWS OBITS 3:580.   NB LOYALISTS, p. 158.


                        FIFTH GENERATION


13 PENELOPE BURTON[5] (Thomas Burton[4], Elizabeth[3] Winslow,
Josiah[2], Edward[1]) b. Duxbury 27 Oct. 1724; living 31 March
1788.[1]
    She m. Pembroke 23 Oct. 1751 SETH JACOB,[2] b.
Bridgewater 6 March 1720/1;[3] living in Sept. 1791;[4] son
of Deacon Samuel and Susanna (Howard) Jacob.
    On 11 April 1787, ack. 31 March 1788, Seth and Penelope
Jacob of Pembroke sold land in Pembroke to Noah Bonney.[1]
On 30 May 1787, ack. 30 July 1787 by Seth and Penelope
Jacob, Seth of Pembroke sold land that was originally owned
by Samuel Jacob, Seth's father.[5]
    On 5 June 1788, ack. same day, Seth Jacob testified in a
suit relating to the estate of his father, Samuel Jacob. At

the Sept. 1791 Court Seth Jacob, husbandman, as executor of
the estate of Samuel Jacob, Gentleman, sued John Turner.[4]
No Plymouth Co. probate record for Seth Jacob was found.

Children (JACOB) b. Pembroke:[6]

   i  SAMUEL[6] b. 11 April 1752; m. Pembroke 13 Oct.
      1778 MARY HATCH.[7]
  ii  PENELOPE bp. 13 Sept. 1761

References:    1. Plymouth Co. LR 75:255(Seth & Penelope
              Jacob). 2. VR PEMBROKE p.296. 3. MD 15:87
4. PLYMOUTH CO CT RECS 10:202.    5. Plymouth Co. LR 67:54,
68:123(Seth Jacob). 6. VR PEMBROKE p. 115.    7. VR PEMBROKE
p. 296. Also: BRIDGEWATER BY MITCHELL, pp. 198,210.


14  ELEANOR BURTON[5] (Thomas Burton[4], Elizabeth[3] Winslow,
Josiah[2], Edward[1]) b. Duxbury 4 May 1728; d. Pembroke 27 Oct.
1751 in 24th year.[1]
    She m. Pembroke 5 Feb. 1746/7 NATHANIEL BISHOP,[2] bp.
Scituate 3 July 1715;[3]    living 18 June 1778;[4] son of
Hudson and Abigail (Keene) Bishop.
    On 24 July 1758, ack. same day, Nathaniel Bishop, of a
place called Miscongres Island in the County of York in the
Province of Massachusetts Bay, [now Maine], sold to Josiah
Keen of Pembroke, land in Pembroke which "my grand father
James Bishop deceased gave to my father Hudson Bishop."[5]
    Hezekiah Eggleston, on 28 Aug. 1771, sold to Nathaniel
Bishop of Muscogus Island "the place where he now
lives."[6] And on 18 June 1778 Nathaniel Bishop sold to Wm.
Solomon Loud a lot on Muscongus Island.[4]
    There is no Plymouth Co. or Maine PR for Nathaniel
Bishop.

Children (BISHOP) b. Pembroke:[7]

   i  NATHANIEL[6] b. 14 Oct. 1747; m. Pembroke 6 June
      1779 ABIGAIL BEARCE.[8]
  ii  ELIPHALET b. 23 Sept. 1751; m. Pembroke 16 May
      1776 ELIZABETH TUBBS.[8]

References:    1. MD 9:6.    2. VR PEMBROKE p. 239. 3. VR
              SCITUATE 1:35.    4. Lincoln Co. ME LR 13:8;
29:122(Nathaniel Bishop).    5. Plymouth Co. LR 46:154
(Nathaniel Bishop).    6. Lincoln Co. ME LR 8:122(Hezekiah
Eggleston). 7. VR PEMBROKE pp. 36-7. 8. Ibid. p. 239.


15  ELIZABETH BURTON[5] (Thomas Burton[4], Elizabeth[3] Winslow,
Josiah[2], Edward[1]) b. Pembroke 9 May 1737; d. there 17 May
1807, age 70 yrs.[1]

She m. Pembroke 15 May 1766 DANIEL BONNEY,[2]  b.
Pembroke 2 July 1739;[3]   d. there 13 Aug. 1813, age 74
yrs.;[1] son of Elisha and Elizabeth (Lincoln) Bonney.
     Daniel Bonney of Pembroke was called housewright and
yeoman in several deeds, but there is no deed indicating his
children.[4] Daniel Bonney was 1-0-2 in the 1790 census of
Pembroke. No Plymouth Co. probate record for him appears.

     Children (BONNEY) b. Pembroke:

     i   SETH[6]*;  m.  Plympton  29  March  1798  DEBORAH
         WESTON.[5]
     ii  JONATHAN b. ca. 1768. (He had a child Pelham
         Winslow Bonney, b. Pembroke 15 July 1798,
         indicating he prob. was a Winslow descendant.)
         He m. Pembroke 28 Oct. 1787 PEGGY TORREY.[6]

*The births of all of Seth's children in VR PEMBROKE show
Seth as son of Daniel.

References:   1. VR PEMBROKE p. 390.  2. Ibid. p. 240.
              3. Ibid. p. 59.  4. Plymouth Co. LR 74:119;
78:279(Daniel Bonney).  5. VR PLYMPTON p. 260.  6. VR
PEMBROKE p. 241.


16 PELHAM[5] WINSLOW (John[4], Isaac[3], Josiah[2], Edward[1]) b.
Marshfield 8 June 1737; d. Brooklyn NY 13 Aug. 1783.[1]
     He m. Marshfield 18 Nov. 1770 JOANNA WHITE,[1]  b. ca.
1744; d. Plymouth 2 May 1829, age 85 yrs;[2]  daughter of
Gideon and Joanna (Howland) White; a descendant of Pilgrims
John Howland and William White.  The will of Gideon White
dated 1 May 1766 named wife Joanna and dau. Joanna (no
surname).[3]  Joanna White, in her will, dated 11 March
1806, named dau. Joanna Winslow.[4]
     Pelham Winslow graduated from Harvard in 1753.[1]  He was
a Loyalist and a Major in the British Army in the Revolutionary War.[1]  In March 1776 he left Boston with the
British Army, and a short time later was in New York with
those troops. In 1778 he was assigned by the British to
duty at Newport RI, but by Aug. 1779 had returned to New
York, where he remained until he died.[1]
     On 1 Oct. 1779 Joshua Thomas of Plymouth, Esq. was
appointed agent of the estate of Pelham Winslow, who had
absented himself for more than two years with the enemies of
the United States of America.[5]  A 1783 letter from the
widow Joanna mentions her problems in bringing up "two
little girls."[6]
     On 23 April 1784 a petition was filed by Isaac Winslow
and Joanna Winslow, as guardian of the children, for the
division of lands held in common between Isaac Winslow and
the heirs of Pelham Winslow. Letters of administration for

_____

the estate of Pelham Winslow, granted the same day, led to
division of the jointly held property on 6 May 1784.[5] Half
of the Marshfield farm of 650 acres, and half of about 1200
acres lying in the township of Winslow on Kenebeck River in
County of Lincoln, (now ME) were assigned to Isaac Winslow,
the other half to be divided between Pelham Winslow's
children.[5]
    Johanna Winslow of Plymouth, widow, sold 110 acres in
Marshfield to [her sons-in-law] Henry Warren and Nathan
Hayward on 12 March 1797.[7] And on 20 Nov. 1797 Johanna
Winslow, widow, and Hannah White, single woman, both of
Plymouth, sold land in Plymouth which had belonged to their
father and was conveyed to them by their mother Johanna
White of Plymouth.[8]

    Children (WINSLOW) b. Plymouth:[9]

    i    MARY[6] b. 28 July 1771; m. Plymouth 8 Nov. 1791
         HENRY WARREN.[10] [See Fam. #18]
    ii   JOANNA b. 30 June 1773; m. NATHAN HAYWARD.[11]
    iii  child d. 1 Nov. 1775.[12]
    iv   PENELOPE PELHAM* d. bef. 1783(Joanna's letter)[6]

*Daughter Penelope is from (PLYMOUTH) ANCIENT LANDMARKS
2:291. No proof of her existence has been found, although
she could be the child who d. in 1775. There were only two
daughters living in 1783.

References: 1. HARVARD GRADS 13:374-7. 2. PLYMOUTH CH RECS
         2:676. 3. Plymouth Co. PR 25:304;#22553(Gideon
White). 4. Ibid. 43:446(Joanna White). 5. Ibid. 27:150;
29:161,164-5,256,427-8(Pelham Winslow). 6. MASS HIST SOCI-
ETY PROCEEDINGS (2nd series) 2:240. 7. Plymouth Co. LR
82:92(Johanna Winslow) 8. Ibid. 82:93(Johanna Winslow and
Hannah White). 9. MD 23:10. 10. Plymouth VR 2:291.
11. BRIDGEWATER BY MITCHELL p. 189. 12. PLYMOUTH CH RECS
1:405.


17 ISAAC[5] WINSLOW (John[4], Isaac[3], Josiah[2], Edward[1]) b.
Marshfield 27 April 1739; d. there 24 Oct. 1819, age 80
yrs.[1]
    He m. (1) int. Marshfield 25 Oct. 1768 ELIZABETH
STOCKBRIDGE,[2] b. Scituate 6 March 1737/8;[3] d.
Marshfield in Nov. 1801;[4] dau. of Benjamin and Ruth
(Otis) Stockbridge. The will of Benjamin Stockbridge of
Scituate, Esqr., dated 5 June 1784, named dau. Elizabeth
Winslow and grandchildren Ruth Stockbridge Winslow,
Elizabeth Winslow, Sarah Winslow among others.[5]
    Isaac m. (2) Hingham 10 Jan. 1805,[6] int. Marshfield 13
Jan. 1805 (sic)[7] FRANCES GAY, bp. Hingham in April

1763;[6]   d. there 12 Oct. 1846;[6]   dau. of Martin and Mary
(Pinckney) Gay.
    Isaac  Winslow of Marshfield, physician, made his will 25
Aug. 1815,  presented 15 Nov. 1819,  naming his wife Frances
Winslow; son John Winslow, and daus. Elizabeth Whitman, Ruth
S. Dingley and Sarah  Clapp.[8]  Division of the  estate was
made  5 March 1822  to  the  four  children: John Winslow;
Elizabeth Whitman, wife of Kilborn Whitman; Ruth S. Dingley,
wife  of Thomas Dingley;  and Sarah Clapp,  wife of Ebenezer
Clapp.[8]

    Children (WINSLOW) b. Scituate, all by first wife:[9]

        i   ELIZABETH[6] b. 14 Nov.  1769; m. Marshfield 5 June
            1788 KILBORN WHITMAN.[10]
        ii  RUTH  STOCKBRIDGE   b.   17  Dec.   1771;  m.   (1)
            Marshfield 12 March 1793  JOSIAH CROCKER SHAW;
            [11]  m. (2)  Marshfield  23 March 1801 THOMAS
            DINGLEY.[12]
        iii JOHN b.  14 July 1774; m.  Northboro 28 Dec. 1800
            SUSAN BALL.[13]
        iv  SARAH b. 14 Aug. 1775; m. Marshfield 21 June 1812
            EBENEZER CLAPP "of Bath."[14]
        v   ISAAC  b. 12 April 1777; d. 1778

References:  1. VR SCITUATE 1:337.  2. MARSHFIELD VR p. 390.
           3. Ibid. p.  130.  4. NEHGR 135:36-41.  5. Suf-
folk  Co. PR  File #12996(Benjamin  Stockbridge). 6. HINGHAM
HIST 2:265.  7. MARSHFIELD VR  p. 184.   8. Plymouth Co.  PR
File #23186; & 50:396,56:73(Isaac Winslow).   9. VR SCITUATE
1:412.   10. MARSHFIELD VR   p.   153.   11. Ibid.   p.  136.
12. Ibid.  p. 114.  13. NEHGR  135:40.  14. MARSHFIELD VR p.
265.


    18  JAMES  WARREN[5]  (Penelope[4]  Winslow,  Isaac[3],  Josiah[2],
Edward[1]) b.  Plymouth 28 Sept. 1726; d.  there 28 Nov. 1808,
ae 82.[1]
    He  m.  Barnstable 14 Nov.  1754 MERCY OTIS,[2]   b.
Barnstable 14 Sept. 1728;[3]  d. Plymouth 19 Oct.  1814, age
86  yrs.;[4]   dau.  of  James and  Mary (Allyn)  Otis,  a
descendant of Pilgrim  Edward Doty.   James Otis of Barnstable,  in his  will dated  21 April  1774 named dau. Mercy
Warren  and  five  grandsons,  sons of James Warren, Esqr.,
namely: James Warren, Junr., Winslow Warren, Charles Warren,
Henry Warren and George Warren.[5]
    James  Warren  graduated  from  Harvard  in 1745.  He was
president  of the Provincial  Congress of Massachusetts, and
was an American  General during the Revolutionary War.  His
wife Mercy was  a noted author  and a sister  of James Otis,
the patriot. [6]

The will of James Warren of Plymouth, Esqr., dated 8 June
1792, proven 28 Dec. 1808, named wife Mercy Warren; sons
James Warren, Henry Warren and George Warren. [7]

Children (WARREN) b. Plymouth: [8]:

i   JAMES[6] b. 18 Oct. 1757;  d. Plymouth 5 Aug. 1821
    ae 64.[9]  James  Warren of  the State  of MA,
    wrote  his  will  1 Aug.  1820, proved 20 Aug.
    1821,  naming nephews and  nieces, the children
    of brother  Henry Warren,  namely: Marcia  Otis
    Torrey, Winslow Warren, Pelham  Winslow Warren,
    Charles Henry Warren, Mary  Ann Warren, Richard
    Warren,  George Warren  and Edward  Warren; and
    niece Charlotte Marcy.[10]
ii  WINSLOW b.  24 March 1759; killed  by Indians at
    the Forks  of the  Miami River  in Ohio  4 Nov.
    1791.[6]  No Plymouth PR.
iii CHARLES  b. 14 April 1762; d. St. Lucar, Spain 30
    Nov. 1784.[8]  No Plymouth Co. PR.
iv  HENRY  b. 21 March  1764; m. Plymouth 8 Nov. 1791
    MARY WINSLOW.[11]  [See Fam. #16]
v   GEORGE  b. 20 Sept. 1766; m. MARY ILSLEY.[12]

References:   1. MD  13:201.   2. MD  31:10    3. MD 32:154.
          4. PLYMOUTH CH  RECS 2:661.   5. Barnstable Co.
PR 20:224(James Otis).  6. WARREN GEN pp. 25-8.  7. Plymouth
Co.   PR   #21876;42:419(James   Warren).     8 MD   19:151.
9. PLYMOUTH CH RECS  2:669.  10. Plymouth Co.  PR 53:535(son
James Warren).  11. Plymouth VR  2:291.  12. MAYFLOWER INDEX
(1960  ed.),  #36,407 &  36,408.   See also: (PLYMOUTH) ANC
LANDMARKS 2:196.


19 SARAH  WARREN[5] (Penelope[4]  Winslow, Isaac[3], Josiah[2],
Edward[1]) b. Plymouth 23 May 1730; d. Kingston 15 March 1797,
age 67 yrs.[1]
    She  m. int. Plymouth 16  Aug. 1755 WILLIAM SEVER,[2]  b.
Kingston 12  Oct. 1729;[3]  d. there  15 June  1809, ae  80
yrs;[1]  son  of Nicholas  and Sarah  (Warren) Sever,  a
descendant of Pilgrims Edward Doty and Richard Warren.  He
m. (2) int. Kingston 25 May 1798 Mercy (Foster) Russell.[2]
    William Sever  of Kingston,  Esquire, wrote  his will  30
April 1802, probated  14 Aug. 1809, mentioning  his marriage
contract with Mercy Russell,  now his wife;  naming grandson
William James Sever, son of William Sever late of Worcester,
deceased;  granddaughters Penelope  Winslow  Sever and  Anne
Warren Sever, daus.  of son William Sever;  dau. Mary Sever,
the widow of son William Sever;  granddau. Sarah Russell, the
dau of Thomas Russell, late  of Boston deceased and of Sarah
Russell,  late wife of  sd Thomas Russell,  my dau; and sons
James Sever and John Sever of Kingston.[4]

Children (SEVER) b. Kingston:[3]

   i   SARAH[6] b. 3 Oct. 1757; m. Kingston 12 Aug. 1784
      THOMAS RUSSELL.[5]
  ii  WILLIAM b. 23 June 1759; m. int. Kingston 25 May
      1798, m. 19 June 1798 MARCY RUSSELL.[6]
 iii  JAMES b. 3 Nov. 1761; m. int Kingston 6 Feb.
      1796, m. 22 Feb. 1796 JANE RUSSELL.[7]
  iv  ANN WARREN b. 25 Sept. 1763; d. Kingston 19 Jan.
      1788, ae 25 yrs; unm.[1] No Plymouth Co. PR.
   v  JOHN b. 7 May 1766; m. int Kingston 15 April 1790
      NANCY RUSSELL.[8]

References:   1. VR KINGSTON  pp. 379-80.   2. Ibid. p. 227.
        3. Ibid.   pp.   131-2   4. Plymouth   Co.   PR
#17842; 43:18(William Sever)  5. VR KINGSTON p. 276.   6. VR
KINGSTON int p. 277 & Bible Record.  7. Ibid. p. 276.   8. VR
KINGSTON p. 276.


20  BENJAMIN MARSTON[5] (Elizabeth[4] Winslow, Isaac[3], Josiah[2],
Edward[1]) b. Salem 22 Sept. 1730; d.  Island of Bolame on the
West Coast of Africa 10 Aug. 1792.[1]
    He m.  Marblehead 13 Nov.  1755 SARAH SWETT,[2] bp.
Marblehead  23 Feb. 1734/5;[3]  d. in the summer of 1775.  A
letter of 8 Jan.  1776 from William  Brown to Samuel Curwen
mentions "About 2 months ago  Mr. Marston of Marblehead came
here by night,  from Col. Fowles's  farm.  He knows  nothing
about Salem.  His wife died  last summer." [4].  On 28  July
1788 a bond for Sarah's estate  was signed.[5]  She was dau.
of Joseph and Hannah (Negus) (Strahan) Swett.  Joseph Swett,
in his will dated 20 March  1744, named wife Hannah and dau.
Sarah Swett.[6]
    Benjamin Marston graduated  from Harvard in  1749.[1]  On
19 Jan. 1774 he sold to Richard James a house and land which
was set off to Benjamin and Sarah Marston in the division of
the real estate of Jos. Sweet, Esq. deceased.[7]
    A Loyalist, he was forced to evacuate to Halifax, NS with
the British forces in 1776,  and was proscribed as a traitor
and banished from Massachusetts  in 1778.[1]  He settled  in
Northumberland Co. NB for a time, where he served as Sheriff
ca. 1785-7.   In New Brunswick he  was also Surveyor-General
of the King's Woods.  About 1787 he returned to  Boston via
Windsor and Halifax, NS; and in 1788 removed to London, England,  where he  lived  in  poverty.  In  1792  he went as
surveyor  for  a  private  company  to the Island of Bolame,
Portugese Guinea, where he died of a fever.[1,8,9]
    No record of any children has been found.

References: 1. HARVARD GRADS 12:439-54; NEHGR 13:324.  2. VR
        MARBLEHEAD 2:278.  3 Ibid. 1:499.   4. NEHGR 27:
392-3.  5. Essex Co. PR #17859.  6. Ibid.  #26963.  7. NEHGR

27:392.    8. NB  LOYALISTS p.   93.   9.  LOYALISTS OF  MA pp.
210-11. See  also NEHGR 27:390-403; and SWETT GENEALOGY, pp.
16-7.


21  ELIZABETH  MARSTON[5],   (Elizabeth[4]  Winslow, Isaac[3],
Josiah[2], Edward[1])  b. Salem  4 March  1731/2; d.  Plymouth 2
Sept. 1798 in her 66th yr.[1]
    She  m.  Salem  22  Sept.  1756  WILLIAM  WATSON,[2]   b.
Plymouth 6 May 1730;[3]  d. there 27  April 1815;[4]  son of
John and Priscilla (Thomas) Watson.
    William Watson graduated from Harvard in 1751.[5]  He was
appointed  Justice  of  the  Peace  in 1762 and held various
offices  in  the  town  of  Plymouth.   In  May  1775 he was
appointed by the Provincial Congress as the first postmaster
of Plymouth.  On  28 Sept.  1782 he became  Naval officer for
the Port of Plymouth,  and was collector of customs there in
1789.[5]
    Letters of administration dated 19 June 1815 were granted
to Benjamin M. Watson [#23,iv] of Plymouth to administer the
estate of William Watson of Plymouth.[6]

    Children (WATSON), b. Plymouth:[7]

        i   WILLIAM[6] b. 18 Aug. 1757; d. 4 March 1781, age 24
            yr.[8] No Plymouth Co. PR.
       ii   ELIZABETH b.  17 Feb.  1759; m.   int. Plymouth 28
            Oct. 1787 NATHANIEL NILES.[9]
      iii   BENJAMIN b. 8 Feb. 1761; d.  24 June 1781 in 21st
            yr.[8]
       iv   ELLEN  b. 12 April 1764; m. Plymouth 17 June 1786
            JOHN DAVIS.[10]

References:    1. (PLYMOUTH)  BURIAL  HILL BY  KINGMAN p. 79.
               2. VR  SALEM  4:441.   3. MD 12:223.  4. (PLY-
MOUTH)  BURIAL  HILL  BY  KINGMAN  p.  125  5. HARVARD GRADS
13:149-53.  6. Plymouth Co.  PR File #22247;  46:108(William
Watson) 7. MD 19:6.  8. (PLYMOUTH) BURIAL HILL BY KINGMAN p.
53.  9. MD 29:129.  10. PLYMOUTH CH RECS 2:503.


22  PATIENCE MARSTON[5] (Elizabeth[4] Winslow, Isaac[3], Josiah[2],
Edward[1]) b. Salem  2 Jan. 1733/4; d. Plymouth  20 April 1767
in her 34th yr.[1]
    She  m.  Manchester  7  Nov.  1754 ELKANAH WATSON,[2]  b.
Plymouth 27  Feb. 1732;[3]   d. there  7 Sept.  1804 aged 73
yrs;[4]  son of  John and Priscilla (Thomas)  Watson.  He m.
(2) prob. Plymouth  ca. 1792 Fanny (Lee) Glover,[5]  by whom
he had Charles Lee and Lucia.[5]
    Elkanah Watson  of Plymouth, gentleman,  in his will dated
21  July  1804,  proved  14  Nov.  1804, mentioned wife (not
named, but Fanny Watson was  executrix); daughters Priscilla

Watson and Patty Watson;  son Charles Watson, land in Maine,
etc.; dau.  Lucia Watson; son Elkanah  Watson, Jr. living in
the state of New York;  twelve children of son Marston, (not
named).[6]

Children (WATSON) b. Plymouth to Patience:[7]

    i   MARSTON[6] b. 28 May 1756;  m. Manchester 30 March
          1779 LUCY LEE.[10]
   ii   ELKANAH b. 22  Jan. 1758; m. Plymouth 1784 RACHEL
          SMITH.[11]
  iii   PRISCILLA  b. 30 Sept. 1760;  m. Plymouth 13 Nov.
          1808 JOSIAH COTTON.[12]
   iv  PATTY    b. 16  Oct. 1762;  unm. 21  July 1804. No
          Plymouth Co. PR found for her.
    v  LUCIA b.  11 Nov.  1765;  d.  Freetown 20 March
          1792,[8]; bur. Plymouth, ae. 26y, unm.[9].

References: 1. PLYMOUTH CH RECS 1:396.    2. VR MANCHESTER p.
        223.    3. MD 12:223  4. PLYMOUTH CH  RECS 2:630.
5. (PLYMOUTH)  ANC  LANDMARKS  2:277.  6. Plymouth Co.  PR
#22232;  40:106(Elkanah  Watson).  7. MD 18:212.  8. BOSTON
NEWS OBITS 3:522.  9. (PLYMOUTH)  BURIAL HILL BY KINGMAN  p.
67. 10. VR MANCHESTER p. 223.  11. (PLYMOUTH) ANC. LANDMARKS
2:277.  12. PLYMOUTH CH RECS 2:648.


23 LUCY  MARSTON[5] (Elizabeth[4]  Winslow,  Isaac[3], Josiah[2],
Edward[1]) b.  Manchester 4  Feb.  1748; d. Plymouth 25 Oct.
1793, age 45 yrs.[1]
    She m.  Plymouth 15  April  1769  JOHN  WATSON,[2]    b.
Plymouth 26 Aug.  1747;[3]  d. there 1 Feb. 1826;[1]  son of
John and  Elizabeth (Reynolds)  Watson; a  descendant of
Pilgrim  Thomas Rogers.   He m.  (2) Plymouth  19 March 1796
Eunice (Marston) Goodwin,[4] by whom he had Edward  Winslow,
Eliza Ann and Albert Mortimer.
    John Watson graduated from Harvard in 1766.[5]  On 20 May
1770  Lucia Watson,  wife of  John Watson,  confessed sin of
fornication.[6]
    Letters  of administration for the  estate of John Watson
of Plymouth,  gentleman, was granted to  Benjamin M. Watson,
Esq. of Plymouth  20 March 1826.   An allowance was  made to
Eunice  the  widow  on  19  June  1826.   On 10 April 1837 a
committee  was  to  set  off  to  Albert Watson, son of said
deceased, one ninth part, being his share and on 25 May 1837
Albert Watson, son  of John Watson received his share of the
homestead farm.[7]

Children (WATSON) b. Plymouth:[8]*

    i   JOHN[6] b. 1769; bp. 8 July 1770; m. int. Plymouth
          23 Dec. 1793 PAMELA HOWARD.[9]

```
ii   GEORGE b.  1771; bp. 28 April  1771; m. Boston 14
     June 1801 ELIZABETH LEACH.[10]
iii  SARAH (SALLY) MARSTON  b. 1772; bp. 8 Nov. 1772
iv   BENJAMIN  MARSTON b.  15 Nov.  1774(g.s.); bp. 20
     Nov. 1774; m.   Fairfield CT Church 7  Oct 1804
     LUCRETIA-BURR STURGES.[11]
 v   LUCIA b.  1776; bp. 17 May 1778; m. int. Plymouth
     25 May 1799 JOHN TAYLOR.[12]
vi   DANIEL b.  1779; bp. 12 Dec.  1779; m. 1810 SUSAN
     (____) SUDLAR, widow of Emery Wells Sudlar.[13]
vii  WILLIAM bp. 14 Oct. 1781; d.y.
viii WILLIAM  b. 1783; bp.  5 Oct. 1783;  m. Duxbury 1
     Jan 1809 HULDAH DELANO.[14]
ix   WINSLOW b. 1786;  bp. 16 April 1786;  m. Plymouth
     19 Oct. 1812 HARRIET LOTHROP GOODWIN.[15]
 x   BROOKE  bp. 22 June 1788
```

*Births are not in Plymouth VR: reference for baptisms only.

References:    1. (PLYMOUTH)  BURIAL  HILL  BY  KINGMAN pp.
      151-2.   2. MD  26:140.    3. MD  14:239.   4. MD
30:117.   5. HARVARD GRADS 16:428-30.  6. PLYMOUTH  CH RECS
1:374.   7. Plymouth  Co.   PR #22238; 60:373; 61:16; 79:341
(John  Watson).   8. PLYMOUTH  CH RECS  1:458-9,461-7; 2:478.
9. MD 30:78.   10. BOSTON VR 30:267.   11. FAMS  OF OLD FAIR-
FIELD  2:2:935,1009.    12. MD  30:190.   13. (PLYMOUTH) ANC.
LANDMARKS 2:277,351.  14. VR DUXBURY, p. 328.  15. PLYMOUTH
CH RECS 2:649.   Also (PLYMOUTH) ANC  LANDMARKS 2:278, &  MF
2:278.

24  EDWARD[5] WINSLOW (Edward[4], Isaac[4], Josiah[2], Edward[1])  b.
Plymouth 20 Feb. 1746;  d. at his  residence "King's Wood,"
Kingsclear, New Brunswick, Canada,  13 May 1815, aged 69.[1]
   He m. before  1776 MARY SYMONDS, [2]  b. ca. 1754;[3]  d.
Kingsclear, NB 21 Nov. 1808, ae 54.[3]  Her identity has not
been learned.
   Edward  Winslow  was  a Loyalist  during  the  American
Revolution, joining the British  army in Boston by  1775.[2]
On 30 July  1776 he was in New York,  where the British high
command    appointed    him    Muster-Master   General   to  the
Provincial Troops, with the rank of Lt. Colonel.[2]  In 1778
he was proscribed  a traitor and banished from  the State of
Massachusetts.[2]  After the war, in April 1783, he took his
family to  Nova Scotia where  they remained two  years, then
moved  to  New Brunswick  to  take  up  land granted by the
British crown for his  war service.[4]  Edward Winslow  held
several  positions   of  public  trust   in  New  Brunswick,
including member of Council, Surrogate-General  and Judge of
the Supreme Court.[5]
   In  a letter dated  4 Oct. 1784  from Nova Scotia, Edward
Winslow wrote: "I lost my sweet little boy 'Chip' soon after

my arrival in this country, and I've had a fine daughter
since."[6] In a letter of 2 Oct. 1805 from George Leonard
to Edward Winslow he mentions the "death of your dear
Catherine."[7]

On 17 May 1815 administration was granted on the estate
of Edward Winslow, Parish of Fredericton, York Co., NB, who
died intestate: to John Jenkins and Edward Winslow Miller,
with fellow bondsmen Garret Clopper and James Fraser, all of
Fredericton.[8]  Ten years later, 22 Dec. 1825, on complaint
by John Wentworth Winslow, the Court commanded Edward
Winslow Miller, the surviving administrator, to file an
inventory by 1 Feb. 1826.[9]

It appears that the assets of the estate were mainly in
land, with little cash. In a letter dated AD 1815 Judge
Ward Chipman mentioned "There are three daughters unmarried,
Hannah, Sarah Ann and Eliza, all grown up, left entirely
unprovided for." On 7 March 1816 the House of Assembly of
New Brunswick voted 100 pounds to Misses Hannah and Eliza
Winslow, the unmarried daughers of the late Hon. Edward
Winslow.[10]

Children (WINSLOW) last eight b. in that part of Nova
Scotia that became New Brunswick:

   i   DANIEL MURRAY[6] b. MA or NY bef. 1 Nov. 1777, when
       his father left NY to recruit Loyalists in
       Philadelphia; on 15 Feb. 1778 Ward Chipman
       wrote Edward Winslow that "Polly [E.W.'s wife]
       and Murray have been in high health since you
       sailed;"[11]   Murray d.s.p. bef. 20 March 1814
       on Capt. Barcly's British ship on the Great
       Lakes during the War of 1812.[12]
  ii   MARY b. prob. Springfield, LI, NY ca. 1778; m.
       EDWARD WINSLOW MILLER.
 iii   THOMAS ASTON COFFIN b. prob. Springfield, LI, NY
       ca. 1779; d. unm. West Indies 1810.[13]
  iv   WARD CHIPMAN, "Chip" b. prob. Springfield, LI, NY
       ca. 1781; d. Nova Scotia in 1783.[6]
   v   PENELOPE b. Nova Scotia, prob. Granville, late
       1783 or early 1784; m. (1) 10 Jan. 1814 JOHN
       JENKINS;[15]   m. (2) 16 Nov 1824 JOHN WINTER-
       BOTTOM.[16]
  vi   EDWARD b. ca. 1785; d. unm. in shipwreck 12 May
       1820 off the coast of Cape Negro, near
       Barrington, NS.[14]
 vii   HANNAH b. ca. 1787; living unm. 19 June 1820.[14]
viii   SARAH ANN b. ca. 1789; m. 1815 LAWRENCE BRAD-
       SHAW RAINSFORD.[10]
  ix   CHRISTIANA BANNISTER b. ca. 1791; d. unm. 22 Nov.
       1814 age 22. [10,17]
   x   JOHN FRANCIS WENTWORTH b. Kingsclear, NB in 1793;
       m. 25 Sept. 1823 JANE CAROLINE RAINSFORD.[1]

          xi   ELIZA CHIPMAN  b. ca. Dec.  1794; m. 10  May 1817
                  Dr. JAMES SAMPSON.[18]
         xii   CATHERINE WELTDEN d. bef. 2 Oct. 1805.[7]
        xiii   BROOKE WATSON  prob. d.y.*

*Brooke  Watson is from (PLYMOUTH) ANC LANDMARKS.  He is not
mentioned in WINSLOW PAPERS, so must  have  d.y.  He would be
named for Edward Winslow's good friend Brooke Watson.


References:  1. WINSLOW  PAPERS,  pp. 5,9.  2. HARVARD GRADS
            16:274-91.    3. NB   VITAL   STATISTICS   FROM
NEWSPAPERS 1:59,  #971, from  "The True  Briton" for  1 Dec.
1808.   4. WINSLOW PAPERS p. 9 & numerous others. 5. Ibid.
pp. 8-9.   6. Ibid. pp.  112-3.  7. Ibid.  p. 537.   8. York
Co.,  NB PR 1:184-5(Edward Winslow)  9.  EARLY NB PROB RECS,
p.  496.   10. WINSLOW  PAPERS p.  696.  11. Ibid.  p. 23.
12. Ibid. p. 688.   13. Ibid. p. 657. 14. Ibid.  pp. 704-5.
15. Ibid. p. 687.  16. ARMY  LIST for 1836, p.  226.  17. NB
VITAL STATISTICS FROM NEWSPAPERS  8:5.  18. ROLL OF OFFICERS
IN MEDICAL SERVICE, p. 218, #3286.  See also: (PLYMOUTH) ANC
LANDMARKS 2:289;  NB LOYALISTS p.  158.  LOYALISTS OF MA
p. 300. AMERICAN LOYALIST CLAIMS 1:531-2.

# JOHN BILLINGTON

of the

# MAYFLOWER

*Compiled by*

Harriet Woodbury Hodge

Harriet Woodbury Hodge, a native of Kansas City, Missouri, is a member of the Illinois Society of Mayflower Descendants, serving on their Board of Assistants 1977-1990. She is a descendant of Pilgrims John Alden and John Billington, one through each of her grandmothers. Both ancestral families migrated to the middle west before 1825. Mrs. Hodge has a B.A. degree from Wellesley College, and became a Certified Genealogist in 1977. She has written three published family genealogies, as well as the John Billington Mayflower Families in Progress pamphlet in 1988. She began work on the Billington family for the Five Generations Project in 1980, using research notes left by the late Claude Barlow, who was originally assigned to the family, but died before completing his task. Mrs. Hodge takes particular pride in having been for twenty years a member of the volunteer staff in the genealogy department of the Winnetka, Illinois Public Library, helping others find their ancestry, as well as doing personal research there.

JOHN BILLINGTON

John Billington, his wife Elinor, and two adolescent
sons, John and Francis, were passengers on the Mayflower.
According to Bradford's History, "they came from London, and
I know not by what friends shuffled into their company."[1]
There is evidence, however, that the Billingtons had
connections to the gentry in Lincolnshire.[2]

The English Crown granted, on 7 Feb. 1612, a lease of 29
acres of land in the village of Cowbit, near Spaulding,
Lincolnshire to Francis Longland, gentleman, then about 32
years of age. This "lease for three lives" allowed Mr.
Longland to select two heirs, or successors to the lease
after his death. He chose two small boys: Francis
Billington, son of John Billington and Francis Newton, son
of Robert Newton. [2,3] The children were very probably
related to Francis Longland, cousins or nephews, perhaps his
namesakes. If nephews, then Longland's sisters were the
mothers of Francis Billington and Francis Newton. Proof of
any relationship has yet to be found.

A survey of Crown lands was made in February 1650 to
ascertain the condition of the land and whether the primary
lessee or either of his two successors were then living. It
was determined that the original lessee and immediate
tenant, Francis Longland, then aged 70 years, was still
living at Welby, Lincolnshire; Francis Newton, aged 40, was
living at Swayfield in that county; and Francis Billington
"was living a year since in New England aged forty years or
thereabouts."[2] Whether Francis Billington actually
inherited the lease is unknown. The parish registers of
Lincolnshire contain many baptism and marriage entries for
persons of the surnames Longland, Billington and Newton, but
so far these individuals have not been identified.[4]

William Bradford was critical of the Billingtons from the
beginning, and his references to them almost invariably
chronicle their misconduct. John Billington may well have
been one of the dissidents among the passengers on the
Mayflower who wanted to be independent of the Separatist
church group from Leiden, but he accepted and signed the
Mayflower Compact 11 November 1620 O.S. on board ship while
anchored in Provincetown Harbor.[1] A few days later, 5
December 1620, one of the Billington sons, we are not told
which one, in his father's absence, fired a gun near an open
half-keg of gunpowder in the crowded cabin of the Mayflower,
endangering ship and passengers, "and yet, by God's mercy,
no harm done."[5] In March 1621, "The first Offence since
our arrival is of John Billington...and is this month

convented before  the whole company for  his contempt of the
Captain's  [Miles Standish] lawfull command with opprobrious
speeches, for  which he  is adjudged  to have  his neck  and
heels  tied together.  But upon humbling himself and craving
pardon, and it being the first offence, he is forgiven."[6]

Early  in  January,  shortly  after  the  settlement  at
Plymouth,  son Francis Billington saw from the top of a tree
on a  high hill "a great  sea as he thought"  which he later
explored with one  of the ship's crew.  The two  lakes thus
discovered  have  ever  since  been  known  as  "Billington
Sea."[5]  John Billington, Jr. lost  himself in the woods in
May of 1621,  but was found and cared for by Indians on Cape
Cod.   Chief  Massasoit  sent  word  to  Plymouth that young
Billington  was safe,  and in  June ten  men set sail in the
Pilgrim company's shallop  toward Nauset (Eastham)  to bring
the boy home.  With  this encounter the colony began  a long
and beneficial friendship with the Cape Indians.[1,5]

In  the  Division  of  Land  at  Plymouth  in  1623, John
Billington received  three acres "on  the South side  of the
Brooke to  the baywards."[7]  Why the  Billingtons, who all
four miraculously survived the first bitter winter, received
only three  acres is a  mystery.  Families were allotted one
acre  for  each  household  member,  including  servants.
Possibly John, Jr. had been indentured as a  servant to some
other family.  In the 1627  Division of Cattle,  young John
Billington was  listed with  the Warren  and Soule families,
while his parents and  brother Francis were grouped with the
Hopkinses.[7]

Bradford described  at length  the 1624  confrontation of
the  Governor's Council  with John  Oldham and the minister,
John Lyford.  The two  culprits had written highly  critical
accounts  of  affairs  at  Plymouth,  and their letters were
intercepted by Governor Bradford and his associates from the
ship Charity as it sailed for England.  "After the reading of
[Lyford's] letters before the whole company, he was demanded
what he  could say to  these things.  But  all the answer he
made was,  that Billington and some  others had informed him
of  many things and  made sundry complaints,  which they now
denied....  And this was  all the answer they could have, for
none  would take [Lyford's] part  in anything but Billington
and any  whom he  named denied  the things  and protested he
wronged  them and  would have  drawn them  to such  and such
things which  they could  not consent  to, though  they were
sometimes drawn to his meetings...."[1]

After  this trial,  Oldham and  Lyford were banished from
Plymouth Colony.  A  number  of other  disgruntled settlers
left  voluntarily about  this time.  One wonders that John

Billington was not expelled or at least urged to depart, but
he remained at Plymouth, an outspoken critic and persistent
rebel. On 9 June 1625 William Bradford, in a letter to
Robert Cushman in England, wrote: "Billington still rails
against you and threatens to arrest you, I know not
wherefore. He is a knave, and so will live and die."[8]

The story of John Billington's execution for murder has
often been embellished with fanciful details in prose and
poetic fiction. But the only contemporary eyewitness
account was written by Bradford: "1630--This year John
Billington the elder, one that came over with the first, was
arraigned, and both by grand and petty jury found guilty of
wilful murder, by plain and notorious evidence. And was for
the same accordingly executed. This, as it was the first
execution amongst them, so was it a matter of great sadness
unto them. They used all due means about his trial and took
the advice of Mr. Winthrop and other the ablest gentlemen in
Bay of the Massachusetts, that were then newly come over,
who concurred with them that he ought to die, and the land
to be purged from blood. He and some of his had been often
punished for miscarriages before, being one of the profanest
families amongst them; they came from London, and I know not
by what friends shuffled into their company. His fact was
that he waylaid a young man, one John Newcomen, about a
former quarrel and shot him with a gun, whereof he died."[1]

Tradition that the execution took place in September is
borne out by John Winthrop who wrote merely:
1630--"Billington executed at Plimouth for murdering one."
[9] Inasmuch as Winthrop arrived at Cape Ann 12 June 1630
and at "Mattachusetts" 17 June 1630, he was "lately come
over" that summer when consulted about the legality of the
trial.[10]

John Billington, Jr. died before his father, but the
widow Elinor and son Francis remained at Plymouth, retaining
John Billington's land, and acquiring new grants according
to their rights as original settlers. It is clear that John
Billington, Sr. had some friends, for in the land records
there is, under date of 14 Sept. 1638: "Memorand that
whereas Wllm Tench and John Carman (sic) did bequeath 2
acres of land unto John Billington, dec'd., now Ellinor
Billington his widow and Francis Billington his sonn sell
sd. land, two acres lying in the South side of the second
brook."[11] William Tench and John Cannon (surely the same
man as "Carman") came to Plymouth on the Fortune in November
1621 and were allotted two acres in the 1623 Land Division,
near Billington.[7] Evidently they died or left the colony
before the 1627 Division of Cattle, having named John
Billington their heir.

Elinor, often written "Ellen" or "Helen" by Bradford or by Plymouth court clerks, invariably was called "Ellinor" in her own and her son's land records. Ellinor Billington, widow, on 8 Jan. 1637/8 for "natural love I bear unto Francis Billington my natural son," conveyed to him all her land at Plain Dealing in New Plymouth, reserving enough of the land for her own use during her lifetime.[11] On 28 Aug. 1638 Ellinor Billington, widow, entered into a marriage contract with Gregory Armstrong; and by 21 Sept. 1638 Gregory Armstrong and Ellinor his now wife, with her son Francis Billington, sold land.[11]

On the last date at which Elinor is known to have been living, 2 March 1642/3, Francis Billington of Plymouth, planter, sold three lots of land at Plain Dealing within the township of Plymouth: provided that Ellinor the wife of Gregory Armstrong be allowed to occupy one of the three said lots during her lifetime.[11]

It has often been pointed out that almost all we know about the Billington Pilgrims was written by William Bradford, who obviously disliked and criticized the entire family from the beginning. The Billingtons were not in sympathy with the aims and tenets of the Plymouth church, but one wonders that they were not more cooperative with those in authority who struggled to establish and maintain such a fragile colony on the hostile New England shore. John Billington, however, stoutly supported individual independence and freedom of speech, raising the voice of opposition when he disagreed with the rule of government. He and his descendants surely contributed to that integral part of the American character!

References: 1. BRADFORD'S HIST (1952) pp. 75, 87-8, 156-7, 234, 442. 2. NEHGR 124:116-118, (1970). 3. GENEALOGIST'S MAGAZINE 17:327-329, 376-7; (1973). 4. IGI Recs, Parish records for Lincolnshire, England. 5. MOURT'S RELATION pp. 31,44,69-71. 6. PILGRIM READER pp. 124-5. 7. MD 1:151-2, 228. 8. PILGRIM READER p. 284. 9. NEW ENGLAND HIST p. 43. 10. MA PIONEERS p. 508 11. PLYMOUTH COLONY RECS 11:33-4; 12:28-9, 37, 93-4.

JOHN BILLINGTON

FIRST GENERATION

1 JOHN[1] BILLINGTON  b. England, perhaps Lincolnshire, ca.
1580,  d.  Plymouth,  in  Sept.  1630,  executed  for
murder.[1,2,]
     He  m.  in  England  by  1604  ELINOR _____, b. England,
perhaps  Lincolnshire,  ca.  1580,[1]  d.  aft.  2 March
1642/3.[3]   Although Bradford's History and Plymouth Colony
records often refer to  her as "Ellen" or "Helen,"  when she
and her son stated her name in their own deeds of 1638-1643,
it  is  invariably  written  "Ellinor."   She entered into a
marriage agreement 28 Aug. 1638,[4]  and m.  (2) bet. 14 and
21 Sept.  1638 Gregory Armstrong.[4]  He  d. Plymouth 5 Nov.
1650.[5]
     Although  Bradford  states  that  the  Billington  family
joined the Mayflower Company from  London,  there is evidence
that  they  were  originally  from  Lincolnshire.   In  1612
Francis  Longland,  gent.,  of  Lincolnshire named  Francis
Billington,  son of  John  Billington,  as  one of his  two heirs
in a lease of Crown land.[1,2,6]
     John Billington  and his  family received  three acres in
the 1623 Division  of Land at  Plymouth and in  May 1627 he,
his  wife  and  sons  John  and  Francis  were  named  in the
Division  of  Cattle.   In  1651  Bradford  wrote:  "John
Billington,  after  he had been here  ten years,  was executed
for  killing a man,  and his  eldest son died before him, but
his  second  son  is  alive  and  married  and  hath  eight
children."[2]

     Children (BILLINGTON) b. England, poss.  Lincolnshire:[1]

     i   JOHN[2] b.  ca.  1604;  d.  between  22  May  1627
         (Division  of  cattle  at  Plymouth)  and Sept.
         1630,  [7,2].   In  May  1621  as a boy he lost
         himself  in the woods  near Plymouth, was found
         and cared for by the  Cape Cod Indians, and was
         returned  to  Plymouth  by  a party of Pilgrims
         sent that June to bring him home.[2,8]
2    ii  FRANCIS b.  ca.  1606  or  1609:  In  1650  the
         Lincolnshire survey  of crown lands  determined
         that  Francis  Billington  of  New  England,  a
         secondary  lessee,  was  "aged  forty  years or
         thereabouts" in the previous year, thus  b. ca.
         1609.[1]   In  1674  Francis Billington deposed
         that he was aged 68.[9]

References:  1.  NEHGR  124:116-118,  (1970).  2. BRADFORD'S
          HIST (1952), pp 234,446.  3. PLYMOUTH COLONY
RECS  12:28-9,33-4,37-8,93-4.     4. PLYMOUTH   COLONY   RECS
12:33,37.    5. PLYMOUTH  COLONY   RECS 8:11.  6. GENEALOGIST'S
MAG 17:327-329,376-7.  7. MD 1:151,152.  8. MOURT'S RELATION
(1963), pp. 69-71.  9. MD 2:46.


                    SECOND GENERATION

   2  FRANCIS$^2$  BILLINGTON  (John$^1$)  b.  England,  prob. Lincolnshire, about  1606 to  1609, d.  Middleboro 3  Dec. 1684
"aged 80."[1]
   He m.  Plymouth __ July 1634, CHRISTIAN (PENN) EATON,[2]
b. England ca. 1607, d. Middleboro ca.  1684.[3]  She m. (1)
at Plymouth in 1624 or 1625, Pilgrim Francis  Eaton, by whom
she had three children, Rachel, Benjamin and another, living
in 1651, whose name is unknown.   Francis Eaton, b. England;
d. Plymouth between 25 Oct.  and 8 Nov. 1633.[4]   He  had m.
(1) in England, Sarah_____, b. England; d. Plymouth early in
1621; m. (2)  _____ _____; d. Plymouth ca. 1624.  Christian
Penn came to Plymouth on the ship Anne in 1623.[5].
   Francis Billington lived at Plymouth  until 1669, when he
moved to Middleboro and occupied land granted to him as  one
of the "First  Comers."[6]  He lived there  until his death,
except for a few years during King Philip's War when he fled
to Plymouth for  safety.[3]  On 18  April 1642 his  daughter
Elizabeth  was  apprenticed;[7]   and  14  January 1642/3 he
bound out  son Joseph, "aged  vi or vii"  and two daughters,
probably  Martha and Mary, one five  years old and the other
even  younger.[8]    Bradford  stated  in  1651 that Francis$^2$
Billington had eight children.[9]
   In his old age Francis was dependent on his son Isaac for
support  and  died  intestate.   No  probate  record appears,
although  son Isaac  petitioned the  probate court in 1703/4
for title  to all his  father's Middleboro lands, stating he
had  had sole  care of  his parents  in their old age.[3]   A
Plymouth County Court case of Sept. 1722, brought by Isaac's
daughter Desire$_4$ (Billington) Bonney and her husband, James,
shows that Francis Billington died intestate leaving issue
two sons and  five daughters, viz: sons  Joseph (eldest, who
inherited a double portion) and Isaac;  daughters Elizabeth,
Mary, Dorcas, Mercy and Martha, with a total of eight shares
in the  estate.[10]  A  1719 quitclaim  deed from  Francis's
grandson Francis Billington, (Family #12),  reading  "my
father  Francis and grandfather  (unnamed) Billington" seems
to  imply a  son Francis,  Jr.   But in the  absence of any
mention of  such a son in  contemporaneous Plymouth records,
coupled  with the  fact that  Francis$^4$'s  deed evidently
transferred the  shares of  Joseph Billington, we conclude
that the deed  contains a clerical error.  The original must

have read "my father Joseph and grandfather Francis
Billington."[11]   Indications are that the seven children
named in the Bonney suit and their progeny were the only
survivors of Francis[2] Billington.   A more detailed account
has been published.[12]

Children (BILLINGTON) prob. all b. Plymouth:

3     i   ELIZABETH[3]  b. 10 July 1635,[7]
4    ii   JOSEPH  b. in 1636 (bef. 2 Feb. 1636/7),[8,13]
5   iii   MARTHA  b. ca. 1638
6    iv   MARY  b. ca. 1640
7     v   ISAAC  b. ca. 1644
     vi   child, b.____; d.y.
    vii   REBECCA  b. 8 June 1648;[14]  evidently d.y.
8  viii   DORCAS  b. ca. 1650
9    ix   MERCY  prob. unnamed dau. b. 25 Feb. 1651/2,[15]

References: 1. MIDDLEBORO DEATHS, p. 20.  2. PLYMOUTH COLONY
RECS,   1:31.   3. Plymouth   Co.   PR,   File  #2001  (Isaac
Billington  petition,  1703/4).    4. MF  1:5.   5. MD 1:229.
6. Plymouth  Colony  LR  1:344;  3:129  (Francis Billington)
7. PLYMOUTH COLONY RECS 2:38.   8. PLYMOUTH TOWN RECS  1:12.
9. BRADFORD'S  HIST (1952), p.446.  10. PLYMOUTH CO CT RECS,
1686-1859,  5:145.  11. Plymouth  Co.  LR  14:255.   12. MQ
52:137-44;  & TG 3:231-2.   13. PLYMOUTH COLONY RECS 3:127.
14. MD 15:27.  15. MD 16:237.


                        THIRD GENERATION


3  ELIZABETH[3] BILLINGTON  (Francis[2], John[1]) b.  Plymouth 10
July  1635,[1]  living  at  Providence  RI 22  March 1709/10,
when she signed a deed.[2]
     She m. (1) Rehoboth 21 Sept. 1660 RICHARD BULLOCK,[3]  b.
ca. 1622 in England, d. Rehoboth bef. 22 Oct. 1667.[4,5]  He
m. (1) Rehoboth 4 Aug. 1647 Elizabeth Ingraham, who d. there
7 Jan. 1659 [1659/60].[3,4]    Children by his first marriage
were  Samuel  b.  1648,  Elizabeth  b.  1650,  Mary b. 1652,
Mehitable b. 1655, Abigail b. 1657 and Hopestill b. 1659.[3]
These children were not Billington descendants.
     Elizabeth m. (2)  Rehoboth 25 June  1673 ROBERT BEERE  or
BEERS,[3]   who was killed by  Indians 28 March 1676, during
King Philip's War.[3,4,6] The  marriage in Rehoboth is the
earliest record found for Robert Beere,  but he was probably
related to a family of the name at Newport RI.[4]
     She m. (3) ca.  1679 THOMAS PATEY/PATTE of  Providence RI,
who drowned  when he took  a  canoe on  the Seekonk River 19
Aug. 1695.[7]  There were no children by the third marriage.
     Elizabeth  was  bound  out  as  an  apprentice in 1642 at
Plymouth  before she  reached the  age of  7 years, and this

record states her birthday.[1]  On 13  Feb. 1663/4  Francis
Billington  conveyed  50  acres  of  land at Plymouth to his
daughter Elizabeth Bullock, his son-in-law [Richard] Bullock
and their  son Israel.[8]  This tract was  sold 31 Oct. 1695
by Elizabeth's son John Bullock, of Swansea.[9]

   Thrice  widowed, twice with small  children to rear, many
references  were  made  to  Elizabeth (Billington) (Bullock)
(Beers)  Patey in court records of  the estates of her three
husbands.  A  detailed account  has been  published.[4]  The
inventory  of  Richard Bullock's  estate  was taken 22 Nov.
1667, and a preliminary  division of real estate made 5 July
1670.  The final settlement of the property, to the children
of  both of Bullock's  marriages, was not  made until 5 June
1677.[5,10]  This was  soon after  the inventory  of Robert
Beere's estate was filed 24 May 1677.[11]  Both men lived in
Rehoboth, then part of Plymouth Colony.

   The inventory of the estate of Thomas Patey was presented
at Providence RI 24 Sept. 1695.  By 12 April 1698  the widow
Elizabeth  could not yet procure bondsmen for administration
and the case  was continued.  Four years later,  on 14 April
1702,  Elizabeth  Patey  laid  down  administration  of  her
husband Patey's  estate,  and  her  son  Benjamin Beere was
appointed in her stead.[7]

   On 1 Aug.  1707 Elizabeth Patte (Patey)  of Providence RI
joined her sisters Mary  Sabin, Dorcas May and  Mercy Martin
in  deeding land in Middleboro  inherited from their father,
Francis  Billington  to  their niece  Desire  Billington,
daughter  of  their  brother Isaac.[12]  Elizabeth "Peedy"
(Patey),  widow of Providence,  conveyed to her son  Benjamin
Beere  of  same,  "after  my  decease  a  parcel  of land in
Providence in  the Neck,  formerly belonging  to my  husband
Thomas Peedy,  deceased, and was  his homestead, 6  acres on
the west  side of the  Moshasuch River."  This  was dated 22
March 1709/10, the last record found for Elizabeth.[2]

   Children by first husband (BULLOCK)  b. Rehoboth:[3]

        i   ISRAEL[4] b. 15 July 1661; undoubtedly d. y.[8,9]
        ii  MARCY b. 13 March 1662/3; d. 19 May 1663
   10   iii JOHN  b. 19 May 1664
        iv  RICHARD    b.  15  March  1666/7;  on  the  1688
            Providence tax list, but no  further record has
            been found.

   Child by second husband (BEERE/BEERS), b. Rehoboth:[3]

   11    v  BENJAMIN  b. 6 June 1674

References:  1. PLYMOUTH COLONY RECS 2:38.  2.  Rhode Island
        Land Evidences, 3:27 (Elizabeth "Peedy" [Patey]
to Benjamin Beere).   3. REHOBOTH VR, pp. 67,563,800,806,897

898,900 (Death of Robert Beere miscopied "Robert Boone" in published VR). 4. TAG 39:65-73 (1963). 5. Plymouth Colony PR II:2:47; MD 17:28 (Richard Bullock). 6. EARLY REHOBOTH 3:17. 7. PROVIDENCE EARLY RECS 10:30,76; 11:103; 15:154; (Thomas Patey). 8. Plymouth Colony LR 3:122, (Francis Billington). 9. Plymouth Co. LR 5:75 (John Bullock). 10. PLYMOUTH COLONY RECS 5:27,45,50,123,233 (Richard Bullock). 11. Plymouth Colony PR IV:2:46 (Robert Beere). 12. Plymouth Co. LR 7:326 (Elizabeth Patte and Billington sisters to Desire Billington).


4  JOSEPH[3]  BILLINGTON (Francis[2], John[1])  b. prob. Plymouth in 1636, (bef. 2 Feb. 1636/7),[1]  d. prob. Block Island RI after 7 Jan. 1684/5, when he was granted land there,[2]  and before 1692, when his name no longer appears in the records.[3]

He m. New Shoreham,  Block Island, RI 16 Sept. 1672 GRACE _____,[4]  whose surname is unknown.  She was living on Block Island 13 Oct. 1680, one of two occasions on which she was brought before the court for theft.[5]

On 13 Jan. 1642/3 Joseph was apprenticed at Plymouth to John Cooke the younger until the age of 21 years, "(being now about vi or vii years old)." [1] Presumably he was 21 in 1657, the year he took the oath of fidelity to Plymouth Colony.[6]  Plymouth Colony Court Records contain many entries of Joseph Billington's name.[7]

As a child, he repeatedly ran away from his master to return to his parents; in July 1643 he and they were sternly admonished. He was at least a part-time sailor in 1656, but called "idle and negligent," had no occupation in June, 1657 and was ordered to "take honest employment" or the court would provide one for him. There is no record that his father gave him land at Plymouth, as he did for son Isaac and for daughters Elizabeth and Martha. Joseph was often sued for debt, fined, had his property attached, etc., the subject of numerous court complaints until March 1666/7 when he was fined 3s/4d for striking Jabez Howland. His fine remained unpaid in June, 1667 and he had probably left Plymouth Colony by that date.[7]  His name never again appears in records there during his lifetime. It is noteworthy that Joseph departed Plymouth Colony in 1667, two years before his father, Francis[2] Billington moved from Plymouth to Middleboro in 1669.

That Joseph was still living when his father, Francis[2], died in 1684 appears in the 1722 court suit brought by James and Desire (Billington) Bonney. [8] Undoubtedly this Joseph Billington was the man who appeared in New Shoreham, on Block Island, RI in 1670, when he witnessed a deed. New Shoreham records show that he lived there from 1670 to 1685: listed as freeman in 1678 and 1684, but not mentioned there

in 1692 or subsequently. He was often sued for debt, cited
for not attending town meetings and for failure to plant
corn.[2,3,9] The last record for him on Block Island was 7
Jan. 1684/5 when he petitioned for and was granted the
seven-year lease of a small piece of land to build a
house.[2] It is probable that he died soon thereafter. The
New Shoreham Town records contain no further mention of his
name.

Only one child, Mary, is recorded in Rhode Island for
Joseph[3] Billington.[4] The statements in the 1722 Plymouth
County court suit brought by James and Desire (Billington)
Bonney, for title to the land of all heirs of her
grandfather, show that Francis[2] Billington had just two
surviving sons: Joseph and Isaac Billington. A study of the
Bonneys' land transactions to support their claim indicates
that Francis[4] Billington of Plymouth conveyed the share of
Joseph[3] Billington. The deed reads "my father Francis, son
of my (unnamed) grandfather of Middleborough," but later
transactions show this must be a clerical error for "my
father Joseph, son of my grandfather Francis."[8,10] The
Bonneys acquired the inherited rights of Joseph Billington
from Francis, so he was apparently Joseph's son.[11]

The 1735 deposition of Elisha Billington, of South
Kingston RI, stating that he lived on Block Island as a
child in the 1690s, identifies him almost certainly as a son
of Joseph.[12] The surname Billington appears in early
Rhode Island records only with Joseph and his presumed son
Elisha, but absolute proof of relationship is as yet
lacking.

    Children (BILLINGTON), incomplete, prob. all b. New
Shoreham, Block Island RI:[4,10,11,12]

        i   MARY[4] b. Sept. 1674; nothing more known.
12     ii   FRANCIS b. ca. 1676
13    iii   ELISHA (very probably), b. ca. 1680

References:  1. PLYMOUTH TOWN RECS 1:12.  2. New Shoreham RI
         Town Recs  1:57,95,201, as  shown in  TG,
3:228-248 (1982).  3. NEHGR  105:162-182, (1951).  4. RI  VR
New Shoreham 4:23, as corrected in RIHS Collections 31:79-82
(1938);  Original records 1:45.  (Arnold  read 1690s, where
dates should be 1670s.)  5. New Shoreham RI Town  Recs 1:554
(see Ref. #2).  6. PLYMOUTH COLONY RECS 8:181.  7. PLYMOUTH
COLONY   RECS    2:58-9,   3:110,127,203;   4:69-70,137,140;
8:119-20.  8. PLYMOUTH CO CT RECS 5:145.  9. New Shoreham RI
Town  Recs  1:13,33,36,57,61,65-6,95,558  (see  Ref.  #2).
10. Plymouth  Co. LR 14:255 (Francis Billington). 11. MQ
52:137-44.  12. NEGHR 106:103-5 (1952).

5  MARTHA[3] BILLINGTON (Francis[2], John[1]), b. prob. Plymouth
ca. 1638, d. after 9 June 1704, when Philip Bump, husband of
her dau. Sarah, transferred to his mother (in-law) Martha
Crossman all his estate both personal and real in
Plainfield, CT.[1]
     She m. (1) Plymouth 10 Jan. 1660/1 SAMUEL EATON,[2] who
came with his parents Francis and Sarah Eaton on the
Mayflower. He was b. in England in 1620; d. Middleboro bef.
29 Oct. 1684.[3]   He m. (1) bef. 1646 Elizabeth _____, who
d. aft. 1652 and bef. 1661, when they lived in Duxbury.[4]
There were at least two unidentified married daughters by
the first wife, mentioned, but not named, in the division of
Samuel's estate.[3]
     Martha m. (2), after an ante-nuptial contract 7 Dec.
1687, ROBERT CROSSMAN [5] of Taunton, b. ca. 1621, d. bef.
27 Oct. 1692, (when the inventory of his estate was taken),
aged 71;[6] prob. son of John Crossman.[7]  He m. (1) Dedham
25 May 1652 Sarah Kingsbury,[7] by whom he had children:
Sarah, John, Mary, Robert, Joseph, Nathaniel, Eleazar,
Elizabeth, Samuel, Mercy, Thomas, and Susanna.[8] Martha had
no Crossman children.
     In a deed of 3 January 1663/4, Francis Billington of
Plymouth conveyed land in Plymouth to his son-in-law Samuel
Eaton, "my daughter Martha his wife," and their daughter
Sarah.[9] Philip Bump and wife Sarah (Eaton), on 4 Oct.
1694, sold Sarah's interest in this Plymouth land, given to
her and to her parents, by her grandfather Francis Billington.[10]   On 2 March 1722 son Samuel Eaton[4], of
Middleboro, sold to James Bonney of Pembroke, husband of his
cousin Desire (Billington) Bonney, "all my right, title and
interest of and unto all ye lands...divided and undivided
which did of right belong unto my Hon'd Mother Martha
Crossman, deceased, at ye time of her decease, lying and
being within ye township of Middleboro...."[11] This was
Martha's share of her father Francis Billington's estate.
     Samuel Eaton lived at Duxbury from 1646 until 17 Aug.
1669, when he sold all his lands there.[12]  He moved to
Middleboro, where his name appeared on a list of Freemen
dated 29 May 1670.[13]  The settlement of the estate of
Samuel Eaton of Middleboro 19 Oct. 1684 shows that the
eldest [son] was assigned the house and land after his
mother's decease; the daughter provided for by her
grandfather (Sarah) to have ten shillings; the two younger
children to have twenty shillings at age or marriage; "the
children of the first wife to have twenty shillings a Peece
& such of them as are Dead the sume to be payed amonge
theire Children;" and the widow to have the remainder.[3]

     Children (EATON) prob. b. Duxbury:[3,9,11,12]

14    i   SARAH[4]  b. ca. 1663  (bef. 3 Jan. 1663/4)
15    ii  SAMUEL    b. ca. 1664  (aft. 3 Jan. 1663/4)

16   iii  MERCY   b. ca. 1665
17   iv   BETHIAH  b. ca. 1668

References:  1. Plainfield  CT LR  1:17(Philip Bump).  2. MD
      17:183.   3. MD 2:172-3(Samuel Eaton estate).
4. PLYMOUTH  COLONY  RECS  3:18,12:100,144.  5. NEHGR 62:233
(1908)  6. NEHGR  63:139  (1909)  7. NYGBR  22:77-8 (1891)
(Crossman  Gen.).   8. VR   TAUNTON  1:109-12.  9. Plymouth
Colony  LR  3:47(Francis  Billington).   10. Plymouth Co. LR
1:187  (Philip &  Sarah  Bump).   11. Plymouth Co. LR 20:10
(Samuel  Eaton).   12. DUXBURY  RECS,  p.  22(Samuel Eaton).
13. PLYMOUTH  COLONY  RECS  5:279.   See also: MF 1:5,6,7,9.
(Eaton Family);  MF 1:51,52,53. (Samuel  Fuller  Family)  and
Addendum.


6  MARY[3] BILLINGTON  (Francis[2], John[1]),  b. prob. Plymouth
ca. 1640, d. aft. 28 June 1717 when she acknowledged a Rehoboth  deed selling property of  her deceased husband, Samuel
Sabin, with her son, Israel Sabin.[1]
    She m. Rehoboth 20  Jan. 1663/4 SAMUEL SABIN,[2]   b. ca.
1640, d. Rehoboth  23 Sept. 1699,[2]   son of William  Sabin
and  his  first  wife,  prob.  a  dau.  of Richard Wright of
Rehoboth.[3,4]   The  Sabin(e)  surname,  found  in  ancient
English records, does not  appear among the Huguenots, as is
often said.[5]
    The  family  lived  at  Rehoboth,  where  Samuel Sabin was
called  planter  and  miller.[6]  He  served in King Philip's
War, and in the Phips expedition  to Quebec in 1690.[3]  The
will  of  Samuel  Sabin  of  Rehoboth,  written 14 July 1690,
"called forth  to war against the  French," was presented 16
Oct. 1699. Mentioned in  it were his wife, sons Samuel and
Israel to have the real  estate, daus. Mercy and Sarah  each
to have three pounds, and the same sum to the  youngest dau.
at her marriage.  The son Samuel was named executor with his
mother, but in a lengthy written agreement, Samuel renounced
executorship  in  favor  of  administration  by  his brother
Israel and mother widow Mary Sabin.  The agreement described
property in  the estate inherited  from "grandfather William
Sabin," and land  purchased from "uncle John  Martin." John
Kingsley  was one of  the bondsmen in  the administration of
the estate.[7]
    On 1 Aug. 1707 Mary Sabin  of Rehoboth joined her sisters
Elizabeth Patte, Dorcas  May and Mercy Martin,  wife of John
Martin, in conveying their rights to the Middleboro  land of
their  deceased  father,  Francis  Billington, "for love" to
their  niece  Desire  Billington,  daughter of their brother
Isaac.[8]

    Children (SABIN) all b. Rehoboth:[9]

18      i   SAMUEL[4]  b. 27 Nov. 1664
19     ii   MERCY/MARCY  b. 8 March 1665/6
20    iii   SARAH  b. 10 Aug. 1667
21     iv   ISRAEL  b. 8 June 1673
        v   EXPERIENCE  b. 5 Oct. 1676; bur. 28 Nov. 1676
       vi   MARY b. 4 March 1678/9; living 14 July 1690. Some
            accounts state that this Mary Sabin m. Rehoboth
            8 Dec. 1696 Nathaniel Cooper.  It is much more
            likely that the bride was an aunt of this girl,
            her father's young half sister. Mary Sabin, b.
            8 Sept. 1675 to William Sabin and his second
            wife Martha Allen, was living just one week
            before the 1696 marriage.  Nothing has been
            found to show  that Mary Sabin, dau. of Samuel,
            survived beyond 1690 when mentioned, but not
            named, in her father's will.[3,10]

References:   1. Bristol  Co.  LR 12:300-301 (Israel Sabin et
              al).  2. REHOBOTH  VR pp. 331,  874.  3. NEHGR
36:52,53.    4. NEHGR  99:240  (1945).   5. NEHGR    101:264-9
(1947).  6. EARLY REHOBOTH, 3:159.  7. Bristol Co.  PR 2:7,8
and  Docket  (Samuel Sabin).   8. Plymouth Co.  LR 7:326
(Elizabeth  Patte et al  to Desire Billington). 9. REHOBOTH
VR, pp. 736,737.  10. NEHGR 63:228, 229].


7  ISAAC[3] BILLINGTON (Francis[2], John[1]), b. prob.  Plymouth
ca. 1644, d. Middleboro 11 Dec. 1709 in 66th yr.[1]
    He m. bef. 1675 HANNAH  GLASS,[2] b.  Plymouth 24 Dec.
1651,[3]  dau. of James  and Mary (Pontus) Glass.[4]  Hannah
d.  aft. 30 Aug.  1704,[4]  and bef.  9 Dec. 1709 when Isaac
deeded his land to his sons without providing for his
wife.[5]  On 30  Aug. 1704 Isaac Billington and wife Hannah,
joined in a deed with Joseph Bumpas  and wife Wybory, all of
Middleborough, and  Samuel Hunt and wife Mary of Duxbury, all
the women daus. of Mary Glass  alias Dilleno, deceased, dau.
of William Pontus, deceased.  All six grantors conveyed land
at Plymouth inherited from William Pontus.[4]
    Isaac lived at  Middleboro, then at  Marshfield 1675-1677
during  King Philip's War, but returned to Middleboro at the
urging of  his parents.  In a petition  dated 1 March 1703/4
Isaac and Hannah Billington described their seven years  of
caring for the aged  Francis and Christian, asking the court
to award  them all of Francis  Billington's landed estate in
Middleboro.[6]  This  request was  evidently denied,  for
Isaac's daughter Desire soon  began seeking quit claims  for
the  land  from all  her grandfather Billington's  other
heirs.[7]
    Near death,  on 9 Dec.  1709, Isaac deeded  his homestead
and 50 acres  at Middleborough to  his son Seth,  mentioning
other  land  given  to son  Isaac.[5]  The inventory of his

estate was taken 16 April 1712 and administration given to son Seth 21 June 1712.[8] The records of Seth's own estate provide proof of Isaac's children.

Children (BILLINGTON), b. prob. Marshfield and Middleboro:[9]

22    i   DESIRE[4] b. ca. 1675
23    ii  LYDIA b. ca. 1677
24    iii ELEANOR b. ca. 1683
25    iv  MARY b. ca. 1685
      v   SETH b. perhaps 1687; d. unmarried and without
          issue before 27 May 1718 when the inventory of
          his estate was presented. On 20 June 1718 his
          estate, administered by his brother-in-law
          Samuel Warren, was settled by agreement upon
          Warren, he to pay equal amounts to Seth's
          brother and sisters: Isaac Billington, Desire
          Bonney, to the children of Lydia Washburn
          deceased, to Eleanor Warren and Mary Wood.[9]
          The order in which the sisters are named was
          probably their order of birth.
26    vi  ISAAC b. ca. 1692/3

References: 1. MD 1:223; MIDDLEBORO DEATHS, p. 20, gives date 9 Dec. 1709. 2. MARSHFIELD BY RICHARDS 1:53. 3. MD 16:237. 4. Plymouth Co. LR 6:5 (Isaac Billington, wife Hannah, and Pontus heirs). 5. Plymouth Co. LR 7:314 (Isaac Billington to son Seth). 6. Plymouth Co. PR Docket #2001, (Petition of Isaac and Hannah Billington) 7. MQ 52:137-144. 8. Plymouth Co. PR 3:156 (Isaac Billington). 9. Plymouth Co. PR 4:100 (Seth Billington)


8 DORCAS[3] BILLINGTON (Francis[2], John[1]), b. perhaps ca. 1650, d. aft. 1 Aug. 1707, when as "Dorkes May" of Plymouth she joined three of her sisters in conveying "Middleborough land which did belong to our father Francis Billington," to their niece, Desire Billington.[1] If "Dorkaj Macy," who appears in the undated list of members of the Plympton Church between 31 May 1711 and 20 Feb. 1720/1, was Dorcas May, she was living until at least 1711.[2]

Dorcas m. aft. 29 March 1673 and undoubtedly bef. 20 May 1686, EDWARD MAY,[3,4] whose birth date and parentage are unknown. He d. Plymouth 10 Aug. 1691.[5] He m. (1) prob. bef. 13 Dec. 1670 Hannah King, dau. of Samuel King, Sr. and his wife Anna Finney. Edward May was granted 20 acres in Plymouth 13 Dec. 1670 and the tract was measured out to him 8 Feb. 1670/1, north of Samuel King, Sr. at Monponsett Meadow.[6]

Edward May's first marriage is established by the will of
widow Katheren (Finney) Fallowell of Plymouth dated 29 March
1673, naming her sister Anna Kinge, Anna's sons Samuel,
Joseph and Isaac Kinge and daughter Hannah May.[3] Anna's
brother, Robert Finney of Plymouth, in his will of 20 May
1686, named Charity May as a kinsman.[4] Charity thus was
certainly a child of Edward May's first marriage to Hannah
King, and apparently Hannah had died by 1686.

Dorcas Billington was fined five pounds and whipped for
committing fornication 7 June 1672, her partner seemingly
unknown to the authorities.[7]    Evidently Dorcas had an
illegitimate son. A Middleboro town meeting of 20 July 1683
agreed that "Goodman [Francis²] Billington being in present
want and for his relief they have left it to ye wisdom and
discretion of ye selectmen...also to ye disposing of his
daughter Dorcas her lad [i.e. Dorcas's lad] as they shall
see cause.[8]  Clearly this boy was not a son of Edward May
of Plymouth, whom Dorcas eventually married; but if born in
Middleboro, the illegitimate child would be the responsibi-
lity of that town.  The child's name, the identity of his
father, or what became of him are all unknown.

The inventory of Edward May's estate was taken 5 Oct.
1691, with administration given to widow Dorcas May on 16
March 1691/2. Distribution was made to the widow, to the
eldest son two-thirds of the real estate, to the other son
one-third, the two sons to pay each of the two daughters the
value of one-fifth or one share.[9]  None of the children
was named and there are no birth records.  Edward May of
Plymouth sold 8 acres [2/5 of 20 acres] of his father Edward
May's farm in Plymouth to John Curtis 12 May 1703.[10]  On 1
Dec. 1707 Israel May sold to Thomas Tomson one-fifth part of
a 20-acre lot in Plymouth that did belong to his father,
Edward May.[11]

    Child of Dorcas born out of wedlock:

    i   Son⁴, name unknown, b. prob. 1672, living at
        Middleboro in 1683.

Because Charity May was the only child of Hannah (King)
May named in the will of Robert Finney, possibly Edward
May's other children were by Dorcas Billington, but their
mother is not proven; Children (MAY):

   ?ii   EDWARD b. by 1680; he appears in several Plymouth
         Co. land records beginning in 1702, but no
         family has so far been found. He may well have
         been a son of the first wife.[10]
  ?iii   ISRAEL b. by 1686; of age when he sold land in
         1707. He had wife and children; lived in
         Plympton and Halifax.[11]
   ?iv   Daughter, whose identity is unknown.

References:  1. Plymouth  Co.  LR  7:326  (Elizabeth  Patte,
           Dorkes May, et al).  2. PLYMPTON BY WRIGHT,  p.
84.  3. Plymouth Colony PR 3:2:43, (Katheren Fallowell); see
also MA PIONEERS pp. 160-1.  4. Suffolk  Co.  PR, Old Series,
#1624,  (Robert  Finney);  also  MA  PIONEERS p. 166.  5. MD
16:62.  6. PLYMOUTH TOWN RECS 1:115,120.  7. PLYMOUTH COLONY
RECS 8:137.  8. MIDDLEBORO PROPRIETORS' RECS  (1858), p. 43.
9. MD 31:104; Plymouth Co.  PR 1:127 (Edward May).  10. Plymouth Co. LR 8:57 (Edward May).  11. Plymouth Co. LR 14:248;
MD 25:180 (Israel May).


9  MERCY[3]  BILLINGTON  (Francis[2],  John[1]),  probably  the
unnamed  daughter  of  Francis  and  Christian Billington, b.
Plymouth 25 Feb. 1651/2,[1]  d. Rehoboth 28 Sept. 1718.[2]
     Mercy  m.  Rehoboth  27  June  1681  JOHN MARTIN,[3]  bp.
Ottery St. Mary,  Devonshire,  England 20 Jan. 1652/3,[4]  d.
Rehoboth  28  Aug.  1720;[2]   son  of Richard and Elizabeth
(Salter) Martin.[4]   John m.  (2)  Rehoboth  28  May 1719
Abigail Read,[3]  who d. there 17  April 1721; widow of John
Martin, Sr.[2]
     John Martin  came to  Rehoboth from  England between 1660
and 1664 with his  father, Richard, who died in  1695.  John
inherited the  homestead and other property  in Rehoboth and
continued to reside  there.[5]  During King Philip's  War in
1676 John paid his father's tax and was himself a soldier in
that  conflict,  from  Rehoboth.   In  1740  his  son,  John
Martin[4], of Rehoboth was  awarded  bounty  land  for  his
father's service.[6]   John Martin,  son  of  Richard, was
always of Rehoboth, never of Swansea.[7,8]
     On 1 Aug. 1707  John and Mercy Martin of Rehoboth and her
sisters Elizabeth Patte, Dorcas May and  Mary Sabin conveyed
"for  love" to  their niece  Desire Billington,  daughter of
their brother Isaac, their  rights to the Middleboro land of
their father, Francis Billington, deceased.[9]
     The  inventory of  the estate  of  John  Martin, Sr. of
Rehoboth  was  taken  6  Sept.  1720,  and presented by John
Martin,  eldest son, who was  appointed administrator of the
estate 4  March 1722/3.[10]  In  a deed dated  29 July 1725,
acknowledged 11 March 1733/4  and  recorded  16 Oct. 1761
(sic),  the son  John  Martin[4] of Rehoboth, taylor, sold the
home lot  of  his  father  John Martin, deceased, to Jotham
Carpenter, husband of his sister Desire.[11]

     Children (MARTIN), all b. Rehoboth, [12]:

27    i  JOHN[4]  b. 10 June 1682
      ii ROBERT  b. 9 Sept. 1683; d. 16 Sept. 1705
28   iii DESIRE  b. 20 March 1684/5
      iv FRANCIS b. 7 May 1686; an incompetent person,  he
         was being cared for by the family in 1725.[13]

References:  1. MD   16:237.      2. REHOBOTH    VR,  p.  848.
3. REHOBOTH VR p. 239.      4. OTTERY ST. MARY CH,
1601-1837,  p.  283.   5.  NEHGR  63:79  (Richard  Martin).
6. KING PHILIP'S WAR, p. 427.  7. MQ 49:170-178.  8. MARTIN
GEN pp. 53-59, (which confuses the early  Martin families of
Swansea and  Rehoboth).  9. Plymouth Co. LR 7:326 (Elizabeth
Patte,  et al.  to Desire  Billington).  10. Bristol Co.  PR
4:166,167  (John Martin).  11. Bristol  Co.  LR 45:322 (John
Martin).  12. REHOBOTH VR, pp. 670, 848.  13. Bristol Co. PR
Files (John Martin).


FOURTH GENERATION


10  JOHN BULLOCK[4] (Elizabeth[3] Billington, Francis[2], John[1]),
b. Rehoboth 19 May 1664, d.  Barrington (then Massachusetts,
now  Rhode  Island)  20  June  1739,  in his 76th year; bur.
Little  Neck  Cemetery,  at  Bullock's  Point  Cove, then in
Rehoboth MA,  now  in Riverside, an  area of East  Providence
RI.[1]
    He m. Swansea 29 Jan. 1695 ELIZABETH BARNES,[2]  b. there
14 Feb.  1674/5,[2]  d. Barrington 20 July  1761 in her 87th
year;[3]    dau. of Thomas and  Prudence (Albee) Barnes.  She
is buried with her  husband in Little Neck Cemetery,  as are
most of their children.[1]   Thomas Barnes of Swanzey, in his
will dated 7 May  1705, named (among others) dau. Elizabeth
wife  of  John  "Bullick" at  Providence;  and John Bullock
receipted 7 Nov.  1706 for the  legacy of "my  Hon'rd father
Thomas Barnes of Swanzey."[4]
    John Bullock was of Swanzey 31 Oct. 1695 when he sold one
acre of meadow in Plymouth, given to him by his grandfather,
Francis  Billington;  and  the  same  day  sold  50 acres of
Plymouth property, also from grandfather Francis Billington,
evidently that conveyed to  John's parents and his  brother,
Israel, 13 Feb. 1663/4.[5]  John  was of Providence RI on 28
Dec. 1703 when he  sold 50 acres of land in Rehoboth.[6]  He
moved  to  Barrington from  Providence  between  1718  and
1724.[7]
    John Bullock  of Barrington, in his will written 10 March
1735/6,  probated  17 July 1739, named  wife Elizabeth; three
sons:  Israel, John and Richard Bullock who were to have the
real  property;  three  daus:  Elizabeth Bullock,  Prudence
Bullock  and  Mary  Bullock,  each  to  have  50 pounds; and
granddaughter Ann Brown to  have 20 pounds at her  full age.
The sons Israel, John and Richard were executors  with their
mother, Elizabeth.[8]

    Children (BULLOCK), b.  prob. Swansea and Providence, not
recorded but reconstructed from grave records and  from John
Bullock's will:[1,7,8]

29     i    ANN[5]  b. ca. 1697
30    ii    ELIZABETH  b. ca. 1699
     iii    ZERVIAH b. ca. 1700; d. 10 June 1718 in 18th yr.,
            unm.
      iv    ESTHER  b. ca. 1702; d. 3  Sep. 1728 in 26th yr.,
            unm.
31     v    ISRAEL  b. ca. 1704
      vi    PRUDENCE  b. ca.  1706; d.  10 July  1736 in 30th
            yr., unm.
32   vii    MARY b. ca.  1711
33  viii    JOHN  b. ca.  1714
34    ix    RICHARD  b. ca. 1718

References:  1. Little  Neck  Cem.    2. SWANSEA  VR Bk A pp.
            5,94.  3. RI VR: King's Church, now St.  John's
Church, Providence:  10:148.    4. Bristol  Co., PR 2:161-2;
3:208 (Thomas Barnes).  5. Plymouth Co. LR 4:93; 5:175 (John
Bullock).  6. Bristol Co.  LR 15:118 (John Bullock).  7. TAG
39:65-73.  8. Bristol Co. PR 9:231-2 (John Bullock).


11  [1]BENJAMIN BEERE/BEERS[4] (Elizabeth[3] Billington, Francis[2],
John[1]) b.  Rehoboth 6  June 1674,  d. Providence  RI 3  July
1714.[1,2,3]
     His  wife  was  RACHEL  PRATT, dau.  of  Daniel and Anna
(_____) Pratt, a descendant of Pilgrim Degory Priest.[4]   In
a record of administration of Benjamin Beere's estate 14 May
1715,  there  is  reference  to  "his wife Rachel also being
dead."[1,3]  Whether she died before or after her husband is
unknown.  Rachel's identity is established  in a series of
deeds involving her children, as will be shown.
     Benjamin lived  at Providence, his name spelled variously
Beere, Beers, Bears, etc.  He succeeded  his  mother as
administrator of the estate of his stepfather, Thomas Patey,
14 April 1702.  He was appointed  constable at Providence  7
June  1708.[3,5]   On  22  March  1709/10 Elizabeth "Peedy"
[Patey], widow of Thomas, deeded  Providence land to her son
Benjamin Beere.[6]
     Benjamin Beere  died  intestate.  The  inventory of his
moveable  estate was  taken 5  July 1714, and administration
given to his  [half] brother John  Bullock 14 May  1715.  In
1717 and 1719 the Providence Town Council ordered Bullock to
appear, questioned  his supervision of  the  Beere children,
and  assigned  the  real  property  to another  manager. The
estate records mention only two minor children, both of whom
were apprenticed to  other families: Charles Beers  by 1720,
and Benjamin Beers by  1721 when the latter was adjudged non
compos mentis.[1,3,5]  Charles Beers evidently inherited all
his father's  real property in Providence,[7] but deeds show
there were at least two other children.
     In  a  deed  dated  22 Oct.  1744,  Charles  Beers,  of
Providence, husbandman, with Patrick "Furrell"  [Farrell] of

--------------------------------------------------------

Newport, cooper, and his wife Rachel [Rachel (Beers)
Farrell], all of Rhode Island, sold one full ninth part of
the 300-acre farm of Phineas Pratt, who had died at
Charlestown [MA] in 1680. This ninth part of the estate had
been settled on Daniel Pratt, son and heir to Phineas; and
Charles Beers and Rachel "Furrell" are described as heirs of
said Daniel Pratt's part.[8]

     Children (BEERS), births not recorded but prob. b.
Providence RI; although only Benjamin and Charles were
mentioned in their father's estate records, two others
appear in family deeds:[3,4,5]

          i    JOB[5] b. ca. 1705; living 1719 at Providence, but
               evidently died before reaching maturity. On 10
               Sept. 1715 Anna Turpin, widow of William
               Turpin, "formerly Anna Pratt," (her first
               husband Daniel Pratt), deeded Providence land
               to her grandson Job Beers, to be his when he
               came of age. Anna (_____) (Pratt) Turpin was
               living in 1719 when she sold the land she had
               conveyed to grandson Job Beers, explaining it
               was unsuitable for his use. In this deed she
               stated her intention to use money from the sale
               to buy other land for Job, but there is no
               record that she did so.[4,9]
    35    ii   RACHEL b. ca. 1707,[3]
          iii  BENJAMIN b. ca. 1710; declared non compos mentis
               as a youth 16 Dec. 1721. He was living 18 Feb.
               1722/3, but evidently did not survive to
               maturity, the only later records being of his
               brother Charles and sister Rachel.[3]
    36    iv   CHARLES b. ca. 1712 (bef. 1714)

References: 1. PROVIDENCE EARLY RECS 6:162,169 (Benjamin
            Beere's estate and death date).   2. RI VR:
Providence 2:261.   3. TAG 39:65-73.   4. Providence RI LE
2:245, 429-430; 4:19-20 (Anna Pratt/Anna Turpin).   5.
PROVIDENCE EARLY RECS, Vol 12, passim.   6. RI LE 3:27;
(Elizabeth "Peedy" [Patey]).   7. Providence RI LE 10B:97
(Charles Bears).   8. NH Colony Deeds in Rockingham Co. NH
Deeds 37:80. (Charles Beers with Patrick and Rachel
"Furrell" [Farrell].)  9. RI GEN DICT, pp. 209-210.


12  FRANCIS[4] BILLINGTON (Joseph[3], Francis[2], John[1]), b.
perhaps Block Island RI ca. 1676, d. aft. 3 Dec. 1719 and
bef. 29 July 1724 when his wife Abigail was called "widow"
in church records.[1,2]
     He m. Plymouth 17 May 1702 ABIGAIL CHURCHILL,[3] b.
Plymouth ca. 1680, d. aft. 1726; dau. of Eleazer and Mary

(Bryant?) Churchill.[4] Abigail m. (2) Plymouth 25 Jan.
1725/6, Nathaniel Howland,[5,6] b. perhaps ca. 1670; d.
Plymouth 20 Dec. 1746, son of Joseph and Elizabeth
(Southworth) Howland.[7] He was a descendant of Pilgrim John
Howland. Nathaniel had m. (1) Plymouth 16 March 1696/7
Martha Cole,[6] who d. Plymouth 11 Aug. 1718.[7]
    Francis Billington served in the militia at Plymouth in
1699.[8] On 27 Jan. 1702/3 his wife Abigail was called
before the First Church of Plymouth and chastised for
fornication before marriage with her new husband Francis
Billington.[9]
    Francis was a mariner and fisherman. He perhaps followed
the sea from Rhode Island to Plymouth as a youth. He
frequently sailed in and out of Boston: Suffolk County
records show he was master of the sloops Fisher in 1711 and
the Mary in 1715. He was often sued for debt, had his house
attached, etc. The last Suffolk County record for Francis
was 28 July 1719, when he was arrested for debt.[10]
    By a deed dated 13 Jan. 1709/10, Francis Billington of
Plymouth, with wife Abigail, sold Plymouth land with a
dwelling house at Willingsley.[11] Two years later, on 8
Feb. 1711/2, Francis Billington of Plymouth, mariner, sold
Plymouth land "where I have built a dwelling house."[11]
    Finally, on 3 Dec. 1719, in the last record of this
Francis of Plymouth, he sold for five pounds to James Bonney
(husband of his cousin Desire Billington) "all my right,
title and interest in all ye lands both uplands, meadows and
swamps, divided and undivided which of right belong unto my
Honoured Father Francis Billington, deceased, and did of
right belong unto my Honoured [unnamed] Grandfather,
deceased, at ye time of his decease lying and being within
ye township of Middleborough, excepting such as they had
disposed of in their Life time by deeds."[1]
    There is evidence that the clerk's copy of the deed cited
above contains a clerical error and the original read "my
father Joseph" and "grandfather Francis Billington." The
original landholder at Middleboro was plainly the
grandfather, Francis Billington. In a 1722 court suit
brought by James and Desire (Billington) Bonney, grandfather
Francis was shown to have had only two surviving sons:
Joseph and Isaac.[12] No provision was made for the heirs
of a deceased son Francis, nor is there any record that such
a son existed. Subsequent deeds show that the Bonneys actually acquired the shares of Joseph Billington through the
Middleboro deed cited from this Francis[4] Billington.[1,13]


    Children (BILLINGTON) recorded Plymouth to "ffrances
(sic) and Abigail Billenton."[14] Children Sarah, Marcy,
Francis, Jemima and Content were baptized together at
Plymouth 17 June 1716:[15]

37      i   SARAH[5]  b. 11 Dec. 1702
38     ii   MARCY/MERCY  b. 1 Jan 1704 [1704/5]
      iii   FRANCES/FRANCIS (son), b.  16 Feb.  1708; living
            1716; nothing more known.
39     iv   JEMIMA  b. 12 June 1710
40      v   CONTENT  b. 2 Feb. 1712/3
       vi   ABIGAIL  b. 21 Oct. 1716; d. 14 Aug. 171_
      vii   JOSEPH  b. 11 Jan. 1718/9; nothing more known.

References:  1. Plymouth Co.  LR 14:255  (Francis Billington
            to James Bonney).  2. PLYMOUTH  CH RECS, 1:228.
3. MD  13:207.  4. TAG  36:8,9  (1960).  5. MD 14:71  6. MD
13:206; 27:41.   7. (PLYMOUTH) BURIAL HILL, BY DREW #650 and
#651 (Nathaniel & Martha  Howland).  8. PLYMOUTH TOWN HIST,
p. 75.   9. PLYMOUTH  CH  RECS,  1:196-7.    10. TG 3:228-248
(1982).  11. Plymouth Co.  LR 13:156,  9:181 (Francis Billington).   12. PLYMOUTH CO CT  RECS, 5:145 (Bonney).  13. MQ
52:133-40.  14. MD 13:33.  15. PLYMOUTH CH RECS, 1:214.


13  ELISHA[4] BILLINGTON (prob. Joseph[3], Francis[2], John[1])  b.
prob.  New Shoreham, Block  Island, RI perhaps  ca. 1680, d.
prob. South Kingstown RI bef. 13  April 1741 when his estate
was filed there.[1]
     He m. at an  unknown date JANE _____, who was living in
1741.   Her identity has not  been learned, but the frequent
use of  her  name  among  later  Rhode  Island  Billingtons
supports  the  belief  that  she  was  mother  of  Elisha's
children.[1]
     The  presumption  that  Elisha  was  a  son  of  Joseph[3]
Billington  hinges  on  a  court  deposition  given  at  South
Kingstown RI 18 Nov. 1735, Elisha stating that  "about three
or four  and forty  years ago  this deponent  lived at Block
Island  alias New Shoreham,...saw William Tosh and Penelope
Niles  joined  in  marriage...and  afterward lived with said
Tosh...."  Further testimony in the case showed  that Elisha
Billington "hath  bin  a  servant  to Mr. Niles this thirty
years...and  the influence Mr. Niles  hath over his being on
the least offence liable to be turned off his  land and hath
no other place to subsist on."[2]
     Elisha Billington, described as  a servant, owned no land
of  record.   Called  "husbandman  alias  laborer  of  South
Kingstown" Elisha was sued for debt  in Jan. 1734 and again
in  Jan. 1736.[3]   At South  Kingstown 13  April 1741 "Jane
Billington of  this town  appeared before  this Town Council
and  prayed to be granted  administration upon the estate of
Elisha Billington her husband, late  of this town deceased."
The widow, granted administration upon  the personal effects
of  the deceased,  posted bond  of 100  pounds with sureties
Joseph Billington and Thomas Parr.[1]  No heirs are named in
the account.

There are no birth records or other absolute proof of the children of Elisha Billington. But there can be little doubt that Joseph, bondsman in Elisha's estate, was a son; or that Daniel of East Greenwich RI and this same Joseph of South Kingstown, involved in buying and selling the same two lots of land in East Greenwich between 1742 and 1755,[4] and later living near each other in South Kingstown, were brothers.[5] The marriages of Sarah and Mary in South Kingstown at appropriate dates strongly suggest that they were daughters, for there is no evidence of any other Billington family in Rhode Island at this time.[6]

Children (BILLINGTON), highly probable but unproven; evidently b. South Kingstown RI:

41    i   DANIEL[5]  b. by 1713 or earlier
42    ii  JOSEPH  b. by 1716
43    iii SARAH  b. perhaps 1718
44    iv  MARY  b. perhaps 1720

References:  1. South Kingstown RI Town Council and Probate Records, 3:122-3.  2. NEHGR 106:103-5 (1952). 3. Washington Co. RI Court of Common Pleas, [LDS Film #937654] Bk A:143,231.  4. East Greenwich RI LE 6:151-3; 7:193,252-4, 258,259,294, 335 (Daniel and Mary Billington; Joseph and Abigail Billington).  5. NEHGR 127:129-30. 6. SOUTH KINGSTOWN RI MARRIAGES; pp. 9,10.


14  SARAH EATON[4] (Martha[3] Billington, Francis[2], John[1]) b. prob. Duxbury in 1663 (bef. 3 Jan. 1663/4); d. aft. Feb. 1725/6.[1]
     She m. ca. 1685 PHILIP BUMPUS (or BUMP), b. prob. Marshfield ca. 1648;[2] d. Plainfield CT 20 Jan. 1724;[3] son of Edward and Hannah (_____) "Bompasse."[4]
     In his first recorded deed, 1681, Philip was called "of Marshfield."[5] Shortly after their marriage, Philip and Sarah moved to Bristol (then Plymouth Colony, now RI), where he took the oath of fidelity 17 May 1685.[6] They moved to Middleboro in 1688, but returned to Bristol bef. April 1692. Philip was among the subscribers, on 13 Nov. 1699, who purchased land in Quinebaug [now Plainfield, CT]. He was still in Bristol in April 1702 when he bought about 300 acres of land in Plainfield, CT where he was living by Dec. 1702.[7]
     An agreement of heirs of Philip Bump of Plainfield, dated 24 Feb. 1725/6, included: Sarah Bump, widow; Samuel Bump of Bolton, CT; Philip Bump, Josiah Bump, Thomas Herd and wife Lydia, Peleg Ballard and wife Bethia, dau. Sarah Bump all of Plainfield; and Thomas Smith and wife Jemima of Preston, CT.[1]

Children (BUMP or BUMPUS), six recorded Bristol, others prob. b. there also:[8]

```
45     i   JEMIMA⁵ b. 7 Jan. 1686/7
46    ii   SAMUEL  b. 16 Feb. 1687/8
47   iii   PHILIP b. 13 Feb. 1689/90
48    iv   LYDIA  b. 2 April 1692
       v   MATTHEW    b.  8  June  1695;   d.  bef.  24  Feb.
           1725/6.[1]
49    vi   JOSIAH b. 9 April 1698
50   vii   BETHIA b. ca. 1700
    viii   SARAH b. ca. 1702; unm. in 1726,  she was called
           "Sarah Harris" in her  brother Josiah's will in
           1757. Her husband is unknown. A Stephen Harris
           with wife Sarah ____ was suggested,  but noth-
           ing was found to connect them to this family.
```

References: 1. Windham  CT Dist.  PR  1:2:117(Philip  Bump). 2. BUMPUS FAM, pp. 36-40. 3. CLS Barbour Index Plainfield 1:34.  4. PLYMOUTH  COL.  RECS 2:54,177; 3:70. 5. Plymouth  Colony  LR  5:28  (Bumpus).  6. Bristol Co. LR 5:160(Philip  Bump).   7. Plainfield CT LR  1:13(Fitch  to Bump). 8. RI VR Bristol pp.  66-7,100; and original Bristol VR in town vault,  1:21,45.  See also: MF 1:7-9  & Addendum, p.3; and TAG 23:228; 43:151.

15  SAMUEL EATON⁴ (Martha³ Billington, Francis², John¹) b. prob. Duxbury  ca. 1664 (aft. 3  Jan. 1663/4); d. Middleboro 8 March 1723/4 in his 61st yr.[1]
    He m.  Middleboro 24  May 1694  ELIZABETH FULLER,[2]   b. prob.  Plymouth ca. 1663 to 1666;[3]  d. before her husband. She was  dau.  of Samuel  Fuller, but whether  her mother was Fuller's first wife or second wife Elizabeth (Nichols) Bowen is unknown.[4]  In Oct. 1695 Samuel Eaton and wife Elizabeth with  other  "children  of Mr.  Samuel  Fuller"  signed an agreement with widow Elizabeth Fuller concerning the  Fuller estate.[5]  Elizabeth (Fuller) Eaton  was a granddaughter of Pilgrim Samuel Fuller.
    In  June  1724 Barnabas and  Elizabeth Eaton  filed an agreement for division of the estate of their father, Samuel Eaton,  "Whereby all  His Estate  falls unto  us by Right of Inheritance."[6]

Children (EATON) b. Middleboro:[7]

```
     i   MERCY⁵ b. 6 Dec. 1695; d. bef. 3 June 1724
    ii   KEZIAH b. 16  May 1700; d. 7 Feb. 1709/10 in 10th
         yr.[8]
```

51    iii   ELIZABETH  b. 26 July 1701
52    iv    BARNABAS  b. 12 April 1703

References:     1. MD 4:74.    2. MD 26:36,38.    3. MD 5:65-72
                (Samuel   Fuller    estate).    4. MD 39:85-7.
5. Plymouth  Co.  PR  1:223,246  (Samuel  Fuller).    6. MD
12:227-9(Samuel  Eaton estate).    7. MD 2:42.    8. MD 2:159.
See also MF 1:9, 51-3 and Addendum, p. 3.


16  MERCY EATON[4] (Martha[3] Billington, Francis[2], John[1]) b.
prob. Duxbury ca. 1665;  d. aft. 27 Feb. 1704, date her last
child was born.[1]
    She  m. Plymouth 7  Jan.  1685/6  SAMUEL FULLER,[2], b.
Plymouth ca.  1658; d.  Plympton 6 Sept. 1728  in his  70th
year.[3]   He  was  son  of  Samuel  Fulller  and his first
unknown wife,[4]   and grandson of  Samuel Fuller, Mayflower
passenger.
    Samuel Fuller  probably lived  in that  part of  Plymouth
that later became Plympton.  In July and August 1728 he made
deeds of gift of  his lands in Plympton and  Kingston to his
sons Nathaniel, Seth,  Ebenezer, Benjamin,  John, Jabez and
James.  On 15 Aug. 1728 he made a deed of  gift "to my two
daughters, viz: Elizabeth  Rayment and Mercy Rayment  of all
my   household   stuff...the   remainder   of   my personal
estate...to  be equally divided among  all my children, sons
and daughters...."[5]

    Children (FULLER), recorded Plymouth:[1]

53     i    NATHANIEL[5]  b. 14 Nov. 1687
       ii   SAMUEL  b.  30  Aug.  1689;  d. Plympton 18 April
            1728.[3]   His  estate  was  administered by his
            brother,  Nathaniel Fuller of  Plympton, 1 Dec.
            1728.[6]
       iii  WILLIAM  b. 14 Feb. 1691; d. 26 Aug. 1692
54     iv   SETH  b. 30 Aug. 1692
55     v    EBENEZER  b. 24 March 1695
56     vi   BENJAMIN  b. 7 March 1696
57     vii  ELIZABETH  b. 30 March 1697
58     viii JOHN  b. 19 Dec. 1698
59     ix   JABEZ b. "sometime in the beginning of June" 1701
60     x    MERCY  b. 3 Oct. 1702
61     xi   JAMES  b. 27 Feb. 1704

References: 1. MD 3:14.    2. MD 13:204.    3. VR PLYMPTON p.
480.  4. MD 5: 65-72(PR Samuel Fuller, father).  5. Plymouth
Co.  LR 23:111,  119;   24:55,116,131,178;   27:138;  28:122
(Samuel Fuller).   6. Plymouth  Co. PR 5:407 (Samuel  Fuller,
son). See also MF 1:53-4.

17  BETHIA EATON[4] (Martha[3] Billington, Francis[2], John[1]) b.
prob. Duxbury ca. 1666; d. bef. 12 Jan 1735/6, when she was
omitted from her husband's will.[1]
    She m. Taunton 5 Nov. 1691 JOSEPH BASSETT,[2]  b. Bridge-
water ca. 1664; d. there 8 Nov. 1736, son of Joseph and Mary
(Lapham) Bassett.[3,1]
    Joseph Bassett of Bridgewater, husbandman, in his will
dated 12 Jan. 1735/6 and proved 1736/7, named oldest dau.
Bethia Bassett; 2nd dau. Mehetabell Holloway living at Middleboro; 3rd dau. Lydia Phillips of Norton. The inventory
of Joseph Bassett's estate gives his death date.[1]

    Children (BASSETT) b. Bridgewater:[4]

62     i   BETHIA[5]  b. 25 Dec. 1693
63    ii   MEHITABLE  b. 22 June 1697
64   iii   LYDIA  b. 29 April 1703

References: 1. Plymouth Co. PR 7:265-6, 345(Joseph Bassett).
            2. VR TAUNTON 2:164.  3. BRIDGEWATER BY MITCHELL
p.111.  4. MD 15:46.  See also MF 1:9-10 and Addendum, p. 4.


18  SAMUEL SABIN[4] (Mary[3] Billington, Francis[2], John[1]) b.
Rehoboth 27 Nov. 1664, d. there 7 Oct. 1746.[1]
    He m. ca. 1695 GRACE ORMSBY, b. Rehoboth 27 Nov.
1669,[2]  d. there 13 April 1747;[1]  dau. of John and Grace
(Martin) Ormsby.  The will of John "Ormsbee" of Rehoboth,
dated 31 Oct. 1717, named one of his daughters Grace
Saben.[3]
    Samuel Sabin, a cordwainer, lived on inherited land
except for a small plot granted by the town of Rehoboth 17
Jan. 1698/9.  In a deed of 1719 he is called Samuel, Sr.,
but when he sold in 1724 his name appears without the
suffix, indicating his son Samuel, Jr. had come of age by
1719, but probably was dead by 1724.[4] On 18 May 1730
Samuel Sabin came before the Town Meeting of Rehoboth,
"informed them of his low circumstances and requested sum of
the money belonging to the poor of the town." From then on,
until their deaths, the town voted each year to expend
several pounds for the maintenance and medical treatment of
Samuel Sabin and his wife Grace.[5]
    In Rehoboth, at that time, such support payments were
regarded as a debt owed the town by the pauper's estate.[5]
Accordingly, in a deed after Samuel's death, his widow Grace
Sabin, with Experience Robinson, Mary Sabin and Patience
Sabin, children of Samuel Sabin, all of Rehoboth: "whereas
the town of Rehoboth on 17 Jan. 1698/9 by vote did give
Samuel Sabin 1/2 acre on the northeast side of Mill River,
on which Samuel Sabin built a house and in which he dwelt

until his death;  and whereas there might arise some dispute
that said land should descend to his heirs, considering what
the town has done  in providing for and maintaining  him for
divers past [years], do yield it up to said town...," dated
17 Feb. 1746/7.[6]  At this time Grace Sabin and her
daughter Patience had been living with another family for
five months at town expense, and the people of Rehoboth paid
for the funeral and  burial of widow Grace Sabin  two months
later.[5]  Understandably, there is no probate record.

        Children (SABIN)  b. Rehoboth:[7]

  65     i   ISAAC[5] b. 2 Feb. 1695/6
  66    ii   SAMUEL  b. 29 Aug. 1697
  67   iii   GRACE  b. 5 April 1699
  68    iv   EXPERIENCE    b.   22  May 1700
  69     v   PATIENCE    b.  3 Oct. 1704
        vi   EBENEZER  b. 15 Aug. 1705; d. __ Sept. 1705.
       vii   MERCY/MARY b. 19  Aug. 1706; living Rehoboth unm.
             1747.

References:  1. REHOBOTH VR p.  874.  2. REHOBOTH VR  p.693.
3. Bristol  Co.  PR  Files  (John Ormsbee), LDS
Film #577,919.  4. Bristol Co. LR 12:509-510; (Samuel Sabin,
Sr., 1719); 21:490  (Samuel Sabin, 1724).  5. Rehoboth Town
Meeting   Records,   LDS   Film  #562,561:   1:252,261,   281;
2:8,9,26,38,49,57,68,78,82,86  (Samuel  and  Grace   Sabin).
6. Bristol  Co. LR 36:39 (Grace  Sabin et al.).  7. REHOBOTH
VR p. 737.


19  MERCY/MARCY SABIN[4] (Mary[3] Billington, Francis[2], John[1])
b.  Rehoboth  8  March  1665/6,  d.  aft.  18 June 1728, undoubtedly in Connecticut.[1]
        She m.  Rehoboth 9 Nov.  1683 JAMES WELCH of Swansea,[2]
who d. Plainfield CT bef. 22 Nov. 1726, when  his estate was
filed.[1]  The  origin  of  this  James Welch* has not been
learned.
        This  family lived  in Swansea  until 1686/7, in Rehoboth
until  1701,  briefly  in  Bristol, MA (now  RI) and were in
Plainfield  CT by  1704.  The  births of  their children are
recorded variously in Swansea, Rehoboth, Bristol  and Plainfield, [3,4,5,6].
        On 8  and 9  March 1723/4  James Welch,  Sr. deeded  "for
love" to  sons John  Welch  and  Ebenezer  Welch,  land at
Plainfield.[7]  Administration on  the estate of James Welch
was  granted  to  eldest  son,  James  22  Nov. 1726.  The
inventory, taken  by Joshua Whitney, Philip  Bump and Joseph
Lawrence,  was recorded  10 Feb.  1726/7.  The  widow's third
was set  off to "Relick Marcy" 18 June  1728, and shares to

James, eldest son; Samuel, 2nd son; Thomas, 3rd son; and daus. Elizabeth Lawrence, Mercy Spaulding and Martha Welch, the others having had their portion.[1] A Voluntown CT deed of 18 June 1728 shows that James Welch of Voluntown, Thomas Welch of Windham, Thomas Spaulding and wife Mercy of Plainfield, Daniel Lawrence and wife Elizabeth of Killingly, and Martha Welch of Plainfield CT conveyed "for love to our brother Samuel Welch of Voluntown, 100 acres where said Samuel now lives, being land of which our father James Welch died seized."[8]

Children (WELCH):[3,4,5,6]

|       | i    | JOHN[5] b. Swansea 25 June 1685; d. 14 Aug 1685 |
|-------|------|------|
| 70    | ii   | ELIZABETH b. Rehoboth 27 Sept. 1688 |
| 71    | iii  | MERCY b. Rehoboth 1 March 1689/90 |
| 72    | iv   | JAMES b. Rehoboth 27 July 1692 |
| 73    | v    | SAMUEL b. Rehoboth (also rec. Bristol) 15 Oct. 1693 |
| 74    | vi   | THOMAS b. Rehoboth (also rec. Bristol) 1 March 1694/5 |
| 75    | vii  | EBENEZER b. Bristol 13 Feb. 1697; d. without issue; his 1759 will named all his brothers and sisters.[9] |
| 76    | viii | JOHN b. Bristol 17 April 1699 |
|       | ix   | MARTHA b. Plainfield 25 Oct. 1704; living 1759 when mentioned in brother Ebenezer's will; unm. in 1728; said to have m. Joseph Robson or Robinson, but no record found. |

*Note: This James Welch was not the soldier of King Philip's War, awarded bounty land at Voluntown CT, with a son James who lived and died at Colchester, CT. The two entirely different families with the same names have often been confused.

References: 1. Windham CT Dist. PR 1:pt.1:141,154,156; pt. 2:88 (James Welch). 2. REHOBOTH VR p. 381. 3. SWANSEA VR, Bk. A, 24-27. 4. REHOBOTH VR, p. 767. 5. RI VR: Bristol: 6:111. 6. CSL Barbour Index, Plainfield. 7. Plainfield CT LR 1:113 [2 deeds] (James Welch, Sr.). 8. Voluntown CT LR A1:388 (James Welch et al). 9. Plainfield CT Dist. PR 3:249,251,253,268,287 and CSL PR File #2206 (Ebenezer Welch).

20 SARAH SABIN[4] (Mary[3] Billington, Francis[2], John[1]) b. Rehoboth 10 Aug. 1667, d. Windham CT 9 March 1709.[1]
    She m. Rehoboth 1 July 1686 JOHN KINGSLEY,[2] b. Rehoboth 6 May 1665,[3] d. Windham CT 17 March 1732/3, aged

about 68;[1] son of Eldad and Mehitable (Mowry) Kingsley.
He m. (2) Mansfield CT 11 March 1712 Elizabeth Storrs,[4] by
whom he had Ebenezer Kingsley, b. Windham 5 April 1714, d.
there 22 July 1714; and Lydia Kingsley, b. 20 July 1717,[1]
not Billington descendants.

John Kingsley moved to Windham CT from Rehoboth by 1704.
He conveyed land "for love" to sons John and Ezra 10 May
1720. Eldad Kingsley deeded to brother Ezra 18 June
1733.[5]

John Kingsley, in his will dated Windham 17 March 1733,
probated 10 April 1733, named wife Elizabeth executrix; gave
sons Josiah and Amos the homestead, son John his gun and
sword, son Ezra his carpenter tools and named son Eldad.
Dau. Tabitha Broughton received his cattle. His
grandchildren, children of dau. Sarah Hix, deceased, were to
have a mare. Bequests were made to daus. Lydia and
Elizabeth Kingsley, singlewomen. All of the named children
and John Broughton signed an agreement that widow Elizabeth
should have all the moveables in the estate except those
specifically bequeathed to others, dated 13 Aug. 1733.[6].

    Children (KINGSLEY), b. to Sarah, first eight b.
Rehoboth, last two b. Windham CT:[3,1]

|      | i    | MARY[5] b. 1 March 1686 [1686/7];d. Windham, CT 7 March 1706 |
|------|------|-------------------------------------------------------------|
| 77   | ii   | TABITHA b. 23 Sept. 1688                                     |
| 78   | iii  | SARAH b. 9 Oct. 1690                                         |
|      | iv   | ELIZABETH b. 29 Dec. 1692; d. unm. very aged.               |
| 79   | v    | JOHN b. 26 Feb. 1694                                         |
| 80   | vi   | JOSIAH (twin) b. 18 Jan. 1696/7                             |
| 81   | vii  | AMOS (twin) b. 18 Jan. 1696/7                               |
| 82   | viii | EZRA b. 10 Dec. 1698                                        |
|      | ix   | ELIPHALET b. 2 Feb. 1704; d. 9 May 1721                     |
| 83   | x    | ELDAD b. 8 Jan. 1707                                        |

References: 1. CSL Barbour Index, Windham. 2. REHOBOTH VR
            p. 331. 3. REHOBOTH VR p. 661. 4. CLS Barbour
Index, Mansfield. 5. Windham CT LR E:413; G:248 (Kingsley
deeds). 6. Windham CT District PR 1:465-7; 2:86,87 (John
Kingsley).


21 ISRAEL SABIN[4] (Mary[3] Billington, Francis[2], John[1]) b.
Rehoboth 8 June 1673, d. aft. 25 March 1718, then living in
Barrington, (then Massachusetts, now Rhode Island).[1]
    He m.(1) Rehoboth 20 May 1696 MARY ORMSBY,[2] b.
Rehoboth 4 Apr. 1677,[3] d. Swansea 8 Dec. 1715;[4] dau.

of John and Grace (Martin) Ormsby. In his will of 31 Oct.
1717, John Ormsbee bequeathed some household furnishings to
"two oldest daughters of Israel Sabin, the share that would
have been my daughter Mary's part or portion."[5]
    Israel m. (2) Swansea 29 Jan. 1716 ELIZABETH WILLIAMS,
who has not been identified.[4]
    Israel Sabin lived in Rehoboth continuing the family
trade as miller until he and his mother sold their share of
the mill and homestead in 1700.[6] Styled husbandman or
yeoman in later deeds, he moved to Swansea ca. 1712. He,
"of Swanzey" on 7 May 1717, with wife Elizabeth and mother
Mary Sabin sold Rehoboth land that had been part of the
estate of Samuel Sabin, Sr.[7] In the last record found,
Israel Sabin was of Barrington 25 March 1718 when he sold
his rights of commonage in Rehoboth.[1] It is probable that
he died soon afterward, for his children scattered at an
early age. No probate record in Bristol County has been
discovered.

    Children (SABIN) all by wife Mary, first ten b. Rehoboth,
last two b. Swansea:[8,4]

|    |      |                                                      |
|----|------|------------------------------------------------------|
|    | i    | SARAH[5] b. 26 March 1697; living 31 Oct. 1717, when mentioned but not named in her grandfather Ormsby's will. |
|    | ii   | ELIZABETH* b. 31 March 1698; living 31 Oct. 1717.    |
| 84 | iii  | SAMUEL b. 21 Jan. 1699/1700                           |
|    | iv   | ISRAEL b. 8 Oct. 1701; with brothers Samuel and Jeremiah, he went to Maine where he and Samuel served in the militia 1724-5 during an Indian war.[9] On 23 Oct. 1729 Israel Sabin, fisherman, of the town of York [ME] gave a power of attorney to "my loving friend Edward Carpenter, glazier, of Falmouth, York Co.," [ME] recorded in Bristol County [MA] 14 Jan. 1729/30.[10] No further record has been found. |
| 85 | v    | JEREMIAH b. 26 Aug. 1703                              |
| 86 | vi   | JOSIAH b. 3 June 1705                                 |
| 87 | vii  | MARGARET b. 5 Feb. 1706/7                             |
| 88 | viii | WILLIAM b. 14 Oct. 1708                               |
|    | ix   | ELEAZER b. 21 Feb. 1709/10; d.y.                      |
| 89 | x    | MARY b. 1 June 1711                                   |
| 90 | xi   | ELEAZER b. 21 July 1713                               |
|    | xii  | MARTHA b. 30 Nov. 1715; d. 29 Nov. 1715(sic) See **[4]. |

*Note: No evidence was found to identify this Elizabeth as
the wife of Peter Robinson of Rehoboth, as suggested by some
descendants.

References:  1. Bristol  Co.  LR  16:77  (Israel  Sabin).
2. REHOBOTH VR p. 331.  3. REHOBOTH VR  p. 693.
4. Swansea  Original  VR,  Bk  B,  p. 138/257 (LDS Microfilm
#903,395)  **The  death  record  of  the infant Martha Sabin
follows that of her mother on the same page.  5. Bristol Co.
PR  Files (John  Ormsbee).  6. EARLY  REHOBOTH  3:171.
7. Bristol  Co.  LR  12:300-301.  8. REHOBOTH  VR p.  737.
9. EARLY  REHOBOTH  2:97;  and  MASS SOLDIERS 1723-1743, pp.
217-8.  10. Bristol Co. LR 19:140.


22  DESIRE[4]  BILLINGTON (Isaac[3],  Francis[2], John[1]) b.  prob.
Marshfield or Middleboro ca. 1675, d. aft. 25 June  1730 and
bef. 30 Dec. 1736.[1]
    Between  1714 and 1718 she m.  JAMES BONNEY, b.  ca. 1672,
d. Pembroke 24 Jan. 1723/4, aged 52; son of Thomas and  Mary
(Hunt?)  Bonney.  He  m.  (1)  Duxbury 12 June 1695 Abigail
Bishop, who d.  Pembroke 12 April 1714.  By Abigail,  James
had Elisha, Sarah, Abigail,  David, Ebenezer, Elijah, James,
Job and  Abiah.  The  widow's dower  in the  estate of James
Bonney was set off to Desire Bonney 20 May 1725.[2]
    Desire m.  (2) Middleboro 5 March  1729/30 Deacon THOMAS
PRATT  of  Easton,  in  a  double  ceremony with her brother,
Isaac Billington.[3]  Thomas  Pratt  d.  Easton  1 Dec.
1744.[4]  He  had  m.  (1) Deborah _____, mother  of  his
children.
    As Desire Billington,  on 1 Aug. 1707  she obtained, by a
deed from four of  her Billington aunts, all their  claim to
land  in Middleboro  in the  estate of  their father Francis
Billington.[5]  In Sept.  1722, Desire  and husband James
Bonney, having bought the rights of two other heirs, sued in
Plymouth County  court for title  to  the Middleboro property
of Desire's grandfather Francis[2] Billington.  His heirs were
thus established  as two  sons: Joseph  and Isaac;  and five
daughters: Elizabeth, Martha, Mary, Dorcas and Mercy.[6,7]
    There is no evidence that Desire had issue from either of
her marriages.

References:  1. TG 3:238.  2. NEHGR  89:220-223; see also MD
8:232 and  VR PEMBROKE.  3. MD 8:250  4. EASTON
HIST p. 46.  5. Plymouth Co. LR 7:326 (Elizabeth Patte et al
to Desire Billington) 6. PLYMOUTH  CO CT RECS 5:145.  7. MQ
52:133-140.


23  LYDIA[4]  BILLINGTON  (Isaac[3],  Francis[2], John[1]) b. ca.
1677, d. Plymouth 22 or 23 Sept. 1716, in childbirth.[1,12*]
    She m. ca. 1698 JOHN  WASHBURN, b. ca. 1672, d. Kingston
17 or  27 June  1750 in  his 79th  year; son  of Philip and

Elizabeth (Irish) Washburn.[2]  He was not a descendant of a
Mayflower  Pilgrim.[3]    He  m.   (2)   ca. 1717 Wybra/Wiborah
Bumpus,[4]  b. Plymouth 15 May  1672;[5]  d. Kingston 6 Feb.
1743/4 in her 72nd year, dau. of Joseph and Wiborah  (Glass)
Bumpus.[6]   He m.   (3)  Plympton 13  June or 13 Dec. 1744
Mehitable (Barrow) Wright, dau. of Robert  and Ruth (Bonum)
Barrow of Plympton  and widow of Adam  Wright.[7]   There was
no issue by the second or third wife.

     John  Washburn lived at Plymouth,  then at Kingston where
he was deacon of the church.  After the death of his  second
wife,  on  20  March  1743/4,  in  two  separate deeds, John
Washburn of Kingston conveyed all his property "for love" to
his sons  Ephraim Washburn and Barnabas  Washburn.  This was
followed  4 April 1744  by a deed  from Ephraim and Barnabas
Washburn  to  John  Washburn,  leasing  to  their father his
homestead and adjacent property for his natural life.[8] His
estate  being thus disposed  of in his  old age, there is no
probate for John Washburn.

     Because Lydia (Billington) Washburn's  children inherited
her part of the estate  of her brother, Seth Billington, who
died in 1718, there were guardianships 22 Sept. 1721 for the
children of  John  Washburn.   Ichabod, Elisha, Ephraim and
Barnabas  Washburn, minors over  the age of  14 years, chose
Francis  Adams, clothier of Plymouth,  guardian.  Adams was
also appointed the same day for Jabez, Ebenezer and Thankful
Washburn,  minors under age  14.  Presumably, John Washburn,
Jr. aged  22 and Mercy  Washburn aged 19  were considered of
age,  having  attained  their  majorities  at ages 21 and 18
respectively.[9]

     Children  (WASHBURN),  b.  Plymouth,  first  seven bp. 27
March 1709: [10,11]

91     i    JOHN[5]  b. 19 April 1699
92     ii   ICHABOD  b. 7 Feb. 1700/1
93     iii  MERCY/MARSEY  b. 21 April 1702
94     iv   ELISHA  b. 5 Nov. 1703
95     v    EPHRAIM  b. 6 June 1705
96     vi   BARNABAS  b. 12 Feb. 1706/7
97     vii  JABEZ  b. 10 April 1708
98     viii EBEN/EBENEZER  b. 18 Aug. 1709
99     ix   THANKFUL  b. 24 Feb. 1714/5
       x    Child stillborn in Sept. 1716 [12]

References: 1. PLYMOUTH CH  RECS 1:215.  2.  VR KINGSTON p.
            390 and  MD  7:223.   3. TG 3:238; corrected TG
4:202-3.  4. TAG 43:71.  5. MD 18:69.  6. VR KINGSTON p. 391
and  MD 7:223.   7. GEN ADVERTISER 3:22,51;  MF3  p. 14; MD
4:239-40;  11:242-7;  TAG 59:167.   8.    Plymouth  Co.  LR
36:160,161,162 (John, Ephraim, Barnabas Washburn).   9. Plymouth Co.  PR  4:288-291 (Guardianships  of Washburn chil-

dren). 10. MD 2:165. 11. PLYMOUTH CH RECS 1:209. *12. MD
16:85: "Desre wife of John Woshbon d. 23 Sept. 1716 being
delevered of a child both deceased," in Plymouth VR.
Evidently Lydia (Billington) Washburn's name was confused
with that of her sister Desire Billington. The date of
death differs by one day with the church record, and no
Desire Washburn is to be found.


24  ELEANOR[4]  BILLINGTON (Isaac[3], Francis[2], John[1]) b. ca.
1683, d. aft. 3 Aug. 1752, when distribution of her
husband's estate was made.[1]
    She m. Middleboro 26 Jan. 1703/4 SAMUEL WARREN,[2] b.
Plymouth 7 March 1682/3,[3] d. Middleboro bef. 4 Feb. 1750,
when administration on his estate was granted.[1] He was a
son of Richard and Sarah (Torrey) Warren and a descendant of
Pilgrim Richard Warren.[4,5]
    Samuel Warren was administrator of the estate of his
brother-in-law Seth Billington in 1718.[6] On 4 Feb. 1750
administration of the estate of Samuel Warren of Middleboro
was granted to his son, Samuel Warren. The inventory was
filed 21 Feb. 1750, containing an account of the value of
property already given by Samuel Warren to each of his
children. Distribution of the remaining estate was ordered
3 Aug. 1752 to the widow, to sons Samuel, James, Nathan,
Josiah, Benjamin and the heirs of Cornelius Warren; to daus.
Priscilla Warren, Joanna Barlow and Sarah Reed.[1]

    Children (WARREN), b. Middleboro:[7]

        i    PRISCILLA[5] b. 12 Dec. 1704; living unm. 1752
        ii   JABEZ  b. 3 Feb. 1705/6; d. 10 May 1717 in 12th
             year.[8]
100     iii  SAMUEL  b. 9 Aug. 1707
101     iv   CORNELIUS  b. 12 June 1709
102     v    JAMES  b. 24 Feb. 1710/11
103     vi   NATHAN  b. 5 March 1712/13
        vii  JOSEPH  b. 21 Feb. 1714/15; d. 22 July 1732
104     viii JOANNA  b. 25 March 1717
105     ix   BENJAMIN  b. 30 July 1720
106     x    SARAH  b. 9 Feb. 1721/2
107     xi   JOSIAH  b. 9 May 1724

References:  1. MD 21:104-6 (Samuel[4] Warren's Estate) 2. MD
             2:43.  3. MD 21:111.  4. MD 21:76.  5. NEHGR
55:165-6.  6. Plymouth Co. PR 4:100 (Seth Billington).
7. MD 2:104,105,201; 3:84,86,234; 4:68; 6:226.  8. MD
2:160.

25  MARY[4] BILLINGTON (Isaac[3], Francis[2], John[1]) b. ca. 1685,
d. Middleboro 30 May 1733 in her 48th year.[1]
    She m. Middleboro 13 Feb. 1711/2  ELNATHAN WOOD,[2]  b.
Middleboro 14 April 1686,[3]  d. there  20 April 1752  aged
66 years,  13 days;[1]   son  of  Abiel  and  Abijah (Bowen)
Wood.  Elnathan  Wood  m.  (2)  Middleboro  23  April  1735
Patience (Holmes) Cushman,[4]   b.  Plymouth  3  Nov. 1690,[5]
d. Middleboro  8 Sept. 1755, in 65th  year;[1]   dau. of John
and Sarah Holmes and widow of Ichabod Cushman.  There was no
issue by the second marriage.
    Elnathan  Wood  of  Middleborough,  yeoman,  in  his will
written  1  April  1752,  probated  15  May 1752, named wife
Patience; son Ephraim Wood and his son, my grandson Elnathan
Wood, under 21;  five daughters: Jemima Ellis, Jedidah Eddy,
Mary Conant,  Lydia Tomson, and Judah  Washbourne.  Mentioned
were  sons-in-law Jonathan  Washbourne  and  John Tomson, the
latter appointed executor.[6]

    Children (WOOD), b. Middleboro:[7]

108      i    JEMIMA[5]  b. 21 July 1712
109      ii   JEDIDAH  b. 27 March 1715
110      iii  EPHRAIM  b. 8 May 1716
111      iv   MARY  b. 5 Oct. 1719
112      v    LYDIA  b. 1 July 1722
113      vi   JUDAH  b. 11 April 1728

References:   1. MIDDLEBORO  DEATHS  p.232.   2. MD  2:158.
              3. MD 2:106.   4. GEN ADVERTISER  1:112.   5. MD
5:56.   6. Plymouth  Co.  PR  13:34  (Elnathan Wood).   7. MD
4:68; 7:242.


26  ISAAC[4]  BILLINGTON  (Isaac[3],  Francis[2],  John[1])  b.
Middleboro  ca. 1692/3,  d. there  19 June  1779 in his 87th
year.[1]
    He  m. Middleboro 5  March 1729/30 MARY DONHAM/DUNHAM,[2]
b.  ca.  1706,  d.  Middleboro  24  July  1777  in  her 72nd
year.[1]   She may  have been  a dau.  of Nathaniel and Mary
(Tilson) Donham of Plymouth:  in  1750 she petitioned the
Bristol  County  judge  of  probate  to  appoint "my brother
Nathaniel Donham" administrator of the estate of "my son Job
Eddy,"  deceased.  Job, apparently  an illegitimate son born
before  her  marriage  to  Isaac  Billington, was of Norton.
[3,4,5,6]
    Isaac Billington lived at Middleboro.  On 17 June 1752 he
bought from  Lemuel Donham part  of the 7th  lot in the last
allotment of  hundred acre lots  in the 26 Men's Purchase  in
Middleboro,  the  deed  witnessed  by  Joseph  Warren  and

Nathaniel Billington, his son.  Later, a deed of 13 May 1777
shows that  Seth Billington of Middleboro  sold to Nathaniel
Billington of same [both sons of Isaac] part  of the 6th and
part of the 7th lot in the hundred acre lots in the 26 Men's
Purchase, probably part of the land conveyed in the previous
deed.[7]  We have found no probate  record for  Isaac
Billington.

    Children (BILLINGTON) b. Middleboro:

     i  ISAAC[5]  b.  14  Feb.  1730/1;[8]  nothing further
        known.
114  ii  NATHANIEL  b. 7 Feb. 1732/3;[9]
115  iii SETH  b. 11 May 1735;[10]
116  iv  ICHABOD  b. 23 May 1737;[11]
117  v   MARY  bp. 3 Oct. 1739;[12]

References:  1. MIDDLEBORO  DEATHS  p.  20.   2. MD  8:250.
             3. Bristol Co.  PR  Files (Job Eddy);   4. EDDY
GEN p. 1222.  5. TAG 30:15. 6. TG 3:239.  7. Plymouth Co. LR
59:27; 67:130  (Isaac, Seth,  Nathaniel Billington).   8. MD
9:48.    9. MD   12:131.    10. MD   13:3.    11. MD  8:249.
12. Middleboro 1st Cong. Ch Recs, p. 34.


27 JOHN MARTIN[4]  (Mercy[3] Billington,  Francis[2], John[1])  b.
Rehoboth 10 June 1682, d. there 3 Nov. 1759.[1]
    He m.  (1) Rehoboth 17 July  1710 SARAH WILLMARTH,[2]  b.
Rehoboth 21  Dec. 1682,[3]  d. there 27 March 1728;[1]  dau.
of John and Ruth (Kendrick) Willmarth.
    He  m. (2) int. Rehoboth and Attleboro 13 June 1730,[4,5]
ELIZABETH (_____) FULLER, b._____, d. bef. 28 July 1760,
when her  son Samuel Fuller  of Attleboro  was appointed
administrator of her estate.[6]   She was the widow  of John
Fuller, Jr. of Attleboro who  d. 21 April 1724.[5]  Fuller's
estate was  divided 15  Jan. 1730/1 among "his  Late Widdow
Elizebeth  Martin," their Fuller children Samuel, Mary, John
and Elizebeth and married dau. Hannah Healey.[7]
    John  Martin of  Rehoboth, taylor,  in his  will dated 31
March 1758,  probated 10 Nov. 1759,  provided wife Elizabeth
with her  thirds and the use of the home and land.  Son Amos
received half the land in Attleboro, son Gideon four pounds;
the  heirs of son Timothy,  deceased, viz: Timothy, Abel and
Sarah, were to have two shillings each, their  father having
had his share.  Son Robert was named executor and  residuary
heir.[8]

    Children (MARTIN), b. Rehoboth, first four by wife Sarah,
and probably the fifth also:[9]

---

        i   JOHN[5]  b. 29 Dec. 1712; d. 30 May 1725 [1]
118    ii   TIMOTHY  b. 14 June 1716
119    iii  ROBERT  b. 2 July 1718
120    iv   AMOS  b. 28 April 1722
        v   GIDEON  b._____, living in 1758, in father's
            will. A search of land records, etc. shows
            nothing for him in Bristol Co.

References:  1. REHOBOTH VR p. 848.  2. REHOBOTH VR p.  239.
             3. REHOBOTH VR p. 908.  4. REHOBOTH VR p.  473.
5. VR ATTLEBOROUGH p. 675.  6. Bristol  Co.  PR  17:84-5
(Elizabeth Martin).  7. Bristol Co. PR  4:295-6; 7:249-252
(John Fuller).   8. Bristol  Co.  PR  16:432 (John Martin).
9. REHOBOTH VR p. 671.


    28  DESIRE MARTIN[4] (Mercy[3] Billington, Francis[2], John[1]), b.
Rehoboth 20 March 1684/5, d. there 12 Sept. 1727.[1]
    She  m. Rehoboth 10 July 1707 JOTHAM CARPENTER,[2]  b.
Swansea 1 July 1682,[3]  bp. Dorchester 1 July 1683, son of
Benjamin and Renew (Weeks) Carpenter.[4]  He  d.  prob.
Rehoboth,  before 8 April 1760.[5]  Jotham m.  (2) Swansea 6
June 1728, Isabel Sherman,[6]  by whom he had no  issue.  On
14 April  1760,  her  stepson Jotham  Carpenter was appointed
her  guardian,  "the widow  Izabel,  by old  age and other
difficulties, has  become non  compos mentis."[5]    Isabel's
identity in unknown.
    Jotham  Carpenter  died  intestate.  Distribution of his
estate was  made 17 April  1760 to his  widow Isabel, eldest
son Jotham Carpenter,  son Hezekiah Carpenter and daughters
Hannah,  Renew, Desire  and Esther.  [5] By  a deed dated 29
Nov. 1760, recorded 16 Oct. 1761, Jabez Round  and Renew his
wife,  Hezekiah Hix  and Desire  his wife,  all of Rehoboth;
with David  Round and Hannah his  wife of  Tiverton RI, and
Nathaniel  Bowen and  Esther his  wife of  Warren RI sold to
their  brother Jotham  Carpenter their  rights in the real
estate  of  "our  honoured  father,  Jotham  Carpenter,
deceased."  Hezekiah Hix  also  conveyed  the share he had
purchased from Hezekiah Carpenter of Johnston RI.[7]

    Children  (CARPENTER),  all  but  Esther  recorded  at
Rehoboth:[8,9]

121    i   JOTHAM[5]  b. 1 Aug. 1708
      ii   AMOS  b. 1 Sept. 1710; prob. d.y.; not an heir to
           father's estate.
122   iii  HANNAH  b. 6 June 1712
123   iv   RENEW  b. 6 June 1714
124    v   DESIRE  b. 3 June 1716
125   vi   ESTHER  b. ca. 1718
126   vii  HEZEKIAH  b. 6 Jan. 1724/5

References: 1. REHOBOTH VR p. 809. 2. REHOBOTH VR p. 79.
3. SWANSEA VR Bk A, p. 24. 4. STEVENS-MILLER
ANC p. 267. 5. BRISTOL CO MA PR ABSTRACTS, 2:259; also
Bristol Co. MA PR 17:1-6 (Jotham Carpenter). 6. Swansea
Original VR p. 91/193 7. Bristol Co. LR 45:300 (Jotham
Carpenter heirs). 8. REHOBOTH VR p. 573. 9. MQ 48:67-71.


## FIFTH GENERATION


29 ANN BULLOCK[5] (John Bullock[4], Elizabeth[3] Billington,
Francis[2], John[1]) b. ca. 1697; d. Barrington, then MA now RI,
11 April 1730 in her 33rd year.[1,2,3]
   She m. Bristol, at St. Michael's Episcopal Church, 27
March 1729, OLIVER BROWN, as his second wife.[4] He was b.
Swansea 3 Feb. 1696,[5] d. Barrington between 19 Dec. 1733
and 15 Jan. 1733/4; son of Jabez and Jane (_____) Brown.[6]
He was a descendant of Pilgrim John Howland. Oliver m. (1)
_____ _____, an unknown wife, mother of his daughter
Rebecca, who was baptized at Bristol 8 April 1729, "daughter
of Oliver Brown."[7] He m. (3) Sarah _____, named in his
will.[6] Sarah was living 15 May 1744 when she presented
the executrix's account listing items in Oliver Brown's
estate owed and paid to John Bullock.[6]
   Oliver Brown of Barrington, in his will dated 19 Dec.
1733, probated 15 Jan. 1733/4, gave wife Sarah one-third of
the moveables, the property she brought with her, and use of
the real estate until daughter Rebecca came of age;
appointed his father and mother to bring up and educate his
daughter, Rebecca, a minor. Rebecca was to inherit the
whole of the estate at her age 18, except for one pound to
beloved daughter Anna; wife Sarah to be executrix.[6] It
is evident from the will that Rebecca, baptized a few days
after her father's marriage to Ann Bullock, was not an
infant, and daughter neither of Ann nor of widow Sarah.
   The daughter Ann[a] Brown was also named in the will of
her grandfather, John Bullock.[7]

   Child (BROWN), by wife Ann:[8]

      i  ANNA[6] bp. St. Michael's Church, Bristol, 13 Apr.
         1730 dau. of Oliver and Ann Brown of
         Barrington.

References: 1. RI VR: St. Michael's Episcopal Church,
Bristol: 8:223. 2. Little Neck Cem. 3. TAG
39:65-73. 4. RI VR: St. Michael's Church, Bristol: 8:201.
5. SWANSEA VR, Bk A, p. 41. 6. Bristol Co. PR 8:44,56;
10:426; and Probate Files (Oliver Brown). 7. Bristol Co.
PR 9:231-2 (John Bullock). 8. RI VR: St. Michael's Church,
Bristol: 8:149.

30 ELIZABETH BULLOCK[5] (John Bullock[4], Elizabeth[3]
Billington, Francis[2], John[1]) b. ca. 1699, d. without issue
at Providence RI 2 July 1759.[1]
    She m. aft. 1736 WILLIAM ASHTON, b. Providence ca. 1680,
d. there 14 or 19 April 1765; son of John Ashton.[1,2]
William and wife Elizabeth are bur. in St. John's
Churchyard, Providence.[2]   He m. (1) bef. 1716 Patience
Williams, by whom he had children Joshua, William, Thomas,
Rebecca. There were no children by Elizabeth Bullock.[3]

References:  1. RI GEN DICT p. 5.  2. RI VR: King's Church,
            now St. John's Church, Providence: 10:147.
3. TAG 39:72.


31 ISRAEL BULLOCK[5] (John Bullock[4], Elizabeth[3] Billington,
Francis[2], John[1]) b. Providence RI ca. 1704, d. Rehoboth 16
Feb. 1757 in his 52nd year,[1] bur. Little Neck Cemetery,
Riverside (East Providence) RI with many of his family.[2]
    He m. ca. 1731 SARAH BROWN,[3]   b. Rehoboth 19 Feb.
1698,[4]  d. in 1763;[2]  dau. of Nathaniel and Sarah
(Jenckes) Brown. Nathaniel Brown, in his will of 20 May
1738, probated 13 Dec. 1740, called one of his seven daus.
Sarah Bullock.[5]
    Widow Sarah Bullock was appointed administratrix of the
estate of Israel Bullock, late of Rehoboth, dec'd, 5 April
1757. On 12 Feb. 1760, Sarah Bullock prayed the court for
division of the estate of her late husband, Israel Bullock,
but no record of the distribution has been found.[6]
    By the first of two deeds dated 5 Oct. 1759 and 17 Jan.
1760, Josiah[6] Bullock of Rehoboth, mariner, sold to James
Brown of Warren RI, "one-fifth part of one-sixth acres (sic)
ye same lands and buildings which were late ye estate of my
hon'd father, Israel Bullock, and lyeth in common and
undivided." The second deed corrects the strange wording of
the first thus: "all my right and interest in the estate of
my father Israel Bullock," specifically including "one-third
part of 76 acres at Rehoboth with mansion and buildings
bounded by John Bullock," etc.[7] These deeds seem to
indicate that Josiah, as eldest son, expected to inherit a
double portion of the estate: with five heirs, the estate
would be divided into six parts, two-sixths or one-third to
Josiah and one-sixth to each of the other four children of
Israel Bullock.

    Children (BULLOCK), b. Barrington:[8]

        i   JOSIAH[6] b. 30 Sept. 1733
       ii   SARAH  b. 8 June 1735
      iii   PRUDENCE  b. 29 Sept. 1736

            iv  ANNA    b. 15 Jan. 1739/40
            v   COMFORT  b. 14 April 1741

References:  1. RI VR: King's Church, now St. John's Church,
            Providence, 10:148.     2. Little   Neck   Cem.
3. TAG 39:72.   4. REHOBOTH VR, p.  555.  5. Bristol  Co. PR
9:300-301 (Nathaniel  Brown).   6. Bristol   Co.  PR   Files
(Israel   Bullock).   7. Bristol  Co.  LR 44:68,83  (Josiah
Bullock).  8. RI VR: Barrington: 6:25.


   32  MARY  BULLOCK[5]  (John  Bullock[4], Elizabeth[3] Billington,
Francis[2], John[1]) b. ca. 1711, d. 14 Jan.  1781 in her 69th
year.[1]
    She  m. Providence RI  21 Aug. 1766  ALEXANDER FRAZIER of
Providence,[2]  as  his second wife.  He  d. 3 Dec. 1769.[2]
He m. (1) Mercy Lumber, who d. 20 June 1763,[2]  by  whom he
had children Elizabeth,  John, Merebah and  Phenix.[3]  Mary
(Bullock) Frazier had no issue.

References:  1. TAG 39:72.   2. RI VR: King's Church, now St.
            John's Church,  Providence, 10:137,150.   3. RI
VR: Providence, 2:224, 266.


   33  JOHN  BULLOCK[5]  (John  Bullock[4], Elizabeth[3] Billington,
Francis[2], John[1]) b.  Providence RI ca. 1714,  d. Rehoboth 11
May  1788  in  his  74th  year,  bur.  Little  Neck Cemetery,
Riverside (East Providence) RI.[1,2]
    John m. (1) Swansea 6 Nov.  1740,[3]  int. Barrington (MA
now RI) 6 Sept.  1740 PATIENCE BOSWORTH,[4]  b. Rehoboth 8
Dec. 1717,[5]  d. 7 April 1747 in her 30th year, bur. Little
Neck  Cemetery;[1]   dau.  of  Jabez  and  Susannah  (____)
Bosworth.  She was a descendant of Pilgrim John Howland.
    He  m. (2) Warren RI 16 March 1748/9 JERUSHA SMITH,[6] b.
ca.  1730,  d.  16  July  1753.[1]   Jerusha  has  not  been
identified.
    John  m.  (3) bet.  1756 and  1768 ANNA  (CHILD) COLE,  b.
Swansea 17 Sept. 1729,[7]  living 11  Jan. 1790;[8]  dau. of
John and Abigail (Eddy) Child and widow of David Cole.
    Administration  of the estate of John Bullock of Rehoboth
was granted 6 June 1788 to his son  Jabez.  Distribution was
made  11 Jan.  1790: to  widow Anna  Bullock, her thirds; to
Capt.  Jabez  Bullock,  eldest  son,  two  shares  or a double
portion;  to the heirs of  Elizabeth Kent, deceased; to John
Bullock, youngest son; to Jerusha Bullock, youngest dau.[8]
Dau. Elizabeth Bullock, deceased, had married Josiah Kent.

Children (BULLOCK), first two by Patience, third by
Jerusha and fourth by Anna:[9,10]

    i   JABEZ[6] b. Barrington 19 April 1741
   ii  ELIZABETH b. prob. Barrington ca. 1745
  iii  JOHN b. Rehoboth 21 May 1751
   iv  JERUSHA b. Rehoboth 1 Aug. 1769; d.s.p.  28 Dec.
       1803 in her 35th year.

References: 1. Little  Neck   Cem.    2. TAG   39:65-73.
3. Swansea Original VR, Bk B, p. 88/190.  4. RI
VR: Barrington:  6:8.   5. REHOBOTH  VR,  p.551.  6. RI VR:
Warren: 6:11.  7. Swansea Original VR, Bk B,  pp. 2/5 and p.
L 91/193; (An erroneous birth date for Anna  appears in COLE
FAM, p. 60;  and copied in Reference #2 above.)  8. Bristol
Co.  PR  30:13;  31:277,478-482  (John Bullock).  9. RI VR,
Barrington,  6:25.  10. Rehoboth Original VR,  Bk. 3, p. 207
gives son John's mother as wife  Jerusha; and dau. Jerusha's
mother as "Nanna."  Arnold, REHOBOTH VR, p. 565, erroneously
shows both John and Jerusha as children of Jerusha.


34  RICHARD BULLOCK[5] (John Bullock[4], Elizabeth[3] Billington,
Francis[2], John[1]) b. Providence RI ca. 1718, d. Warren  RI 10
(or 11--g.s.) March 1764 in his 45th year, bur. Little  Neck
Cemetery, Riverside, (East Providence) RI.[1,2]
    He m.  Warren RI  6 June  1751 ABIGAIL  KINNECUTT,[3]  b.
Swansea 30 Sept. 1730,[4]  d.  28 April  1802, bur. Little
Neck Cemetery;[2]  dau. of John and Anne  (Eddy) Kinnecutt.
She m. (2)  Providence RI, 19  June 1766,[5]  as  his second
wife,  Richard Harding,  who d.  Barrington RI bef. 4 Sept.
1786.[6]  Abigail's father, John Kinnecutt of Warren, in his
will  dated 9 Aug.  1782,  named among others dau. Abigail
Harding, wife of Richard Harding.[7]  Abigail had three sons
by  her second marriage: twins  John and Jonathan Harding b.
1768 and Richard Harding, Jr.[8]
    Widow Abigail Bullock was appointed administratrix of the
estate of Richard Bullock of Warren 2 April 1764.  The heirs
were not  named in  the estate  account.[9]  Joseph Bullock,
their son,  was of Barrington  RI 10 Feb.  1780 when he sold
land there  to his cousin Jabez  Bullock of Rehoboth; Joseph
was of  Guilford, Windham Co.  VT 13  Aug. 1791 when he sold
to John Humphrey, (husband of his sister Elizabeth Bullock),
Barrington  RI  land  and  "all  dower  rights  of my mother
Abigail Harding that will fall  to me after her decease  and
will  come  to  me  by  lineal  descent of my father Richard
Bullock."[10]
    Abigail  (Kinnecutt)  (Bullock)  Harding  was  granted
administration of  the estate of her  second husband Richard
Harding of Barrington 4 Sept.  1786.[6]  Her  son Jonathan

Harding of Attleborough, on 11 Jan. 1794, sold to John
Humphrey, property from father Richard Harding's estate and
"that which will come to me after decease of my mother
Abigail Harding," witnessed by brothers John and Richard
Harding.[11]. The Hardings were not Billington descendants,
but Abigail's sons Richard Bullock and Richard Harding have
led to some confusion.

    Children (BULLOCK) b. Warren, RI, bp. St. Michael's
Episcopal Church, Bristol, RI:[12,13]

        i    WILLIAM[6] b. 27 March 1752; bp. 10 May 1752; d. 24
             Oct. 1753, aged 1y,6m,27d.[2]
       ii    ANN b. 31 Jan. 1754; bp. 14 April 1754; d. 22
             Nov. 1775 in 22nd yr.;[2]  Anne, dau. of
             Richard Bullock, dec'd., of Seekonk, bur. 23
             Nov. 1775.[14]
      iii    JOSEPH b. 8 April 1755; bp. 25 May 1755
       iv    ABIGAIL b. 23 March 1757; bp. 15 May 1757
        v    RICHARD b. 19 Nov. 1759; bp. 10 Feb. 1760; prob.
             d.y. No later record appears, and his mother
             named a Harding son "Richard."
       vi    ELIZABETH bp. 2 May 1762

References: 1. RI VR: Warren: 6:98    2. Little Neck Cem.
          3. RI VR: Warren: 6:11  4. Swansea Original VR,
Bk B, p. 3 or 6.   5. RI VR: King's Church, now St. John's
Church, Providence, 10:137.  6. Barrington RI Town Council &
Probate Recs. 2:113-116 (Richard Harding). 7. Warren RI
Town Council and Probate Records 1:489-492 (John
Kinnecutt).  8. RI VR: Warren: 6:70.  9. Warren RI Town
Council and Probate Records, 1:244; 2:168 (Richard
Bullock). 10. Barrington RI LE 1:244; 2:168 (Joseph
Bullock). 11. Barrington RI LE 2:169 (Jonathan Harding).
12. RI VR: Warren: 6:52. 13. RI VR: St. Michael's Episcopal
Church, Bristol, 8:149. 14. RI VR: Burials, King's Church,
now St. John's Church Providence: 10:148.


    35 RACHEL BEERS/BEERE[5] (Benjamin Beere[4], Elizabeth[3]
Billington, Francis[2], John[1]) b. prob. Providence RI, ca.
1707,[1] living at Newport RI 23 Sept. 1748, when Rachel
Farrel, adult, was bp. at Trinity Church, Newport,[2].
    She m. Newport 14 Jan. 1742 PATRICK FARRELL, whose
identity has not been determined.[3]. He was living at
Newport 22 Oct. 1744.[4]
    In 1737 Rachel Beers of Newport RI, granddaughter of
Daniel Pratt, gave Samuel Pratt, [her cousin and a grandson
of Phineas and Mary (Priest) Pratt], power of attorney to
dispose of her share of the 300 acres of Dunstable,

Middlesex Co. land "belonging to the said Daniel, late of
Providence, deceased."[5] Shortly after Rachel's marriage,
on 11 Sept. 1742, her husband Patrick Farrell [written
"Fazzel" in deed] bought from her brother Charles Beers, the
Providence property inherited by Charles from their father
Benjamin Beers.[6] And in a deed dated 22 Oct. 1744,
Charles Beers of Providence, husbandman, with Patrick
"Furrell" [Farrell] of Newport, cooper, and Rachel his wife,
all of Rhode Island, sold one full ninth part of the
300-acre farm of Phineas Pratt, deceased; this ninth part
had been settled on Daniel Pratt, heir to Phineas; and
Charles Beers and Rachel "Furrel" are described as heirs of
said Daniel Pratt's part.[4].
   Rachel Farrell was baptized as an adult in 1748, but no
record of children has been found.[2]

References: 1. TAG 39:65-73. 2. RI VR: Church Recs 10:498.
          3. RI VR: Newport 4:8. 4. NH Colony Deeds in
Rockingham Co. NH Deeds 37:80 (Charles Beers and Patrick and
Rachel Farrell) 5. PRATT(PHINEHAS) DESC, p. 60. 6. Provi-
dence RI LR 10B:97 (Charles Beers to Patrick Farrell)


   36 CHARLES BEERS/BEARS[5] (Benjamin Beere[4], Elizabeth[3]
Billington, Francis[2], John[1]) b. prob. Providence RI ca. 1712
(bef. 1714), d. aft. 1774 and bef. 1790.[1]
   He m. Providence 1 April 1744 SUSANNA SPENCER,[2] b.
East Greenwich RI 1 July 1721,[3] d. aft. 1790 census when
she was living at Rehoboth;[1] dau. of Benjamin and
Patience (Hawkins) Spencer.[4] Patience Spencer, widow of
Providence RI, in her will dated 18 Sept. 1744, probated 4
Aug. 1748, named dau. Susanna Beers.[5]
   Charles Beers, son of Benjamin, dec'd., was first
apprenticed in Providence to Stephen Arnold, Jr., but Arnold
died and on 30 Sept. 1720 Charles was ordered apprenticed to
Mary Arnold, mother of Stephen.[4]
   As an adult, on 11 Sept. 1742, Charles Bears (sic) of
Providence, laborer, sold Providence land for fifty pounds
to Patrick "Fazzel" [Farrell, his brother-in-law] of
Newport: 30 acres at a place called The Neck; 10 acres on
the west side of the river called Moshasuch; land in
Smithfield, the same being on surveys and returns; and
rights of commonage in Providence that were vested in or did
belong to "my honored father Benjamin Bears, deceased."[6]
In 1744 Charles and his sister Rachel (Beers) Farrell sold
land inherited from their maternal grandfather Daniel Pratt.
[See Fam. #35, Rachel Beers, above.]
   Charles Beers was in the 1774 census at Barrington RI, as
was Spencer Beers. Neither was there in the 1782 census,
but widow Susanna Beers appears in the 1790 census of

Rehoboth.[1]  The family apparently moved from Barrington RI
to  Rehoboth between 1774  and 1782.[1]  No  probate or land
records in Barrington RI or in  Bristol County MA were found
for Charles  Beers.  But a Bristol Co.  deed pertaining to a
1794  sale in the  estate of his  very probable son, Spencer
Beers, is indexed  under "Charles Bears."[7]  And  this deed
shows that Spencer owned half a house, shared with "heirs of
Moses  Blake,"  Blake  being the  father-in-law of Job Beers.
Job was called "son of Charles" in his marriage record.

     Children  (BEERS/BEARS),  Job  a  proven  son,  others so
closely associated as to be virtually certain:[4]

          i   SPENCER[6]  b. 1745-50;  d. bef.  12 Nov. 1787 when
              "widdow Lillis  Bears and  her family,  late of
              Rehoboth, were warned  and ordered removed from
              Barrington."[8]   Spencer  Bears of  Barrington,
              m. Rehoboth 16 Dec. 1773 LILLIS BULLOCK.[9]
         ii   RACHEL  b._____;   of  Rehoboth  when she   m.
              Providence  RI 21 Oct. 1781,[10]  int. Rehoboth
              24   Sept.  1781,[11]   JOSEPH  WHITTEMORE*  of
              Providence.[12]   [Ref. 4*  calls  her husband
              Joseph "Waterman," an error.]
        iii   JOB  b._____,  d. bef. 1790;  "of Rehoboth, son of
              Charles"  m.  Providence  RI  17 Jan. 1783,[13]
              int. Rehoboth 1 Jan.  1783, "both of Rehoboth,"
              MOLLY BLAKE dau. of Moses.[11]

References:  1. RI CENSUS  1774 and  1782; FED  CENSUS 1790.
          2. RI  VR:  Providence  2:15.   3. RI  VR: East
Greenwich 1:148.   4.*TAG 39:65-73.   5. RI GEN  DICT p. 187
(Patience  Spencer).   6. Providence  RI  LR 10B:97 (Charles
Bears).   7. Bristol  Co.  LR  73:571  (Lillis  Bears, admx.
estate  of Spencer  Bears).   8. Barrington  Town  Council
Records 2:138.   9. REHOBOTH VR,  p. 26.  10.  RI VR: Provi-
dence, 2:15.   11. REHOBOTH  VR  p.423.    12. NEHGR  108:90
(Whittemore  Gen.).  13. RI  VR:  Congregational Church West
Side of Providence, 10:199.


37  SARAH[5] BILLINGTON  (Francis[4], Joseph[3], Francis[2], John[1])
b. Plymouth 11 Dec. 1702, d. there 27 Dec. 1748.[1]
     She m. Plymouth 3 May 1723 JAMES HOWARD,[2]  int. 22 Dec.
1722 to  James Howard* "a  strainger,"[3]  who has  not been
identified; he d.  Plymouth 12 April 1763.[4]    James m. (2)
Plymouth 15 April 1752  Mercy (Ward) Warren,[5]  b. Plymouth
8 March 1708/9,[6]   d. aft. 20 Oct. 1770.[7]   She was dau.
of Nathan  and Elizabeth (Pope) Ward  and widow of Cornelius
Warren, Family #101.

By deed dated 11 April 1757, acknowledged and recorded the same, James Howard of Plymouth, with wife Mercy releasing dower, sold to his son John Howard, "all my land and dwelling house that I bought 18 Nov. 1743," bounded partly by a fence between land of Thomas and Ebenezer Churchill.[8] No probate record has been found in Plymouth County for this James Howard.

On 24 Sept. 1732, John, James, Mary and Francis Howard, children of Sarah Howard, wife of James, were baptized in the First Church, Plymouth; on 24 Feb. 1734/5 dau. Sarah was baptized.[4]

Children (HOWARD) b. Plymouth by wife Sarah:[9]

   i    JOHN[6]  b. 12 Jan. 1723/4
   ii   MARY  b. 28 Feb. 1725/6
   iii  JAMES  b. 18 Jan. 1727/8;  d.  Jamaica  9  May
        1749.[1]
   iv   FRANCIS  b. 12 Sept. 1731
   v    SARAH  b. 1 Jan. 1733/4
   vi   WILLIAM  b. 10 June 1742

*Note: This James Howard was not James, son of James and Elizabeth (Washburn) Howard, as stated in Heman Howard, Descendants of John Howard, (1903), pp. 11-12. The author himself entered a handwritten correction in the copy now at the Winnetka, Illinois Public Library, stating that James Howard, husband of Sarah Billington, belonged to some other unknown family.

References:  1. MD  16:86.    2. MD  14:40.    3. MD  18:144.
            4. PLYMOUTH  CH RECS 1:393,430.    5. MD 18:141.
6. MD 12:11.   7. NEHGR 55:169.    8. Plymouth Co.  LR 43:267
(James and Mercy Howard to John Howard).  9. MD 13:170.


38 [1]MERCY/MARCY[5] BILLINGTON (Francis[4], Joseph[3], Francis[2], John[1]) b. Plymouth 1 Jan. 1704/5, d. Plymouth 8 Aug. 1758, in her 54th yr.[1]

She m. Plymouth 18 Feb. 1728/9 MATTHEW LEMOTE/LEMATE,[2] b. ca. 1705, d. Plymouth 27 Oct. 1762, aged 57y,0m,20d. [3,1] His origin is not known, but he may have come from Boston.

On 20 Feb. 1767 George Lemote and Richard Holmes were appointed to administer the estate of Matthew Lemote. The real estate was divided 1 Feb. 1768: to the only son, George Lemote, a double share; then shares to Richard Holmes, husband of the eldest dau. Marcy, to Susannah Chambers, Mary Pappoon and Abigail Maxwell.[4]

Children (LEMOTE/LEMATE/LEMONT) b. Plymouth:[5*,1]

   i  MATTHEW[6]  b. 18 Aug. 1730; d. 15 July 1733
  ii  JOSEPH  b. 30 Nov. 1732; d. 22 July 1733
 iii  ABIGAIL b.  6 June 1733  (written over 1734-sic);
       d. 25 Oct. 1734
  iv  MARCY  b. 29 Oct.  1734; m. (1) int.  Plymouth 26
       April 1755 WILLIAM BARNES;[6]  m. (2) int. Ply-
       mouth 31 March 1764 RICHARD HOLMES.[7]
   v  SUSANNAH     b. 30  June 1736;  m. Plymouth 13 July
       1756 WILLIAM CHAMBERS.[8]
  vi  MATTHEW  b. 25 June 1738; d. Sept. 1739
 vii  MARY  b.  17 Feb. 1739 (1739/40);  m. Plymouth 10
       April 1759 DANIEL PAPPOON.[9]
viii  GEORGE  b.  24 Dec. 1741; m. (1) Plymouth 12 July
       1764 CATHERINE NICHOLSON;[10]  m. (2) int. Ply-
       mouth 9 Dec. 1775 THANKFULL WHITTEMORE.[11]
  ix  ABIGAIL  b. 2 Feb. 1743/4; m. int. Boston 2 Sept.
       1765 JOHN MAXWELL.[12]

*Note: Some of the children's birth dates are so close
together as to be impossible, but this is copied  correctly.
Perhaps Joseph was born in 1731?

References:  1. (PLYMOUTH) BURIAL HILL  BY DREW p.  214 (has
            some  death dates and ages at death that differ
slightly from the vital records).  2. MD 14:72.  3. PLYMOUTH
CH  RECS,  1:392.   4. Plymouth Co.  PR  17:178; 19:436,558
(Matthew Lemote).  5. MD 14:241.*  6. MD 25:52.  7. MD 26:43
8. Plymouth VR 2:252.  9. Ibid. 2:256.   10. Ibid. 2:261.
11. MD 27:177.   12. BOSTON VR 30:424.


39 JEMIMA[5] BILLINGTON (Francis[4], Joseph[3], Francis[2], John[1])
b. Plymouth 12 June 1710, d. aft. 3 May 1758.[1]
     She m.  Plympton  17  Oct.  1728 JOSEPH BENT,[2]  b. ca.
1704,  probably  the  Joseph  who  d. Middleboro  13  Jan.
1782;[3]  son of Experience and Abigail (Sampson) Bent.[4]
     Joseph Bent of  Middleborough,  nailer, and wife Jemima
Bent deeded 10 acres at Whetstone Vineyard Brook to son John
Bent of Middleborough,  nailer, 3  May 1758.[1]  On 6 Oct.
1759, John Bent and  wife Bethiah conveyed to  [his brother]
Joseph Bent, Jr.  "part of  the homestead  where Experience
Bent formerly lived, on Whetstone Vineyard Brook."[5]
     Joseph  Bent, Jr.  was somewhat  of a  scoundrel, for the
following year  he was sued for debt by Perez Tilson, Thomas
Mayhew and brother John Bent.  Plymouth court records of the
case for Oct. 1760,  April and July 1761 show  "Joseph Bent,
Jr., Middleborough sailmaker or mariner, absconding."[6]  On
10 and  12 Aug. 1761,  Joseph, Jr.'s property  was attached,

and ceded to the plaintiffs, including part of his farm "where his father Joseph Bent now dwells."[7] Joseph, Sr.'s homestead was preserved however, for on 28 Aug. 1764 John Bent of Middleboro and wife Bethiah deeded to [his father] Joseph Bent, nailer, land in Middleborough "where Joseph now lives and is part of the land he formerly owned." Witnesses were John Briggs and William Bent.[8].

No probate record appears in Plymouth County for Joseph or Jemima Bent. No evidence for a son William Bent, as stated in the Bent genealogy, could be found except for the William Bent who witnessed the deed cited above. He apparently owned no real estate himself.

Children (BENT):[9,10]

     i   SARAH[6] b. Plympton 27 Jan. 1730
    ii  JOHN b. Middleboro 27 Feb. 1731/2
   iii  ALICE b. Middleboro 16 Jan. 1733/4
    iv  JOSEPH b. Middleboro 6 Jan. 1735/6
   ?v  WILLIAM b. ca. 1742,[4] perhaps the William Bent
          who d. at the Pauper House in Middleboro 11
          April 1831.[3]

References: 1. Plymouth Co. LR 45:52 (Joseph and Jemima Bent to John Bent). 2. MD 1:248. 3. MIDDLEBORO DEATHS, p. 19. 4. BENT FAM, pp. 29-30. 5. Plymouth Co. LR 45:247 (John and Bethiah Bent to Joseph Bent, Jr.). 6. PLYMOUTH CO CT RECS 8:16-17, 29,37. 7. Plymouth Co. LR 45:95,96 (3 deeds) (Joseph Bent, Jr. by court order to Perez Tilson, Thomas Mayhew and John Bent). 8. Plymouth Co. LR 55:55 (John and Bethiah Bent to Joseph Bent). 9. MD 1:246. 10. MD 8:248.


40  CONTENT[5] BILLINGTON (Francis[4], Joseph[3], Francis[2], John[1]) b. Plymouth 2 Feb. 1712/3, d. aft. 3 March 1760.[1]

    She m. (1) Plymouth 18 Oct. 1734,[2] FRANCIS MERRIFIELD, b. ca. 1711 prob. in York Co. ME, evidently d. aft. 1742 and bef. 1 Sept. 1753; son of William and Margaret (Frost) Merrifield, who moved from Maine to Barnstable Co. On 29 June 1715 William and Margaret Merrifield, living at "Cape Cod, Barnstable Co.," she "the natural dau. of Mr. Nicholas Frost, deceased of Newcchawanock in Co. of York," [then Massachusetts, now Maine] sold her 1/6 share of property in the estate of Nicholas Frost.[3]

    Content (Billington) Merrifield m. (2) Plymouth 2 Oct. 1753, int. 1 Sept. 1753, SAMUEL RANSOM of Plympton,[4] who was living 3 March 1760.[1] He was prob. the Samuel Ransom b. Plympton 25 Sept. 1718, son of Samuel and Abigail (Rickard) Ransom.[5]

    Plymouth Court Records for March 1729/30 show that

Nathaniel Morton (Plymouth cordwainer) by atty. Elkanah
Leonard, Gent. sued Eleazer Morton (Plymouth cordwainer) and
"Francis Maryfield a minor and dwells with Eleazer Morton,
Jr." for trespass and cutting trees contrary to province
law.[6]

On 6 Nov. 1738 Francis Merrifield of Plymouth, seafaring
man, "son to William Merrifield and Margarett his wife
[which Margarett was] Daughter to Mr. Nicholas Frost late of
Kittery in the County of York" [ME], quit claimed all right
and title to land in Kittery "which fell to me by my mother
Margarett Merrifield, deceased."[7] "Content Merrifield,
wife of Francis," was a member in full communion at First
Church, Plymouth in 1742.[8].

Samuel Ransom and wife Content, "who came from Plympton
about one month ago," were warned out of Plymouth 8 Jan.
1755.[9] On 3 March 1760, Samuel Ransom and Content his
wife of Plympton were appointed administrators of the estate
of Francis Merryfield, late of Plymouth, deceased,
intestate, "having while he lived and at the time of his
death goods, chattels, rights and credits..." The Ransoms
were ordered to make an inventory "on or before the 14 day
of May next ensuing" and to present an account by 14 Feb.
1761. No record of compliance with the court order appears,
presumably because the Merrifield estate contained little or
no property.[1]

Children (MERRIFIELD), baptized at First Church, Plymouth
as "two [unnamed] children of Content Merrifield":[10]

  i   Child[6] b. _____; bp. 6 June 1742
  ii  Child b. _____; bp. 6 June 1742; possibly the
      MARGARET MERRIFIELD who m. Taunton 10 Feb.
      1763, int. Plymouth 1 Jan. 1763, DAVID STOOPS
      of Taunton.[11,12]

References: 1. Plymouth Co. PR 15:459 (Francis Merry-
           field). 2. MD 14:75. 3. YORK DEEDS 8:124-5
(William and Margaret Merrifield); also ME NH GEN DICT,
p.248. 4. MD 16:165,255. 5. VR PLYMPTON p. 160. 6. PLY-
MOUTH CO CT RECS 5:329. 7. York Co., [ME] LR 21:40 (Francis
Merrifield). 8. PLYMOUTH CH RECS 2:528. 9. PLYMOUTH CO CT
RECS 3:118. 10. PLYMOUTH CH RECS 1:443. 11. VR TAUNTON
2:462. 12. MD 26:42.


41 [1]DANIEL[5] BILLINGTON (prob. Elisha[4], Joseph[3], Francis[2],
John[1]) b. prob. South Kingstown RI ca. 1713 or earlier,
(sued for debt Jan. 1734);[1] d. East Greenwich RI 15 Aug.
1799.[2]

He of South Kingstown RI m. East Greenwich RI 10 March
1736 MARY AUSTEN, dau. of John.[3] She was living 28 Oct.
1754 when she signed a deed with her husband at East
Greenwich.[4]
    Daniel poss. m. (2) at South Kingstown RI 14 June 1778
widow SARAH CHAPPEL,[5] although this may have been Daniel,
Jr., a probable son. Daniel, Sr.'s unnamed wife d. East
Greenwich 18 Aug. 1796.[2]
    Daniel Billington, called laborer or boatman of South
Kingstown, was sued for debt in Jan. 1734.[1] He moved to
East Greenwich after his marriage in 1736, and bought a lot
there 9 Sept. 1742. He had several more land transactions
in East Greenwich, including two exchanges with his brother,
Joseph Billington, who continued to reside in South
Kingstown.[4] Daniel and wife Mary sold his land at East
Greenwich RI 28 Oct. 1754, then apparently moved back to
South Kingstown RI where he had been sued at court in Feb.
1753.[1]
    South Kingstown Town Records show Daniel was paid
£ 118.4.8 on 14 March 1751, possibly part of his father's
estate.[6] He was over 60 in the 1777 military census at
South Kingstown,[7] and was head of a family at that place
in the 1774 and 1782 RI censuses.[8,9] In the 1774 Town
Council records of South Kingstown, Daniel Billington was
called "under the care of this town."[10] During the
Revolutionary War Daniel Billington filed a claim for four
pounds, 10 shillings in March 1778 for boarding Thomas
Billington, a sick soldier at his house.[11]
    Daniel Billington and his unnamed wife returned to live
at East Greenwich RI by 24 Feb. 1787 when they first
appeared on the town poor rolls there, and they were
supported at town expense until their deaths in 1799 and
1796 respectively.[2] There are no probate records for
them.
    No vital records for Daniel's children appear. There
were a number of younger Billingtons in Rhode Island, some
of whom have been proved to belong to Daniel's brother
Joseph. It is hoped that proof of Daniel's children will
eventually be found.

Probable children of Daniel were (BILLINGTON):

    i   DANIEL[6], Jr. sued for debt in Washington County
        RI Court of Common Pleas in Aug. 1769 and Feb.
        1773.[1]
    ii  ELISHA m. at South Kingstown RI 22 Jan. 1775
        SARAH TENNANT,[12] and had a family there in
        the 1782 RI census.[9] On 22 Nov. 1785 Elisha
        obtained a certificate from the Town Council
        showing that he, wife and children "belonged"
        to South Kingstown, thus could go to Newport.
        Elisha received Rev. War Pension #S38551.[13]

iii  SARAH  m. at South Kingstown  RI 2 Feb. 1772 JOHN
     CROUCHER (or Croncher).[12]  Sarah was said  to
     have been sister of:
iv   THOMAS  a  Revolutionary War  pensioner,  #S38545,
     the sick soldier boarded at Daniel Billington's
     house in 1778; a highly probable son.[11]

References:  1. Washington  Co.  RI  Court  of Common Pleas
        Recs.,  A:173;  C:252  (Daniel  Billington)
H:40,416 (Daniel Billington, Jr.).  2. Town Council Recs. of
East  Greenwich, n.p., meetings dated  24 Feb. 1787, 27 Aug.
1796,  31 Aug. 1799,  et al (LDS  Film #927,238).  3. RI VR:
East  Greenwich: 1:10.  4. East  Greenwich, RI  LE 6:151-3;
7:193,  252-4,258,259,294,335  (Daniel  and Mary Billington;
Joseph  and  Abigail  Billington).  5. SOUTH  KINGSTON
MARRIAGES,  p.  22.  6.  South Kingstown Town Council and
Probate  Recs,  1743-1754,  p.  370.  7. RI MILITARY CENSUS
1777.  8. RI  CENSUS 1774.  9. RI  CENSUS  1782,  (NEHGR
127:129-30).  10. SOUTH KINGSTON  RI TOWN  COUNCIL RECS, p.
48.  11. RI COL RECS 8:385.  12. SOUTH KINGSTOWN MARRIAGES,
p. 19.  13. SOUTH KINGSTON RI TOWN COUNCIL RECS, p. 188.


42  JOSEPH[5]  BILLINGTON  (prob.  Elisha[4], Joseph[3], Francis[2],
John[1]) b.  prob. South Kingstown RI by  1716 (over 60 in the
1777 RI military census);[1]  d. aft. the 1782  Rhode Island
census, living then at South Kingstown.[2]
    He m. South Kingstown RI 21 Dec.  1746 ABIGAIL BRAMAN,[3]
b. there  23 Dec. 1727,  dau. of Joseph  and Abigail (Allen)
Braman.[4]  She was living  at South Kingstown 10  Nov. 1755
when  she  signed  a  deed  with her husband;[5]  and  was
apparently mother of the twins born in 1768.[4]
    Joseph Billington, called  yeoman, mariner or cordwainer,
lived at South Kingstown RI.  He  was bondsman there 13 Apr.
1741  for Jane  Billington, administratrix  on the estate of
Elisha  Billington,  presumably  his  parents.[6] Joseph was
sued for debt in Washington Co.  RI 1742, 1743,  1753, 1754,
1755, 1756,  1759, 1762, 1764,  1765, 1769 and  1772.[7]  He
bought  17 acres at South Kingstown  5 Oct. 1752; Joseph and
wife Abigail sold the same land back to the original grantor
10 Nov. 1755.[5]
    Joseph Billington of South  Kingstown, on 25 March  1752,
bought  lot  #126  in East  Greenwich RI, near the land of
Daniel  Billington,  his  presumed  brother; Joseph and wife
Abigail, of South Kingstown, sold the same  lot #126 in East
Greenwich  to Daniel  Billington 16 Jan. 1754.[8] Although
Daniel  and  Mary  Billington  shortly  sold  lot  #126  and
returned to  live at South Kingstown,  Joseph Billington, of
South  Kingstown, on  17 July  1755 bought  lot #166 in East

Greenwich, the land first owned by his brother.    This lot,
however was sold at a sheriff's sale 1 July 1756, apparently
attached for debt.[9]
    Evidently both brothers were unsuccessful with land
ownership and neither had another real estate transaction.
The Rhode Island 1774 census, the 1777 military census and
the 1782 census show Joseph Billington living at South
Kingstown.[10,1,2]    He is not found in the 1790 Federal
census.   No probate record for Joseph or his wife Abigail
appears at South Kingstown RI.
    The births of the three youngest children of Joseph and
Abigail are recorded at South Kingstown, RI probably at the
time the Town Council, on 19 Dec. 1774, took action with all
four youngest children, calling the father Joseph "one of
the poor of this town."   There were probably more older
children.

    Children (BILLINGTON), b. South Kingstown, RI:

    i   SARAH[6] (probably); m. South Kingstown 8 Jan. 1775
        WILLIAM TOURJEE.[3]
    ii  JOSEPH, Jr. b. ca.  1754-5; the Town Council in
        1774 ordered the overseer of the poor  "to bind
        out Joseph, Jr., who is an idle, indolent
        person, to some suitable person for one year or
        ship him a voiage to sea."[11]   He was serving
        in the militia in the RI 1777 military
        census,[1]
    iii JANE b. 13 Nov. 1762;[4] in 1774 she was bound as
        apprentice to Rowse Potter until the age of
        eighteen.[11]
    iv  ABIGAIL (twin) b.    24 June 1768;[4] in 1774 she
        was to be cared for by the overseer of the poor
        "and he endeavor to find a suitable place to
        take her as apprentice."[11]
    v   ELISHA   (twin), b. 24 June 1768;[4] apprenticed
        in 1774 to James Gardner until age 21.[11]

References:  1. RI  MILITARY  CENSUS   1777.    2. RI  CENSUS
            1782 (NEHGR  127:129-30). 3. SOUTH   KINGSTOWN
MARRIAGES, p. 11.   4. RI VR: South Kingstown: 5:8.   5. South
Kingstown   RI    LE   1:481;5:525   (Joseph  and  Abigail
Billington).   6. South Kingstown RI Town Council and Probate
Recs., 3:122-23 (Elisha Billington).    7. Washington Co.  RI
Court  of  Common  Pleas:  Index  of  Defendants,  (LDS Film
#937,653)  8. East  Greenwich RI LE 7:252-54,258 (Joseph and
Abigail    Billington).     9. East    Greenwich   RI    LE
7:294-94,333-35 (Joseph  Billington).    10. RI  CENSUS 1774.
11. SOUTH KINGSTOWN RI TOWN COUNCIL RECS, pp. 48-9.

43  SARAH$^5$ BILLINGTON (prob. Elisha$^4$, Joseph$^3$, Francis$^2$,
John$^1$) b. say 1718, prob. South Kingstown RI; d. aft. 1740.
     She m. South Kingstown 20 April 1740 JAMES ROSE,[1]
whose identity has not yet been learned. The will of John
Rose of Block Island dated 17 Dec. 1720 named a son James
Rose under 21, possibly this James.[2]
     The 1774 census of North Kingstown RI shows a James Rose
with 1-2-1-1;[3] and in the 1777 military census, aged
between 16 and 50.[4]  This man was too young for Sarah
Billington's husband: perhaps a son. No recorded children
have been found for them at North Kingstown or elsewhere.

References:  1. SOUTH   KINGSTOWN   MARRIAGES,   RIHS  Coll.
         18:102ff.  2. RI GR 3:111.  3. RI  CENSUS 1774,
p. 81.  4. RI ROOTS, 9:17.


44  MARY$^5$ BILLINGTON (prob. Elisha$^4$, Joseph$^3$, Francis$^2$,
John$^1$) b. prob. South Kingstown RI ca. 1720; living
Hopkinton RI 15 June 1784.[1]
     She m. South Kingstown 2 Feb. 1743 JOHN BENT,[2]  b.
perhaps ca. 1712; (over 60 in the 1777 Military Census of
Rhode Island at Hopkinton.)[3] He d. Hopkinton bet. 15 June
and 13 Sept. 1784 when his will was proved.[1]  He m. (1)
South Kingstown 13 Nov. 1737 Sarah Smith.[4] John Bent has
not yet been identified.
     John Bent of Hopkinton RI, in his will dated 15 June
1784, proved 13 Sept. 1784, mentioned: wife Mary Bent; daus.
Mary Bent, Sarah Helme, Elizabeth Douglas, Catherine
Gardner, son-in-law Thomas Potter Gardner, dau. Jane Bent;
and granddaughters Hannah Bent under 18 and Dorcas
Helme.[1]

     Children (BENT), from marriage dates, prob. were all by
Mary Billington, and b. South Kingstown or Hopkinton RI:

     i    MARY$^6$ b. perhaps 1744; unm. 1784
    ii    JOHN b. poss. 1746; apparently d. bef. 1784 and
          prob. soon aft. 1771. He m. Westerly RI 10 Oct
          1770 HANNAH SAUNDERS; they had dau. Hannah b.
          Westerly 10 July 1771.[5]
   iii    SARAH b. ca. 1748; m. Narragansett RI 9 March
          1769 NILES HELME.[6]
    iv    ELIZABETH b. ca. 1750; m. _____ DOUGLAS bef.
          1784.
     v    CATHERINE b. ca. 1752; m. Hopkinton RI 15 April
          1773 THOMAS POTTER GARDNER.[7]
    vi    JANE b. ca. 1756; unm. 1784.

References: 1. RI GR 4:142(Will of John Bent). 2. SOUTH
            KINGSTOWN MARRIAGES p. 10. 3. RI ROOTS 8:85
(Dec. 1982). 4. RI VR: South Kingstown: 5:8. 5. RI VR:
Westerly; 5:11,79. 6. RI VR St. Paul's Church, Narra-
gansett: 10:137. 7. RI VR: Hopkinton: 5:6.


45  JEMIMA BUMP or BUMPUS[5] (Sarah Eaton[4], Martha[3] Billington, Francis[2], John[1]) b. Bristol 7 Jan 1686/7, d. aft. her
husband's death in 1739;[1] prob. the Jemima Smith who was
a member of the First Congregational Church of Preston CT 14
March 1744.[2]
    She m. Plainfield CT 9 May 1706 THOMAS SMITH of Preston
CT,[3] whose birth and parentage are unknown. He bought
land in Plainfield in June 1701, then resident of
"East_____stable in Mass. Bay" (perhaps "Eastham in the
County of Barnstable").[4] He d. 3 July 1739, according to
the inventory of his estate.[1]
    Thomas Smith, of Preston, left a will dated 23 April and
proved 31 July 1739, bequeathing his estate to wife Jemima,
to "cousin" Sarah Parke, wife of Paul Parke, and to Daniel
Thomas "whom I have brought up."[1] Jemima apparently had
no children.

References:      1. New London CT Dist PR D:403-5.(Thomas
                 Smith). 2. PRESTON CONG CH p. 153. 3. Plain-
field CT VR 1:4. 4. Plainfield CT LR 1:9 (Fitch to Smith).


46  SAMUEL BUMP or BUMPUS[5] (Sarah Eaton[4], Martha[3] Billing-
ton, Francis[2], John[1]) b. Bristol 20 Feb. 1687/8, d. Bolton
CT in 1747.[1,2]
    He m. (1) Bolton CT 4 April 1723 ABIGAIL ROSE (or
ROUSE),[3] b. Rochester 28 March 1693;[4] d. Bolton CT 1
Dec. 1725;[5] dau. of Edward and Rebecca (Bumpus) Rose (or
Rouse).[4]
    Samuel m. (2) Bolton CT 18 May 1727 MARY RAY,[6] b.
_____, d. Bolton CT 8 Feb 1727/8,[5], dau. of James Ray,
Sr.[7] James Ray, Sr. of Haddam CT, in his will dated 14
Jan. 1730/1, probated 28 June 1731, instructed his son James
Ray to pay "my grandson Samuel Bump of Bolton 30 pounds when
he becomes twenty-one."[7]
    "Sam'l Bump of Bolton" made his will 15 April 1730,
inventory 20 March 1747, dividing his property between his
two sons and asking that Edward Rose of Bolton be guardian
to eldest son Mathew, and Lieut. Abel Shaylor be guardian to
son Samuel.[1,2] In 1747/8 Samuel of East Haddam and
Matthew of Bolton sold their inheritances.[8]

Children (BUMP) b. Bolton CT, two by Abigail one by Mary:

   i   PATIENCE[6] b. 23 Jan. 1723/4;[9]    d. there 1 May
        1725.[5]
  ii  MATTHEW  b. 27 Nov. 1725;[10]   living 1747/8;
        apparently Matthew Bump of Dutchess Co., [the
        part that became Fredericksburgh, Putnam Co.]
        NY, who was on tax lists 1747/8 to 1779,[11]
        and was there in the 1790 census.[12]
 iii  SAMUEL  b. 5 Feb. 1727/8;[10]  living 1747/8.

References: 1. MANWARING 3:514 (Samuel Bump) 2. Hartford
        CT PR Dist. File #894 (Samuel Bump) 3. CSL
Barbour Index, Bolton CT VR 1:201. 4. VR ROCHESTER 1:253.
5. CSL Barbour Index, Bolton CT VR 1:279. 6. Ibid. 1:202.
7. MANWARING 3:99 (James Ray). 8. Bolton CT LR
2:523,525,619 (Matthew & Samuel Bump) 9. CLS Barbour Index,
Bolton CT VR 1:213. 10. Ibid. 1:219. 11. Dutchess County
(NY) Tax Lists, pp. 3,24. 12. 1790 Census, NY:82-4. See
also: BUMPUS FAM, p. 43. & TAG 43:151, "The Bumpus Family
of New England."


47  PHILIP BUMP or BUMPUS[5] (Sarah Eaton[4], Martha[3] Billington, Francis[2], John[1]), b. Bristol 13 Feb. 1689/90; living
Sharon CT 3 March 1762.[1]
    He m. (1) Litchfield CT 4 Feb. 1722/3 MARY HORSFORD,[2]
b. Windsor CT 15 Feb. 1690/1;[3]   d. Sharon CT 1 Dec.
1751;[4]  dau. of Samuel and Mary (Palmer) Horsford.[3]
    Philip m. (2) Sharon CT 3 Dec. 1754 ESTHER (_____)
WARNER.[5]
    Philip lived in Plainfield CT from May 1725 to 1733;[6]
he was in Hebron CT from Oct. 1733 to 1736 according to
deeds;[7] in Bolton CT from Dec. 1736 to 1749 when he and
wife Mary sold 117 acres in Bolton;[8] and in Sharon CT by
June 1749 when he bought land, which he "of Sharon" sold 3
March 1762.[9]

Child (BUMP), b. Plainfield CT:[10]

   i   WILLIAM[6] b. 26 Oct. 1723; d. Sharon CT 2 Aug.
        1750.[4]

References: 1. Sharon CT LR 5:183 (Philip Bump); 2. CSL
        Barbour Index: Litchfield VR 1:5. 3. Ibid.
Windsor VR 1:20. 4. Ibid.: Sharon VR 2:22. 5. Ibid. 3:42.
6. Plainfield CT LR 3:75,103,147,153-4, 160(Philip Bump).
7. Hebron, CT LR 3:52,64(Philip Bump). 8. Bolton CT LR
1:553,555,564; 2:24,489; 3:16 (Philip Bump). 9. Sharon CT
LR 2:458; 5:183(Philip Bump). 10. CSL Barbour Index:
Plainfield VR 1:34. See also MF 1:16.

48  LYDIA BUMP or BUMPUS[5] (Sarah Eaton[4], Martha[3] Billington, Francis[2], John[1]), b.  Bristol 2 April  1692; d. Plainfield CT 14 May 1740.[1]
    She m.  THOMAS  HERD  (or Hard,  Heard or Hurd), who d.
Plainfield CT 24 April 1751.[1]
    Thomas Herd made his will dated 19 Dec. 1750, probated 14
May 1751, naming sons Thomas, Josiah, Jacob and  John; daus.
Mary,  Bathyah,  Sarah  and Ame;  brother-in-law Josiah Bump,
executor.[2] Receipts in the estate, dated 18 May 1751, were
signed by Thomas,  Josiah, Jacob,  Bethia, Sarah,  Mary and
Ame; countersigned by Ame's guardian Josiah Bump.[2]

    Children ("HARD" or HERD), b. Plainfield CT:[3]

      i   BETHIA[6]  b. 18 June  1720; m. EBENEZER YERRINGTON
     ii   SARAH  b.  23  March  1722;  living 1751 when she
            signed a receipt with sisters.[2]  n.f.r.
    iii   THOMAS  (twin)  b.  10  Oct.  1724;  m.  KEZIAH
            RICHARDSON
     iv   JOHN  (twin) b. 10 Oct. 1724; m. JEMIMA HUNTER
      v   JOSIAH  b. 23 Sept. 1726; m. PHEBE _____.
     vi   JACOB  b. 7 Feb. 1729; m. AMY WELCH [Fam. #73]
    vii   MARY  b. 20 Jan. 1731; m. OBED BENJAMIN
   viii   AMY  b. 3 Oct. 1735; living 1751.[2]  n.f.r.

References:   1. MF 1:16-8.   2. Plainfield   CT Dist.  PR
              2:149-53 (Thomas Herd);  3. CSL Barbour Index,
Plainfield VR 1:93.


49  JOSIAH  BUMP or BUMPUS[5],(Sarah Eaton[4], Martha[3] Billington, Francis[2], John[1]) b. Bristol 9 April 1698; d. Plainfield
CT 2 Sept. 1757.[1]
    He m.  prob.  Plainfield CT  SARAH HARRIS,[2,3];   b.
Plainfield  CT  10  Aug.  1702;[4]   d.  after 1757; dau. of
Ebenezer  and  Christoble (Crary) Harris.  Ebenezer Harris
mentioned dau. Sarah Bump in his will dated 1750.[2] Josiah
Bump with wife Sarah and her sisters, all daus.  of Ebenezer
and Christoble Harris, signed an agreement in 1754.[3]
    The  will  of  Josiah Bump of Plainfield dated 20 Aug.,
proved 12 Sept. 1757, bequeathed to sisters Sarah Harris and
Bathya  Ballard; and  to "kinsman"  Thomas Heard.  Nephew
Josiah  Heard  and  widow  Sarah Bump shared most  of the
estate.[5]  Josiah Bump apparently had no children.

References:   1. TAG 43:151.  2. Plainfield  CT  PR  2:146
              (Ebenezer  Harris).  3. Ibid. 3:115-6(Josiah
Bump et al.)   4. CSL Barbour Index,  Plainfield CT VR  1:1.
5. Plainfield CT PR 3:176 & File #299(Josiah Bump).

50   BETHIA BUMP or BUMPUS[5], (Sarah Eaton[4], Martha[3] Billington, Francis[2] John[1]), b. prob. Bristol ca. 1700; d. prob.
aft. 1761 and bef. 1790.[1,2]
     She m. Plainfield CT 23 Aug. 1721 PELEG BALLARD,[3] b.
Andover 20 Sept. 1694;[4] prob. d. in 1760 in what became
Fredericksburgh, Putnam Co. NY.[1]   Peleg was son of William
and Hannah (Hooper) Ballard.[4]
     Peleg sold lands and tenements in Plainfield in 1739, and
perhaps moved to NY about this time.[5] William Ballard was
on the Dutchess Co., NY tax lists from 1742/3 to 1765.
Peleg Ballard and Peleg, Jr. were on the tax lists from 1753
to 1760, when they were replaced by "Widow Ballard" in
1761.[1]

     Children (BALLARD) b. Plainfield CT:[3]

       i   WILLIAM[6] b. 29 Nov. 1722; m. Fredericksburgh NY
            bef. 1774 MARY CREED.[6]
      ii   HANNAH  b. 20 Aug. 1726  n.f.r.
     iii   PELEG  b. 6 Dec. 1728; apparently living near
            parents in NY 1753 to 1760.[1]
      iv   JOHN  b. 24 Feb. 1730/1

References:   1. Dutchess County (NY) Tax Lists, p. 1.
              2. 1790 Census, NY:82-4.   3. CSL Barbour
Index: Plainfield VR 1:53.  4. VR ANDOVER 1:50.  5. Plainfield CT LR 3:261,303(Peleg Ballard).  6. MF 1:18-9.


51   ELIZABETH[1] EATON[5] (Samuel Eaton[4], Martha[3] Billington,
Francis[2], John[1]) b. Middleboro 27 July 1701; d. Taunton 5
May 1780.[1]
     She m. Middleboro 21 June 1727 WILLIAM CANEDY,[2] b.
Plymouth 8 March 1689;[3]  d. Taunton 23 or 24 June
1774,[1] son of Alexander and Elizabeth (_____) Canedy.
     Capt. William Canedy of Plympton bought land in Taunton 5
Oct. 1726, and was of Taunton 14 April 1727 when he bought
more land there.[4] William Canedy, called esquire or
gentleman, had many land transactions. Several deeds are
recorded in Bristol and Plymouth Counties, the Canedy
homestead lying in both. He deeded to dau. Mercy Williams
10 Feb. 1763, to son Barnabas 14 March 1763, to son William
16 March 1763; and to both sons 5 April 1771.[5] He gave
land to daus. Hannah Pearce, Thankful Macomber and Fear
Perkins on 11 Dec. 1772, as stated in his will, but these
deeds were apparently never recorded.[6]
     William Canedy, in his will dated 26 Jan. 1773, probated
18 July 1774, named wife Elizabeth; sons William and
Barnabas, executors; and daus. Hannah Pierce, Thankful
Macomber, Fear Perkins and Mercy Williams.[6]

Children (CANEDY), prob. born Taunton:[7,8]

    i   WILLIAM[6] bp. Middleboro 16 Oct. 1729;[7] m.
        CHARITY LEONARD
   ii   NATHAN bp. Middleboro 15 Aug. 1731;[7] d. bef.
        1773; not mentioned in father's will, nor in
        any land record.
  iii   BARNABAS b. _____; m. (1) 1757 BETSEY HATHAWAY;
        m. (2) 1763 ELIZABETH BARNABY.
   iv   HANNAH b. Middleboro in 1737; m. ABIEL PIERCE
    v   THANKFUL b. ca. 1738; m. JOSEPH MACOMBER
   vi   FEAR b. _____; m. 1762 DAVID PERKINS
  vii   MERCY b._____; m. bef. 10 Feb. 1763 JOSEPH
        WILLIAMS. In addition to son Joseph, shown in
        MF1, they also had children: William, Thomas
        and Mercy Williams.[8]

References: 1. VR TAUNTON 3:44.  2. MD 5:39; & MIDDLEBOROUGH
           VR 1:31  3. MD 1:209.  4. Bristol Co LR  17:369,
370(William Canedy). 5. Plymouth Co LR 57:69,71; and Bristol
Co LR  55:61; 56:182,185(William  Canedy). 6. Bristol  Co PR
23:268  (William Canedy, Sr.)  7. Middleboro 1st Cong. Ch.
Recs.  8. MF 1:19-21 and Addendum p. 4


    52  BARNABAS [1]EATON[5] (Samuel Eaton[4], Martha[3] Billington,
Francis[2], John[1]) b.  Middleboro 12 April 1703; d. there Nov.
1790 ae 87y/7m.[1]
     He m. (1) ca. 1729 MEHITABEL ALDEN, b. Bridgewater 18
Oct. 1707;[2]   d. Middleboro 11 April 1739;[1,3] dau. of
Joseph and Hannah (Dunham) Alden; and a descendant of
Pilgrim John Alden.
     Barnabas m.  (2) Middleboro 21 Feb. 1743 ELIZABETH
CLEMENS,[4] b. ca. 1717, d. Middleboro 7 Dec. 1796 in her
80th yr.[5] Her identity is unknown.
     In a series of deeds from 1773 to 1790, Barnabas Eaton of
Middleboro gave land to sons Samuel, Seth, Nathan, Ziba (all
of Middleboro), and Lot of Stoughton; and to "my six
daughters Hannah, Mary, Elizabeth, Welthy, Keziah and
Merebah," (no surnames given for the daus.).[6]

     Children (EATON) b. Middleboro,  five by Mehitable, eight
by Elizabeth: [7,8,9,10,11,12]

    i   HANNAH[6] b. 29 Oct. 1730;[7] m. JOHN CLEMMONS
        (CLEMENTS)
   ii   SAMUEL b. 16 May 1732;[7] m. PATIENCE TINKHAM
  iii   MARY b. 14 May 1735;[8] m. JESSE SNOW
   iv   SARAH b. 16 June 1737;[8] n.f.r.

     v   SETH b. 6 April 1739;[9] m. (1) SARAH DELANO; m.
         (2) BETHIA DELANO
    vi   LOT  b. 9 Nov. 1744;[10]  m. MARTHA COBB
   vii   MEHITABEL  b. 30 April 1747;[10]  n.f.r.
  viii   ELIZABETH b. 22 Feb. 1748/9;[10] m. PEREZ LEONARD
    ix   ZIBA  b. 14 Sept. 1750;[11]  m. RUTH LEONARD
     x   NATHAN  b. 11 Aug. 1753;[11]  m. MARGARET CHERRY
    xi   WEALTHY  b. 19 June 1755;[11]  m. ELIJAH HACKET
   xii   KEZIAH  b. 8 Oct. 1757;[11]  m. DAVID WESTON, Jr.
  xiii   MERIBAH  b.  10  Feb.  1760;[12]  m.  (1)  ANDREW
         MURDOCK; m.(2) GIDEON PERKINS

References: 1. MIDDLEBORO DEATHS,  p. 60.  2. VR BRIDGEWATER
      1:26.  3. MD 15:24.   4. MD 15:220.   5. MIDDLE-
BOROUGH VR 1:267.  6. Plymouth Co. LR  62:64; 64:229; 70:175,
191;  83:18(Barnabas Eaton).  7. MD 12:131.   8. MD 14:244.
9. MD 14:245.   10. MD 16:135.   11. MD 18:156.   12. MIDDLE-
BOROUGH VR 1:117.  See also MF 1:21-4 and Addendum, pp. 4-5.


     53 NATHANIEL[1] FULLER[5] (Mercy Eaton[4], Martha[3] Billington,
Francis[2], John[1]) b.  Plymouth 14 Nov.  1687; d. Plympton  20
April 1750 aged 62y/5m/6d.[1]
     He m. Plympton 24 Jan.  1711/2 MARTHA SAMPSON,[2]  b.
there 25  Oct. 1689;[3]   d. there  8 June  1770 "N.S," aged
80y/7m/3d;[1] dau. of George and Elizabeth (Sprague) Sampson
of Plympton.  This is not a Mayflower Samson line.
     Nathaniel was a housewright and mason.  In his will, made
16 March 1749, probated  7 May 1750,  he named his wife
Martha;  eldest  son Amos  and  son Barnabas;  daus. Sarah
Sturtevant and  Ruth Cobb;  and grandson  William Fuller and
granddaughter Lydia Fuller, children  of son Nathaniel, deceased.[4]

     Children (FULLER), b. Plympton:[5]

     i   SARAH[6] b. 28 Sept. 1712; m. (1) ISAAC STURTEVANT;
         m. (2) AUSTIN BEARSE
    ii   RUTH  b. 4 March 1713/4; m. JAMES COBB, Jr.
   iii   WILLIAM  (twin) b. 20 July 1716; d. in 1716.
    iv   ELIZABETH  (twin) b. 20 July 1716; d. in 1716
     v   AMOS b. 12 Feb. 1718/9; m. (1) ABIGAIL HARLOW; m.
         (2) RACHEL (STANDISH) SAMPSON.
    vi   NATHANIEL  b.26 May 1721;  m. LYDIA PERRY
   vii   BARNABAS  b.  25 Sept.  1723; m. REBECCA CUSHMAN
         [Fam. #93]
  viii   JESSE  b. 18 Feb. 1725/6; d.y.
    ix   SAMUEL  b.  11  Nov.  1729;  d.  Plympton 7 March
         1742/3, aged 13y/3m/26d.[1]

References:   1. VR    PLYMPTON    p. 480.    2. Ibid.   p. 322.
              3. Ibid. p. 177. 4. Plymouth  Co. PR 11:89,91;
12:107(Nathaniel  Fuller).   5. VR PLYMPTON,  pp. 103-8.  See
also: MF 1:57-8 and Addendum, p. 7.


54 SETH[5] FULLER  (Mercy  Eaton[4], Martha[3] Billington,
Francis[2], John[1]),  b.  Plymouth 30  Aug. 1692; d. Plympton
after 30 March 1754 and before 26 Jan. 1758.[1,2]
      He m. (1) Plympton 12  May 1720 SARAH WRIGHT,[3]  b.  ca.
1693, d. Plympton  7 June 1726;[4]  dau. of  Adam and Sarah
(Soule) Wright.[5]  She was a descendant of Pilgrims Francis
Cooke and George Soule.
      Seth m.  (2) Plympton  8 March  1726/7 DEBORAH  (EDWARDS)
COLE,[3]  b. Wenham  22 July 1696, dau.  of John  and Sarah
(Woodin) Edwards.[6]  She m. (1) Rochester, rec. Plympton 12
Sept. 1723, Samuel Cole.[7]  No death record  for her found.
      He m.  (3) after  June 1747,  DEBORAH (____) DOTEN.  On
that date she was appointed an executor of the estate of her
late husband,  Jacob Doten.[2]  On  22 Feb. 1753  a note was
given by Seth  Fuller and his  then wife Deborah  to Solomon
Doten,   executor   of  Jacob  Doten's  estate,  for  "the
improvement of our thirds of the estate of Jacob Doten, late
of Plympton." This note was acknowledged  by Deborah Fuller
alone on 26 Jan. 1758.[2]
      In  1735 Seth  Fuller, then  living in Middleboro, bought
part of  a sawmill in Halifax.  He sold it in  1748 when he
was living  in Plympton, acknowledging  the deed of  sale 30
March 1754.[1]

      Children (FULLER), one by first wife, four by the second,
all but Seth recorded Plympton:[8]

      i    ARCHIPPUS[6] b. 27 May 1721;   m. (1) MARY  PRATT;
           m. (2) MARIA (RIDER) CHURCHILL
      ii   SARAH b. 27 Jan. 1727/8; prob. m. int. Kingston 8
           Dec. 1750 EPHRAIM TINKHAM.[9]
      iii  SETH  b. ca. 1730; m. HANNAH DOTEN
      iv   DEBORAH bp.  4 Nov. 1733; prob.  m. int. Kingston
           15 Sept. 1750 JOSEPH TINKHAM.[9]
      v    SAMUEL bp. 30 April 1738 n.f.r.

References: 1. Plymouth  Co. LR 44:227; 47:251(Seth Fuller).
            2. Plymouth  Co.  PR  10:401  and  Docket  #6587
(Jacob  Doten).   3. VR  PLYMPTON, p. 323.  4. Ibid. p. 480.
5. MD 4:240(Adam Wright's will).   6. TAG 64:152 & VR WENHAM
p.  31.   7. VR PLYMPTON p. 293.   8. Ibid. pp. 103-4, 107.
9. VR KINGSTON p.  291. See also: MFIP Francis Cooke pp.
15,66;  MF 3:14,45(Soule); MF 1:59-60 and Addendum, p. 8.

55  EBENEZER $_1$FULLER$^5$ (Mercy Eaton$^4$, Martha$^3$ Billington, Francis$^2$, John$^1$), b. Plymouth 24 March 1695; d. Kingston 2 May 1759 in 65th yr; bur. there in the old burying ground.[1]

He m. Kingston 21 June 1721 JOANNA GRAY,[2] b. Plymouth 29 Jan. 1695/6;[3] d. Kingston 25 Sept. 1776 ae 80y/7m/18d [MS record unverified]; dau. of John and Joanna (Morton) Gray, and a descendant of Pilgrim James Chilton.[4] John Gray's will of 23 Sept 1728 mentioned dau. Joanna Fuller.[5]

Ebenezer Fuller's will dated 29 ___ 1755, probated 1 Dec. 1772, named his wife Joanna; sons Josiah (to be executor) and Ebenezer; and daus. Rebecca, Lois and Eunice.[6]

Children (FULLER)  first three b. Plymouth [7], others b. Kingston:[8]

   i    JOSIAH$^6$ b. 15 May 1721 (1722?); m. LYDIA CUSHMAN [See Fam. #93]
   ii   SAMUEL  b. 14 Oct. 1723; d. 22 April 1724
  iii  REBECCA  b. 23 April 1725; "spinster" in 1762
   iv  HANNAH  b. 8 June 1727; d. 20 Aug. 1736.[9]
   v   MERCY  b. 29 Aug. 1730; d. 8 Jan. 1733/4.[9]
   vi  LOIS b. 16 Nov. 1733; m. NICHOLAS DAVIS [See Fam. #98]
  vii  EUNICE b. 5 May 1736; m. EBENEZER ROBBINS
 viii  EBENEZER b. 16 Feb. 1737/8; m. (1) LOIS RIDER; m. (2) HANNAH RIDER.

References: 1. VR KINGSTON p. 352. 2. Ibid. p. 226. 3. MD 1: 145. 4. MF 2:37-8,93-4(Chilton).  5. MD 21:62-4; & Plymouth Co. PR 6:191(John Gray's will.) 6. Plymouth Co. PR 21:192(Ebenezer Fuller). 7. MD 13:170. 8. VR KINGSTON, pp. 78-9. 9. Ibid. p. 351. See also: MF 1:60-1 and Addendum, p. 8.


56  BENJAMIN $_1$FULLER$^5$, (Mercy Eaton$^4$, Martha$^3$ Billington, Francis$^2$, John$^1$) b. Plymouth 7 March 1696; living Plympton 4 July 1755 when he sold to (his son) Samuel Fuller of Plympton, laborer, "all my homestead where I now dwell."[1]

He m. bef. 1720 MARY SAMSON, b. ca. 1700, dau. of Samuel and Hasadiah (Eddy) Samson; called "Daughter Mary Fuller" in the will of Samuel Samson dated 31 Aug. 1744.[2] She may have died between that date and 1755 when her husband signed alone in deeding their homestead.[1] No Plymouth Co. probate record for Benjamin Fuller has been found.

Children (FULLER), b. Plympton:

   i    JEPTHA$^6$  b. 26 July 1720;[3]  d.y.

ii  HASADIAH  b.  3  March  1721/2;[3]  m.  JAMES
    STURTEVANT,  Jr.,  a  descendant  of  Pilgrim
    Francis Cooke.
iii SAMUEL b. 14 May  1724;[4]  m. ANN(A) TINKHAM,  a
    descendant  of Pilgrims James Chilton and Peter
    Brown.

References:  1. Plymouth Co.  LR 43:241 (Benjamin  Fuller).
             2. Plymouth Co. PR 9:338(Samuel Samson).  3. VR
PLYMPTON p. 105.  4. Ibid.  p. 107.  See also  MF 1:61-2 and
Addendum, p. 8.


57  ELIZABETH $_1$FULLER$^5$  (Mercy  Eaton$^4$, Martha$^3$ Billington,
Francis$^2$,  John$^1$),  b.  Plymouth  30  March  1697;  d. prob.
Pomfret CT  after 1753,[1]  and bef.  1768 when  her husband
made gifts of  land to their children  without providing for
his wife.[2]
    She  m.  Plymton 30 Jan.  1723/4 JAMES RAYMOND  or
Raiment,[3] of  Middleboro, b.  Beverly 1  June 1689;[4]  d.
CT, prob. Pomfret, after 19 Jan. 1771 when he acknowledged a
deed,[2]  and prob.  later than 19 March 1773  when son James
Raymond called  himself "Jr." in  a deed.[5]  He  was son of
John and  Martha  (Woodin)  Raymond.  James Raymond m. (1)
Middleboro 27 Dec. 1716 Mercy Tinkham,[6]  who d. Middleboro
17 April 1723 aged  31,[7]  by whom  he  had two  children:
Peter  and Mercy.[8]° Mercy was descended from Pilgrim Peter
Brown.
    Elizabeth (Fuller) Raymond was admitted to the Middleboro
Church 19 July 1730.[9]   James and Elizabeth were  admitted
as  communicants to  the  Abington Congregational  Church,
Pomfret CT,  30 Aug.  1753  on recommendation from  the First
Church in Middleboro.[1]
    On 17 March 1753 James Raymond of Middleboro  bought 129
acres  in Promfret CT.  James  Raymond, yeoman  of Pomfret,
deeded separate tracts  of Pomfret land  on 18 Dec.  1760 to
sons James,  Joshua and  Amaziah;  and  on 17 June 1768 he
deeded to son-in-law Silas Rickard, son Amaziah and  to dau.
Martha  Winter.  On 25 May  1770, acknowledged 19 Jan. 1771,
the last date of  record for  him, James  Raymond deeded to
son-in-law William  Plank of  Killingly CT.[2]  No probate
records  for  James  or  Elizabeth Raymond  were  found  in
Connecticut.

    Children (RAYMOND), b. Middleboro:

    i   PATIENCE$^6$ b. 11 Nov. 1724;[10]  m. JAMES BRYANT
    ii  ELIZABETH  b.  13  Jan.  1727/8;[10]      m. SILAS
        RICKARD
    iii MARTHA  b. 21 June 1729;[11]  m. SAMUEL WINTER

    iv  RACHEL b. 9 Sept. 1730;[11] d. Pomfret CT 12 Dec.
        1756.[12]
     v  BATHSHEBA  b.  18  Feb.  1731/2;[11]   m. WILLIAM
        PLANK
    vi  JAMES b.  18  March  1732/3;[11]  m. (1) ABIGAIL
        DOWNING; m. (2) OLIVE PARISH or PARRISH.
   vii  AMAZIAH  b. 27 May 1734;[11]  m. JOANNA CUTLER
  viii  JOSHUA  b. 19 March 1735/6;[6]  m. ABIGAIL SHAW
    ix  ITHAMAR  b. 21  June 1737;[6]    bp. 14 Aug. 1737;
        [13]  n.f.r.

References:  1. CSL  Ch Recs  for Pomfret  (Abington Cong.).
            2. Pomfret  CT  LR  4:395;  5:123,124,205(James
Raymond).  3. VR  PLYMPTON  p.320.    4. VR BEVERLY 1:275.
5. Pomfret  CT  LR  6:66(James  Raymond,  Jr.)   6. MD 4:70.
7. MD  14:84.   8. MD 3:234.   9. Middleboro 1st Cong. Ch.
Recs.   10. MD 7:241.   11. MD   12:131-2.   12. CSL  Barbour
Index,  Pomfret  VR 1:30.   13. Middleboro  1st  Ch  Recs.,
p. 33.   See also MF 1:62-4 and Addendum, p. 8.


 58  JOHN  FULLER[5]  (Mercy  Eaton[4],  Martha[3] Billington,
Francis[2],  John[1]), b. Plymouth 19  Dec. 1698; d. Kingston 25
Sept. 1778 in 80th year.[1]
    He  m. (1) Plympton  7 Feb. 1722/3,  DEBORAH RING,[2]  b.
Plymouth  19  July  1698;[3]    d.  Kingston  8 Nov. 1763 ae.
65y/3m/15d;[1]    dau.  of  Eleazer  and  Mary (Shaw) Ring of
Plymouth, and a descendant of Pilgrim  Stephen  Hopkins.  The
will of  Eleazer Ring, dated  5 June 1738, named dau. Deborah
Fuller.[4]
    John  m.  (2)  Kingston  14  Nov.  1764  MERCY (WASHBURN)
CUSHMAN,[5]  b.  Plymouth 21  April 1702;[6]   d. Kingston 3
May 1796 aged  94y/3d;[7]  dau. of John  and Lydia (Billing-
ton) Washburn, and widow of Robert Cushman, [Fam. #93].
    John Fuller  was a physician and a deacon in the Kingston
Church.   He made  his will  31 Dec.  1761, probated  5 Oct.
1778, naming his sons  Issachar, Ezra, Consider and  Eleazer
and  his daus.  Deborah Prince,  Susanna Dingley  and Hannah
Bisbee.  His son Issachar and his  son-in-law Kimball Prince
were named executors.[8]

    Children (FULLER), all by first wife, b. Kingston:[9]

     i  ELEAZER[6] b.  3  Nov.  1723;  d. Kingston 20 Aug.
        1736,[1]
    ii  ISSACHAR b.  8 July 1725;  m. (1) ELIZABETH DOTY;
        m. (2) LUCY TINKHAM
   iii  JOHN  b. 16 Sept. 1727; d. 30 July 1742.[1]
    iv  DEBORAH  b. 14 Dec. 1729; m. KIMBALL PRINCE

          v   SUSANNA  b. 18 Nov. 1731; m. JACOB DINGLEY
         vi   NOAH  31  May  1734;  d. Kingston  6 Aug. 1756,
              unm.[7]
        vii   EZRA  b. 23 April 1736; m. ELIZABETH WESTON
       viii   CONSIDER  b. 7 July 1738; m. LYDIA BRYANT
         ix   ELEAZER  b. 27 April 1740; m. MARGARET HOLMES
          x   HANNAH  b. 30 April 1743; m. BENJAMIN BISBEE

References:    1. VR  KINGSTON, p. 352.   2. VR  PLYMPTON,
             p. 321.   3. MD  1:208.   4. MD 22:160-2(Eleazer
Ring).    5. VR  KINGSTON,  p. 204.    6. MD 2:165.   7. VR
KINGSTON,  p.  353.   8. Plymouth  Co.  PR  25:96,97,152 and
Docket #8239(John  Fuller).  9. VR KINGSTON,  pp. 80-4.  See
also: MF 1:64-6 & Addendum pp. 8-9.


    59  JABEZ   FULLER$^5$  (Mercy  Eaton$^4$,  Martha$^3$  Billington$^3$,
Francis$^2$,  John$^1$),  b. Plymouth "sometime in  the beginning of
June" 1701; d. Kingston in 1757.[1]
    He m.  int.  Kingston 13  Oct.  1733 MERCY GRAY,[2]  b.
Plymouth 4 Feb. 1703/4;[3]   d.  Kingston 13 Aug. 1782 in her
79th year;[4]  dau. of John and Joanna (Morton) Gray;[5] and
a descendant of Pilgrim James Chilton.[6]
    John Gray, of Kingston, in his will dated  23 Sept. 1728,
named dau.  Marcy Gray; and  on 23 Aug.  1738 Jabez and wife
Mercy  Fuller  signed  a  receipt  for  Mercy's share of the
estate of her father, John Gray. [5]
    Mercy  Fuller,  widow  of  Jabez  Fuller of Kingston was
appointed  administratrix  of  his  estate  20  (or 29) May
1757.[1]

    Children (FULLER) b. Kingston:[7]

          i   THOMAS$^6$  b.  31  Aug.  1734;  d. Kingston 2 April
              1738.[8]
         ii   JOANNA  b. 31 March 1736; m. JAMES FAUNCE
        iii   JAMES  b. 4 Dec. 1737; d. bef. 17 Dec. 1760, when
              his  mother  Mercy  was  appointed adm. of his
              estate.[9]
         iv   JABEZ  b. 24 Feb. 1739; m. RUTH WRIGHT
          v   JOHN  b. 29 Sept. 1741; m. REBECCA ROBBINS
         vi   MERCY  b. 6 July 1747; poss. m. EDMUND WILLIS

References:    1. Plymouth Co. PR 14:238(Jabez Fuller).   2. VR
             KINGSTON,  p. 225.   3. MD 1:145.   4. VR KING-
STON, p. 353.   5. MD  21:62-4, Plymouth PR 6:191, etc. (John
Gray's  estate)  6. MF 2:37-8,93-4;(Chilton)  7. VR KINGSTON
pp. 78-9.   8. Ibid.  p.  351.   9. Plymouth  PR 16:25(James
Fuller).  See also MF 1:66-7 and Addendum, p. 9.

60 MERCY FULLER[5] (Mercy Eaton[4], Martha[3] Billington, Francis[2], John[1]), b. Plymouth 3 Oct. 1702; d. aft. 21 Dec. 1768.[1]

She m. Plympton 28 July 1726 EBENEZER RAYMOND (or Raiment),[2] of Middleboro, b. there 18 Sept. 1703;[3] d. there bef. 5 Dec. 1768;[1] son of John and Martha (Woodin) Raymond.

Settlement of Ebenezer's estate, ordered 5 Dec. 1768, was made 21 Dec. 1768. Named in the settlement were: widow Mercy Raymond (the order gives her name as "Mercy," the settlement reads "Mary"); son Samuel and dau. Mercy.[1]

Children (RAYMOND), b. Middleboro:

    i   SAMUEL[6] b. 26 Dec. 1732;[4] m. (1) DINAH WOOD;
        m. (2) JOANNA (BRYANT) (DOTY) STETSON
   ii   MERCY b. 1 May 1739;[5] unm. in Dec. 1768. In
        the settlement of her father's estate Mercy
        received a piece of land, 1/4 part of a grist
        mill and 8 acres of woodland.[1]

References: 1. Plymouth Co. PR 20:328(Ebenezer Raymond). 2. VR PLYMPTON, p. 322. 3. MD 3:83. 4. MD 12: 131. 5. MD 14:245. See also: MF 1:67-8.


61 JAMES FULLER[5] (Mercy Eaton[4], Martha[3] Billington[3], Francis[2], John[1]) b. Plymouth 27 Feb. 1704; d. bef. 4 April 1769, the date the inventory of his estate was presented, calling him "late of Dartmouth." .[1]

He m. (1) Plympton 19 May 1725 JUDITH (or Judah) RICKARD,[2] b. there 2 Sept. 1705;[3] d. there 23 Feb. 1725/6 in 21st year;[4] dau. of Henry Rickard and his first wife Mary_____.

James m. (2) Plympton 22 May 1729 MERCY (JACKSON) PERKINS,[2] b. Plymouth 28 Nov. 1697;[5] d. aft. 1767;[1] dau. of Eleazer and Hannah (Ransom) Jackson, and widow of John Perkins, by whom she had four children.

On 29 Oct. 1738 James Fuller, bloomer, purchased a parcel of land at the new forge in Dartmouth from Stephen West.[6] James Fuller of Dartmouth, bloomer, made his will 24 Dec. 1767, and it was probated 24 April 1769, calling him "late of Attleboro." The inventory, however, called him "late of Dartmouth." He named his wife Mercy; son Thomas; son Elkanah "in case he be alive"; dau. Judah wife of Thomas Hauth; dau. Hannah; granddau. Olive; and a child of his granddaughter Olive taken in by Thomas Hauth. He gave to sons Elkanah and Thomas, land in Plymouth given to him by his father, Samuel Fuller. [1].

Children (FULLER), one by first wife, three by second
wife:

    i  ELKANAH[6] b. Plympton 9 Feb. 1725/6;[7] living
       1747; n.f.r.
   ii  JUDAH (or Judith) b. ca. 1730;[8] m. 1757 THOMAS
       HORTH.
  iii  THOMAS b. _____; m. 1762 HANNAH WASTE (or West)
   iv  HANNAH b. _____; unm. in Dec. 1767

References:     1. Bristol Co. PR 20:545(James Fuller).   2. VR
                PLYMPTON p. 321.   3. Ibid. p. 164.   4. Ibid.
p. 479.   5. MD 3:123.   6. Bristol Co. LR 28:163(James
Fuller).   7. VR PLYMPTON p. 104.   8. MQ 50:21-30:"Judah
Fuller..."   See also: MF 1:68-9 & Addendum, p. 9.


62  BETHIA BASSETT[5] (Bethia Eaton[4], Martha[3] Billington,
Francis[2], John[1]), b. Bridgewater 25 Dec. 1693;  d. aft. 21
May 1764.[1]
    She m. bet. 12 Jan. 1735/6 and 19 Sept. 1738 WILLIAM
CODDINGTON [2,3]   of Norton, who was living in Norton 24
March 1785.[4]   He m. (1) int. Norton 4 Nov. 1721 Elizabeth
Jones.[5]   An Abigail Coddington, wife of James Verrey, who
d. Norton in 1816 "in 87th year," was thus b. ca. 1730, and
was prob. William's dau. by his first wife.[6]
    William Coddington was of Norton when he bought land
there 19 Sept. 1721 (the earliest record of him.)[7]   William and wife Bethia on 19 Sept. 1738 sold "the homestead of
our  father  Joseph  Bassett  late  of  Bridgewater,
deceased."[3]   In 1742 William and wife Bethia were both
admitted to the Norton Church, she from Bridgewater. They
both acknowledged the sale of swampland in Bridgewater 21
May 1764.[1]   William sold land and dwelling house in Norton
and acknowledged the sale the same day: 24 March 1785.[4]
    There is no evidence that Bethia had any children.

References:     1. Plymouth Co. LR 52:152(William & Bethia
                Coddington).   2. Plymouth Co. PR 7:265,345
(Joseph Bassett).   3. Plymouth Co. LR 37:155 (William &
Bethia Coddington).   4. Bristol Co. LR 63:396(William
Coddington).   5. VR NORTON p. 214.   6. MF 1:9-10 and
Addendum,  p. 4.   7. Bristol Co. LR 41:28 (Blake to
Coddington).


63  MEHITABLE BASSETT[5] (Bethia Eaton[4], Martha[3] Billington,
Francis[2], John[1]) b. Bridgewater 22 June 1697; d. Middleboro
bef. 1754, when her husband remarried.[1]

She m. Middleboro 20 June 1733 NATHANIEL HOLLOWAY,[2]  b.
Taunton ca.  1702; d. Middleboro bef.  13 Oct.  1757;[3]  son
of Nathaniel and  Deliverance (Bobbit) Holloway.  He  m.  (2)
Berkley 25 May 1754 Abiah (Crane) Babbitt.[1]
     No children were found from his first  marriage.  In 1757
his widow  Abiah was appointed administratrix of her husband
Nathaniel  Holloway's estate.   In  a  subsequent  division
Jedidah  and Lois Holloway, two children of his second wife,
are called his only surviving heirs.[3].

References:  1. Index Berkeley  Marr. Bk.  1 (Old  Co. Hist.
             Soc.,  Taunton).   2. MIDDLEBOROUGH  VR,  1:60
3. Plymouth Co. PR 14:419; 20: 448(Nathaniel Holloway).  See
also  MF 1:9-10.


     64  LYDIA  BASSETT$^5$  (Bethia  Eaton$^4$,  Martha$^3$ Billington,
Francis$^2$, John$^1$),  b. Bridgewater  29 April  1703; living at
Norton 17 May 1764.[1]
     She m.  Bridgewater 17 Nov. 1726  SAMUEL PHILLIPS,[2]  b.
Taunton  10  Feb.  1697  to  James  and  Elizabeth  (French)
Phillips.[3]  He was living at Norton 23 April 1771.[4]
     In 1738 Samuel  and Lydia sold  land "by the  meadow that
was  our father  Joseph Bassett's."[5]   They were living in
Norton when  they acknowledged a  deed in 1747.[6]   In 1763
William  Coddington and wife Bethia, and Samuel Phillips and
wife Lydia, all of  Norton, sold their rights to  a swamp in
Bridgewater.  The  Phillipses acknowledged this  deed 17 May
1764.[1]  Samuel Phillips of  Norton sold his dwelling house
and  barn in Norton  to son Daniel  Phillips of Norton on 23
April 1771; the  land was bounded by "land  of my son Joseph
Phillips."[4]

     Children (PHILLIPS) b. prob. Norton:[4]

     i   JOSEPH$^6$ b. bef. 1734; m. MERCY (HODGES) TITUS
    ii   DANIEL b. bef. 1736;  m. (1) ELIZABETH FISHER; m.
         (2) RACHEL LINCOLN,  perhaps dau. of  Nathaniel
         and Elizabeth (Robinson) Lincoln of Rehoboth.
and possibly:
   iii   LYDIA d. Norton  16 May 1826,  ae. 91; m.  GEORGE
         WETHERELL

References:   1. Plymouth  Co.  LR  52:122  (Coddington  &
             Phillips).  2. VR BRIDGEWATER 2:297.  3. VR
TAUNTON,  p.  335.   4. Bristol  Co.  LR  54:100  (Samuel
Phillips).  5. Plymouth  Co.  LR  37:154;(Samuel Phillips).
6. Ibid. 38:250(Samuel  Phillips).  See  also: MF 1:24-5 and
Addendum, p. 5.

---

65  ISAAC SABIN[5]  (Samuel Sabin[4], Mary[3] Billington, Francis[2], John[1]) b. Rehoboth 2 Feb. 1695, d. Norwich CT 15 July 1756.[1]

He m. Norwich CT 2 June 1718 SARAH ORMSBY,[1] b. Rehoboth 4 Jan. 1697/8,[2] prob. the "old Mrs. Sabins" who d. Norwich in 1774;[3] dau of John and Susannah (_____) Ormsby. The Ormsby name was often spelled "Olmsby" in Connecticut records.

A study of the descendants of William Sabin of Rehoboth shows that the only Isaac in the family born early enough to be this Isaac of Norwich CT was the son of Samuel and Grace (Ormsby) Sabin. Isaac's wife, Sarah Ormsby, was his first cousin, dau. of his uncle, his mother's brother, John Ormsby, who moved from Rehoboth to Windham CT in 1703 and was an early settler of Norwich CT, admitted as an inhabitant in 1715. Isaac Sabin was admitted an inhabitant in 1720.[4] Another of Isaac Sabin's uncles, Joseph Ormsby of Rehoboth, bought land on Wawecoas Hill in Norwich 10 May 1720, moved to that town and sold part of the same land to Isaac Sabin of Norwich 4 Oct. the same year.[5] The two men were business partners in a land sale at Norwich 14 May 1724.[6]

Administration on the estate of Isaac Sabin of Norwich CT was granted 8 Oct. 1756 to his son Eldad Sabin. Distribution was made 3 May 1757 to the widow, to sons Isaac (eldest), Eldad, Phinehas, and to daus. Sibel, Marabah, Sarah and Anne.[7]

Children (SABIN), b. Norwich CT:[1]

    i    ISAAC[6]  b. 1 May 1719
   ii    ELDAD  b. 2 Aug. 1722
  iii    MARABAH  b. 26 June 1725; d. 23 June 1803 unm.
   iv    PHINEHAS  b. 22 Oct. 1727
    v    SARAH  b. 17 April 1731
   vi    SAMUEL  b. 28 June 1733; d. 19 Oct. 1733
  vii    SYBIL  b. 1 July 1737
 viii    child  d. 16 June 1741.[3]
   ix    ANN  b. 17 Sept. 1742

References: 1. CSL Barbour Index: Norwich. 2. REHOBOTH VR p. 693. 3. Norwich CT Fifth Ch Recs 3:84. 4. NORWICH CT BY CAULKINS pp.237,240 [See Fam. #66, Samuel Sabin, for his visit to his relations in Norwich.] 5. Norwich CT LR 3A:408 (Joseph Ormsby); 3B:435 (Isaac Sabin). 6. Norwich CT LR 4:176 (Joseph Ormsby and Isaac Sabin). 7. Norwich CT Dist. PR 2:37-40 (Isaac Sabin).

66  SAMUEL SABIN[5]   (Samuel   Sabin[4],   Mary[3]   Billington,
Francis[2], John[1]) b.  Rehoboth 29 Aug. 1697, d. bef. 1730 and
probably bef. 1724.[1,2]
    As Samuel Sabin, Jr., he m. Rehoboth 8 Jan. 1721/2 RUTH
READ,  whose identity is  unknown, despite much research.[3]
She  d. after 4 Oct. 1763.[4]    She was undoubtedly the Ruth
Sabin  received  as  a  member  of the Newman Congregational
Church  1 March  1729/30, two  months before  Elijah, son of
Ruth Sabin was baptized there.[2]    The widow Ruth Sabin was
one of the town poor  for whom funds were voted  at Rehoboth
Town  Meetings each year,  beginning 20 Oct. 1740.  She had
been recently  "taken to the workhouse" by  4 Oct. 1763, the
last mention of her name in these records.[4]
    Samuel Sabin[5]  was probably the man mentioned in the Town
Records of  Norwich CT  as follows:   "July 10, 1720--Samuel
Sabin appeareth before  me Richard Bushnell, Justice of the
Peace, and complaineth against himself that the last Sabbath
at night he  and John Olmsby (Ormsby) went  to Wawecoas Hill
to visit their relations,  and were late home, did  no harm,
and  fears it may be a transgression  of ye law and if it be
is  very  sorry  and don't  allow  himself  in unseasonable
night-walking."[5]   Samuel  was   evidently  a  visitor  to
Norwich, was out with his cousin John Ormsby, Jr. aged 16,
and  visiting  his  brother,  Isaac  Sabin[5] and uncle Joseph
Ormsby, who had recently moved to Wawecoas Hill.  [see Isaac
Sabin, #65].
    From  the circumstance  of Samuel  Sabin[4] calling himself
"Sr." in  a deed of  1719, it appears  that his son, Samuel,
the only other Samuel Sabin who could be of age at Rehoboth,
was  then  living.  By  1724,  a  deed of Samuel[4] omits the
suffix,  showing  probably  that  his  son had died.[1]   The
younger Samuel  had certainly  died by  3 May  1730 when his
son, Elijah, was baptized as "son of Ruth Sabin."[2]

    Child (SABIN) of Samuel, Jr. and Ruth, b. Rehoboth:[3,2]

      i  ELIJAH[6]  b.  9 Feb.  1721/2;  bp. as son of Ruth
            Sabin 3 May 1730

References:  1. Bristol  Co.   LR  12:509-10  (Samuel Sabin,
            Sr., 1719) and   21:490 (Samuel  Sabin, 1724).
2. RI VR: Newman  Cong. Church 9:483, 520.  3. REHOBOTH VR
pp. 331,738.  4. Rehoboth  Town Meeting Records [LDS Microfilm #562,561] 2:9,26,38,49,68,78,86,98,103,113,182,204,227,
237.  5. NORWICH CT BY CAULKINS p. 278.


67  GRACE  SABIN[5]  (Samuel   Sabin[4],  Mary[3]  Billington,
Francis[2], John[1]) b. Rehoboth 5 April  1699, living 1731  at
Providence RI, perhaps d. bef. 1749.[1]

---

She m. Rehoboth 27 March 1718 JEREMIAH ROBINSON,[2]   b.
Rehoboth 20 Aug. 1692,[3] d. aft. 28 Feb. 1749;[1] son of
John and Hannah (Wheaton) Robinson.
Three deeds of 25 June 1728, 25 Nov. 1728 and 7 Jan.
1728/9 show that Jeremiah Robinson sold three pieces of
Rehoboth property and moved to Providence RI. In one deed
he sold 6&1/2 acres "that I purchased of my grandfather,
Jeremiah Wheaton;" in another their homestead was conveyed
by Jeremiah with wife Grace Robinson releasing her dower
rights, and in the third, Jeremiah is called "lately of
Rehoboth, but now of Providence."[4] Their first home in
Providence was a 20-acre tract purchased in 1728 and sold 19
May 1731 with Jeremiah and Grace Robinson both signing.[1]
By June 1740 Jeremiah Robinson and family had returned to
Rehoboth but were warned to depart from the town, as they
then owned no property there.[5] Grace's parents, as well
as Jeremiah's widowed mother Hannah Robinson, were all being
supported by the Rehoboth townspeople at that time.[6] It
was customary to warn out those who might become an
additional burden. Jeremiah Robinson bought a 3/4 acre plot
at Long Cove in Providence 23 Feb. 1743/4, and sold this
homestead 28 Feb. 1749, signing alone.[1] This suggests
that he then had no wife. No further record has been found.

Children (ROBINSON), the births of two recorded at
Rehoboth, two baptized at the Newman Congregational
Church:[3,7]

    i   NAOMA$^6$ b. 22 April 1720
   ii   SARAH b. 14 Aug. 1726; bp. 28 Aug. 1726
  iii   JOHN bp. 23 Oct. 1726 [perhaps should be 1728]

References: 1. Providence RI LE 7:416; 8:453-4; 10B:159;
           12:336 (Jeremiah and Grace Robinson; Jeremiah
Robinson). 2. REHOBOTH VR p. 331. 3. Ibid. p. 731.
4. Bristol Co. LR 18:368,552; 19:36 (Jeremiah and Grace
Robinson). 5. Bristol Co. Court of General Sessions for
June 1740. 6. Rehoboth Town Meeting Records, [LDS Film
#562,561] 1:251,261,281; 2:8,9,26,38,49,57,68,78,82,86.
7. RI VR: Newman Cong. Church 9:519.


68  EXPERIENCE$_1$ SABIN$^5$ (Samuel Sabin$^4$, Mary$^3$ Billington,
Francis$^2$, John$^1$) b. Rehoboth 22 May 1700, d. there 6 Feb.
1774 as widow Experience Robinson.[1]
She m. Rehoboth int. 23 June 1722 EBENEZER ROBINSON,[2]
b. there 5 March 1701,[3] d. Rehoboth __ Oct. 1730;[1] son
of John and Hannah (Wheaton) Robinson. Ebenezer was a brother of Jeremiah Robinson who m. Experience's sister, Grace.

Experience was a widow of Rehoboth when she joined her mother and sisters in ceding her father's land to the town in 1747.[4] No children and no probate or land records have been found for them.

References: 1. REHOBOTH VR  p.  871.    2. Ibid.  p.  332.
            3. Ibid.  p.731.  4. Bristol Co. LR 36:39 (Grace Sabin et al).


69 PATIENCE SABIN[5] (Samuel Sabin[4], Mary[3] Billington, Francis[2], John[1]) b. Rehoboth 3 Oct. 1704, possibly the Patience, wife of Ebenezer Smith who d. Rehoboth 16 Feb. 1772.[1]

Perhaps she was the Patience Sabin who m. Rehoboth 12 Sept. 1748 EBENEZER SMITH "late of Wrentham."[2] He has not been identified.

Patience was living unmarried at Rehoboth and helped to care for her parents while the town supported them.[3] In 1747 she joined her mother and sisters in a Rehoboth deed.[4] If she married the following year, it was late in her life, and no children have been found.

References:  1. REHOBOTH VR p. 877.  2. Ibid. p. 332. 3. Re-
             hoboth Town Meeting Records, [LDS Film #562,
561] passim.  4. Bristol Co. LR 36:39 (Grace Sabin et al).


70 ELIZABETH WELCH[5] (Mercy Sabin[4], Mary[3] Billington, Francis[2], John[1]) b. Rehoboth 27 Sept. 1688, d. Killingly CT 16 Nov. 1730.[1]

She m. prob. bef. 1710 DANIEL LAWRENCE,[2] b. Natick ca. 1686, d. Killingly CT 8 April 1747;[1] son of John Lawrence. He m. (2) by 1732 Mercy or Marcy _____, by whom he had four children: Marcy, John, Elihu, and Asa, not Billington descendants.[1,3]

Daniel Lawrence of Killingly CT, in his will of 2 July 1743, exhibited 8 May 1747, gave dower or thirds to wife Marcy; to four older sons Daniel Lawrence, Joseph Lawrence, James Lawrence and Samuel Lawrence, one pound each, with what they had already received; to daus. Mary Covel and Esther Ballard, five pounds apiece with what they had received; to dau. Abigail Lawrence thirty pounds; to dau. Marcy Lawrence thirty pounds at age 21 or at marriage; to sons John, Elihu and Asa Lawrence, "all housing and lands I now live on," when they are of age. The executors were wife Marcy and son Joseph, they to "take good care and bring up my young children."[3]

The real estate of Daniel Lawrence, dec'd. was set off 17 March 1757 to the heirs of John, dec'd., Elihu and Asa Lawrence, youngest sons. Receipts to executor Joseph Lawrence were signed by James, Daniel and Samuel Lawrence, by Mary, wife of Stephen Covell and by Enoch Ballard, husband of Esther. Other records show that Abigail had married Nathaniel Allen.[3]

Children (LAWRENCE) by Elizabeth, apparently all over 21 in 1743, and thus born bef. 1722, prob. at Killingly CT, births not recorded:

     i   DANIEL$^6$
    ii  JOSEPH.  He was named in the will of his uncle
          Ebenezer Welch 25 Jan. 1759.[4]
   iii  JAMES
    iv  SAMUEL
     v  MARY
    vi  ESTHER
   vii  ABIGAIL

References:  1. CSL Barbour Index: Killingly.  2. Windham CT Dist.  PR 1:pt.1: 141,154,156; pt.2:88 (James Welch).  3. Windham Dist.  PR 3:346,347,348 and CSL File #2379 (Daniel Lawrence).  4. Plainfield CT Dist.  PR 3:249, 251,253,268,287 and CSL File #2206 (Ebenezer Welch).

71  MERCY WELCH$^5$ (Mercy Sabin$^4$, Mary$^3$ Billington, Francis$^2$, John$^1$) b. Rehoboth 1 March 1689/90, d. Plainfield CT 19 Oct. 1784, "aged 96 years."[1]
    She m. Plainfield CT 9 Dec. 1714 THOMAS SPAULDING,[1] b. Chelmsford 2 April 1690,[2] d. Plainfield CT 5 Dec. 1761, aged 72 years;[1] son of Joseph and Mercy (Jewell) Spaulding.
    "My sister Marcy" was named in the 25 Jan. 1759 will of her brother Ebenezer Welch of Plainfield CT.[3]
    In the will of Thomas Spaulding of Plainfield, dated 11 Aug. 1761, probated 16 Dec. 1761, wife Marcy Spaulding was named, as were two sons: Andrew and Hezekiah Spaulding; and seven daus.: Mary Tiler, Unice Bauldwin, Abigal Gallop, Lydia Andreson, Sarah Parker, Elisabeth Spaulding, Hannah Spaulding; and granddaughter, Mehetable French. Son Andrew Spaulding was executor.[4]
    Receipts were given 21 Jan. 1762 from: Benjamin and Lydia Andrus, Ebenezer and Abigail Gallup, John and Eunice Baldwin, John and Mary Tyler, Sarah Parker, Elisabeth Spaulding, the widow Marcy and Hezekiah Spaulding for himself and as guardian to Mehetable French.[4]

Children (SPAULDING) b. Plainfield CT:[1]

   i   MARY$^6$  b. 7 July 1716; m. (1) JOSEPH COIT; m. (2)
       JOHN TYLER
  ii  SARAH  b. 7 Oct. 1717; m. (1) NATHANIEL FRENCH,
       father of Mehetable French; m. (2) JONATHAN
       PARKER.
 iii  ELIZABETH  b. 20 April 1719; d.s.p.
  iv  ANDREW (twin) b. 28 July 1720
   v  EUNICE (twin) b. 28 July 1720
  vi  HANNAH  b. 15 July 1722
 vii  HEZEKIAH  b. 20 Feb. 1724
viii  ABIGAIL  b. 20 Sept. 1727
  ix  LYDIA  b. 9 Dec. 1729

References: 1. CSL Barbour Index, Plainfield. 2. VR CHELMSFORD p. 152. 3. Plainfield CT Dist. PR 3:249,251,253,268,287 and CSL File #2206 (Ebenezer Welch). 4. Plainfield CT Dist. PR 4:266; 5:237-240; and CSL File #2011 (Thomas Spaulding).

72 $_1$JAMES WELCH$^5$ (Mercy Sabin$^4$, Mary$^3$ Billington, Francis$^2$, John$^1$) b. Rehoboth 27 July 1692, d. Bolton CT bef. 21 Nov. 1770.[1]
He m. late in life, ca. 1740, MARY KINGSBURY, b. Plainfield CT 29 Feb. 1719/20,[2] d. aft. 8 March 1784, then living at Bolton;[1] dau. of Samuel and Hannah (_____) Kingsbury of Plainfield. The distribution of Samuel Kingsbury's estate 3 June 1777 included a share to dau. Mary, without surname.[3] On 2 Sept. 1768 James Welch and wife Mary of Bolton CT quit claimed to her brother Ebenezer Kingsbury of Plainfield for her share of her brother Nathaniel Kingsbury's estate.[4]
James Welch lived his adult life at Voluntown CT until 25 Feb. 1743/4 when "James Welch, mason, of Voluntown," with wife Mary releasing dower, sold 100 acres, being lot #8 laid out to the said James Welch in the north end of Voluntown.[5] On 4 July 1744 James Welch "of Plainfield" (evidently a temporary residence) bought 64 acres with "mansion house" in Bolton, and continued to acquire land after moving there.[6] James was named in the will of his brother Ebenezer 25 Jan. 1759.[7]*
Administration of the estate of James Welch of Bolton CT was granted 21 Nov. 1770 to the widow Mary, with James Thrall, her son-in-law, as surety. Distribution of the estate was made 26 March 1783: a double share to James Welch the eldest and only son, a single share to Mary Thrall the only daughter, with dower or "thirds" to the widow Mary.[1]

Children (WELCH), prob. b. Voluntown or Bolton CT:

  i MARY[6] b. ca. 1743; m. JAMES THRALL
 ii JAMES, b. perhaps ca. 1745

*Note: The will  of Ebenezer Welch proves  that James Welch,
son  of  Mercy  (Sabin)  Welch,  was  living  in  1759.  The
Mayflower Society formerly accepted, as the son, a different
James Welch  who  died  at  Colchester,  CT  in  1756.  That
identification has been disproved and the Society closed the
line,  but  two  published  genealogies  continue  to mislead
researchers.

References:  1. Hartford CT Dist.  PR, CSL File #5792 (James
      Welch).  2. CSL  Barbour  Index:  Plainfield.
3. Plainfield   CT  District  PR  7:21,  149,154,193,239,294
(Samuel Kingsbury).  4. Plainfield CT  LR 5:502  (James and
Mary  Welch).  5. Voluntown  CT LR  2:65,66  (James  and Mary
Welch).  6. Bolton  CT  LR  2:405,406;  3:45 (James Welch).
7. Plainfield  CT  Dist.  PR  3:249,251,253,  268,287 and CSL
File #2206 (Ebenezer Welch).


 73 SAMUEL  WELCH[5]  (Mercy  Sabin[4],  Mary[3] Billington,
Francis[2], John[1]) b. Rehoboth  15 Oct. 1693,  d. aft. 17 May
1769 when he conveyed land at Plainfield CT, and bef.  7 May
1774  when his  son Samuel  called himself  Samuel, Sr. in a
deed.[1,2]
 He m.  by 1725 AMY WILLIAMS, b. Plainfield CT 15  Nov.
1707,[3]  d.  aft. 1748; dau.  of Robert and  Hannah (_____)
Williams.  By deed dated 17 June 1740, Samuel Welch and wife
Amy  of Voluntown CT  sold their one-sixth  share of a tract
that  "our  honoured  father  Robert  Williams"  bought  in
1722.[4]
 Samuel  Welch  lived  at  Voluntown  before 1728 when his
brothers and sisters conveyed to him Voluntown land that had
belonged to his  father James Welch, and where "Samuel Welch
now  dwells."[5]  Samuel  Welch of  Voluntown sold  40 acres
there to John  Dixson 17 March 1753;[6]  and on 16 July 1757
Samuel Welch of Plainfield bought 10 acres in that town from
his  son,  Samuel  Welch,  Jr.[7]  The same 10 acres Samuel
Welch  deeded back  to Samuel,  Jr., both  of Plainfield, 31
Oct. 1768,  acknowledged 17  May 1769.  This was  the older
man's last land transaction.[1]
 Ebenezer Welch named brother  Samuel and the latter's son
Samuel  in  his  will  dated  25 Jan. 1759.[8]  There is no
probate record  for Samuel Welch in  Plainfield CT District,
which  included  Voluntown.  Samuel Welch, Sr. and  wife
Jerusha  sold Plainfield land  7 May 1774,  witnessed by

Ebenezer Robinson, Jr. and David Welch.[2] This was son Samuel Welch, who with wife Jerusha moved to Vermont.[9] Samuel Welch also sold 14 acres at Plainfield 7 May 1774 to David Welch, his reputed brother, who married but died without issue.[10]    Dau. Amy Welch m. Plainfield 18 Aug. 1750 Jacob Herd/Heard, a descendant of Pilgrim Francis Eaton, as well as of John Billington.[11]

    Children (WELCH) b. to Samuel and Amy at Voluntown CT:[12]

      i    MARY[6]  b. 21 (___) 1726; d.y.
     ii    SAMUEL  b. 16 April 1730
    iii    EZEKIEL  bp. 15 July 1733
    iv    AMY  b. 25 July 1735; m. JACOB HERD. [Fam. #48]
     v    MARY  b. 2 June 1747
 ?vi    DAVID  b. 1748; no birth record found.

References: 1. Plainfield CT LR 5:437 (Samuel Welch to Samuel Welch, Jr.). 2. Ibid. 6:218 (Samuel, Sr. and Jerusha Welch). 3. CLS Barbour Index: Plainfield. 4. Voluntown CT LR 2:179 (Samuel and Amy Welch). 5. Voluntown CT LR A1:388 (James Welch et al to Samuel Welch). 6. Voluntown CT LR 4:33A (Samuel Welch). 7. Plainfield CT LR 4:444 (Samuel Welch, Jr. to Samuel Welch). 8. Plainfield CT Dist. PR 3:249,251,253,268,287 and CSL File #2206 (Ebenezer Welch). 9. CT NUTMEGGER 10:4:615. 10. Plainfield CT LR 6:209 (Samuel Welch to David Welch). 11. MF 1:17. 12. CSL Barbour Index: Voluntown.


    74 THOMAS WELCH[5] (Mercy Sabin[4], Mary[3] Billington, Francis[2], John[1]) b. Rehoboth 1 March 1694/5, d. Windham CT 14 Aug. 1781 in his 87th year.[1]
    He m. (1) bef. 28 June 1714 HANNAH ABBE, b. prob. Wenham 13 Aug. 1693, but recorded Windham CT;[1] d. Windham 24 March 1769, aged 74 years;[1] dau. of John and Hannah (___) Abbe. By a deed dated 25 April 1709, recorded 31 May 1720, all of the children of John Abbe, deceased, quit claimed their shares of his estate to their brother, Richard Abbe. Acknowledgements were made as each child came of age to sign, with Thomas Welch and wife Hannah acknowledging 28 June 1714.[2]
    Thomas m. (2) Windham CT 31 Oct. 1769 RACHEL (WALCOTT) (HUNTINGTON) BINGHAM,[1] widow of Daniel Huntington and of Joseph Bingham.[3] There was no issue by the second marriage.
    Thomas Welch, in his will dated Windham 1 Feb. 1770, probated 24 Aug. 1781, named wife Rachel; sons Jeremiah, John and Daniel and negro woman Jene.[4] Jeremiah Welch, son

of Thomas, was the executor and principal heir in the 1759 will of his uncle Ebenezer Welch.[5]

Children (WELCH), all by first wife Hannah, b. Windham CT:[1]

     i   JEREMIAH[6] b. 14 Nov. 1714
    ii  JOHN b. 8 July 1717
   iii  DANIEL b. 20 March 1726

References: 1. CSL Barbour Index: Windham. 2. Windham CT LR E:476(Richard Abbe). 3. HUNTINGTON FAM pp. 75,371. 4. Windham CT District PR 10:427 (Thomas Welch). 5. Plainfield CT Dist. PR 3:249,251,253,268,287 and CSL File #2206 (Ebenezer Welch).


75. EBENEZER[1] WELCH[5] (Mercy Sabin[4], Mary[3] Billington, Francis[2], John[1]) b. Bristol 13 Feb. 1697, d. testate without issue Plainfield CT 29 Jan. 1759.[1]
He m. (1) Lebanon CT 12 May 1725 LYDIA DIBBLE,[2] who d. Plainfield 5 Oct. 1754;[1] prob. dau. of Benjamin and Mary (Benjamin) Dibble.[2]
Ebenezer m. (2) at Second Preston (Griswold) Church 17 July 1755 SARAH MacQUITHEY/MacWITHY, who was living in 1759.[3]
In his will dated 25 Jan. 1759, probated 7 Feb. 1759, Ebenezer Welch of Plainfield, mentioned wife Sarah; brother Samuell and his son Samuell; brother James; sister Marcy; sister Martha; John Welch son of my brother John Welch, dec'd.; Joseph Lawrence, son of my sister Elezebeth, dec'd.; friend David Downing; brother Thomas Welch's son Jeremiah to have the residue of my estate, to be executor, and to support my mother-in-law Mary Dibell during her natural life.[4] Ebenezer Welch had no known children.

References: 1. CSL Barbour Index, Plainfield. 2. CT MARR 2:39. 3. CT MARR 4:39. 4. Plainfield CT Dist. PR 3:249,251,253,268,287 and CSL Probate File #2206(Ebenezer Welch).


76 [1]JOHN WELCH[5] (Mercy Sabin[4], Mary[3] Billington, Francis[2], John[1]) b. Bristol 17 April 1699, d. Plainfield CT bef. 19 Dec. 1754, when the inventory of his estate was taken.[1]
He m. (1) Plainfield CT 11 Sept. 1722 ABIGAIL DIBBLE,[2] b. Simsbury CT 16 March 1699/1700,[3] d. bef. April 1729; dau. of Benjamin and Mary (Benjamin) Dibble.[3]
John m. (2) Plainfield 11 April 1729 SARAH ABBE,[2] b.

Windham CT 11 March 1699,[4] living in 1754; dau. of John and Hannah (_____) Abbe.

John Welch of Plainfield, in his will dated 16 Nov. 1754, probated 7 Jan. 1755, gave wife Sarah all household goods and the use of one-half the real estate during her widowhood; to son John the whole of the real estate and personalty, except that given to his mother, he to pay debts and legacies; to dau. Mary 100 pounds within three years and to dau. Hannah 150 pounds within four years. Son John was named executor.[1]

"John Welch, son of my brother John Welch, dec'd" was named in the 25 Jan. 1759 will of Ebenezer Welch.[5]

Children (WELCH) b. Plainfield CT, first by Abigail, two by Sarah:[2]

    i   MARY[6]  b. 2 (or 16) July 1723
   ii  HANNAH  b. 11 Dec. 1730
  iii  JOHN  b. 12 June 1732

References: 1. Plainfield CT Dist. PR 3:25,27,58 (John Welch). 2. CSL Barbour Index: Plainfield. 3. CSL Barbour Index: Simsbury. 4. CSL Barbour Index: Windham. 5. Plainfield CT Dist. PR 3:249,251,253,268, 287 and CSL File #2206(Ebenezer Welch).


   77 TABITHA KINGSLEY[5] (Sarah Sabin[4], Mary[3] Billington, Francis[2], John[1]) b. Rehoboth 23 Sept. 1688, d. aft. 13 Aug. 1733 when she and her husband were named in the settlement of her father's estate.[1]

She m. Windham CT 10 May 1709 *JOHN BROUGHTON, [2] b. Northampton 9 March 1680/1,[3] or 7 Jan. 1680,[4] d. aft. 13 Aug. 1733;[1] son of John and Elizabeth (Woodruff) Broughton.[5*]

In the 1731 settlement of his father's estate, John Broughton was called of Windham now of Ashford, CT, but no records for them have been found in Ashford. In 1720 John Broughton sold land at Windham to (his brother-in-law) Ezra Kingsley.[6] There is no probate record for John Broughton in Windham CT District or in Pomfret CT District, which included Ashford after 1752.

Children (BROUGHTON) b. Windham CT:[2]

    i   MARY[6]  b. 12 June 1710
   ii  TABITHA  b. 10 Jan. 1712
  iii  AMOS  b. 23 May 1718
   iv  ELIZABETH  b. 9 March 1720
    v  PHEBE  b. 15 March 1721

*Note: John Broughton had no first wife Hannah, as stated by
Bowen, Ref. #5.  John's father, John, and step-mother Hannah
(Allis) Broughton also lived at Windham, the  probable cause
of confusion.

References:   1. Windham    CT   District    PR   I:465-7(John
Kingsley).    2. CSL  Barbour  Index:   Windham.
3. Judd   Manuscript   at   Farley   Library,   Northampton.
4. DEERFIELD  BY  SHELDON  2:92.    5. *WOODSTOCK CT BY BOWEN
2:658.   6. Windham  CT  LR  E:429  (John  Broughton to Ezra
Kingsley).


78  SARAH  KINGSLEY[5]   (Sarah   Sabin[4],   Mary[3] Billington,
Francis[2],  John[1]) b. Rehoboth 9 Oct.  1690, d. there __ Oct.
1727.[1]
     She m. Swansea 10 Feb.  1708/9,[2]   int. Rehoboth 18 Dec.
1708, EPHRAIM HIX/HICKS,[3]  b.  prob. Swansea ca. 1687,  d.
aft.   21 Oct.  1765  when  he  acknowledged   a  deed  at
Rehoboth;[4]   son  of  Ephraim  Hix  of  Swansea  and
Rehoboth.[5]  He m. (2) Swansea 28 Aug. 1728 Johanna Luther,
b.  Swansea  16  Aug.  1687,  dau.  of  Theophilus and Lydia
(Kinnecutt) Luther.[2]   He  m.  (3)  Eunice ____, who d.
Rehoboth 25 Feb.  1748/9 as "wife of Deacon Ephraim Hix."[1]
Deacon  Ephraim Hix m. (4)  int. Rehoboth  22 April 1749 Ann
Peirce, probably a widow.[3]
     Ephraim  Hix  was  a  deacon  of  the  Baptist  church at
Rehoboth.  He  appears  on  the  1759  and  1765 tax lists:
"Deacon Ephraim Hix and son Barnard," as one household unit.
Barnard Hix was taxed in 1769, but his father Ephraim is not
listed,  apparently  having  died  or  moved  away  in  the
interim.[6]  No death or probate record for this Ephraim Hix
was found in Bristol County.
     On 10 June 1746, Ephraim  Hix, for 200 pounds old  tenor,
sold to Barnard Hix [his son] half his dwelling house and 20
adjoining  acres.[7]    That  Barnard  continued to share the
homestead  with  his  father  until  1765  is  shown  by the
Rehoboth tax lists.  Finally,  in his last land transaction,
on 6 Aug. 1765,  acknowleged 21 Oct.  1765, Ephraim Hix
conveyed "for  love  to  my  son  Benjamin Hix," the  eldest
child, whose birth was not recorded in town records.[4,8]

     Children (HIX/HICKS) b. Rehoboth, by wife Sarah:[4,8,9]

     i    BENJAMIN[6]  b. ca. 1709/10, from age at death.
     ii   JOHN  b. 10 May 1712
     iii  EPHRAIM  b. 28 May 1714
     iv   BARNARD  b. 11 Apr. 1719
     v    ALETHEA  b. 18 Feb. 1723/4

References:   1. REHOBOTH VR p. 833.   2. Swansea Original VR,
             Bk B, p. 84/178.      3. REHOBOTH VR p. 460.
4. Bristol  Co.   LR  48:419  (Ephraim  Hix  to son Benjamin
Hix).   5. HICKS/HIX FAMS pp.  16-18.  6. EARLY   REHOBOTH
4:94,101,109.   7. Bristol  Co.   LR  48:418 (Ephraim Hix to
Barnard Hix).  8. MQ 42:98 (1976).  9. REHOBOTH VR p. 634.


    79  JOHN   KINGSLEY[5]  (Sarah   Sabin[4],  Mary[3]  Billington,
Francis[2], John[1]) b. Rehoboth 26 Feb. 1694/5,  d. aft. 9 Feb.
1754, then living at Windham CT.[1]
    He  m.  Windham  25  Dec.  1717  ELIZABETH  BASS,[2]   b.
Braintree 5 Sept. 1696,[3]  apparently d.  Windham between 8
Nov.  1753 and  9 Feb.  1754;[1] dau.  of John and Elizabeth
(Neale)  Bass.[4]   The  will  of  John  Bass  of Windham CT
written 16 April 1752, probated 15 Oct. 1753, included as an
heir,  dau.  Elizabeth,  wife  of  John  Kingsley.  Elizabeth
signed  for her  share of  father's estate  8 Nov. 1753, but
husband John Kingsley receipted alone for John Bass's legacy
9 Feb. 1754 calling Elizabeth "my former wife."[1]
    John  Kingsley  sold  33  acres  in the Second Society in
Windham to Benjamin Bidlack 17 Jan. 1749/50.[5]  There is no
probate  record for  him in  Windham District,  and no death
record has been found.

    Children (KINGSLEY) b. Windham CT:[2,6]

       i   JONATHAN[6]  b. 24 Dec. 1718
      ii   EBENEZER  b. 17 Oct. 1720
     iii   JERUSHA  b. 17 Sept. 1723
      iv   ABIGAIL  b. 14 Oct. 1725
       v   SARAH  b. 6 Sept. 1727; bp. 10 Dec. 1727
      vi   JOHANNAH  b. 3 Sept. 1729; bp. 26 Oct. 1729
     vii   ANN  b. 9 Nov. 1731; bp. 2 April 1732
    viii   IRENIAH/IRENE  b. 20 May 1734; bp. 14 July 1734
      ix   ENOCK  b. 10 Oct. 1736; bp. 28 Nov. 1736

References:   1. Windham CT Dist. PR 4:297-299, 385-387 (John
             Bass).     2. CSL   Barbour   Index: Windham.
3. BRAINTREE RECS p. 674.  4. BASS GEN pp. 21-2, 32-3, 36-7.
5. Windham CT LR  I:373.  6. WINDHAM CT FIRST  CH pp. 13,15,
18,21,23.


    80  JOSIAH  KINGSLEY[5]  (Sarah  Sabin[4],  Mary[3]  Billington,
Francis[2], John[1]) twin of Amos,  b. Rehoboth 18 Jan. 1696/7,
d. aft. 13 Aug. 1757.[1]
    He  m.  Windham  CT 10  Dec. 1718  DOROTHY BINGHAM,[2]  b.

Norwich, CT 24 Jan. 1699/1700, d.    aft.  1743; dau. of Thomas
and Hannah (Backus) Bingham.[3]
     Josiah Kingsley   lived at Windham CT, in Scotland Parish,
although one child was baptized   in the Lisbon CT church.[4]
On 13 Aug.  1757 Josiah Kingsley  of Windham sold  "the land
that I  live on,"   to  Josiah Kingsley, Jr.[1]  No probate
record for him has been found in Connecticut.

     Children (KINGSLEY) b. Windham CT:[2,4]

          i    MARY[6]  b. 11 Oct. 1719
         ii    ELIPHALET  b. 3 Dec. 1721
        iii    JOSIAH  b. 31 March 1724
         iv    JABEZ  b. 19 Aug. 1726
          v    DOROTHY  b.  17  Sept.  1729;  bp.  28 Sept. 1729
               Lisbon Church
         vi    SARAH  b. 28 Oct. 1731
        vii    ADONIJAH  b. 3 April 1734
       viii    JEREMIAH  b. 3 April 1738
         ix    ELIPHAS  b. 8 Feb. 1740
          x    ELISHA  b. 7 Aug. 1743

References:   1. Windham  CT   LR  N:20   (Josiah  Kingsley).
              2. CSL Barbour Index: Windham.   3. CSL Barbour
Index, Norwich.   4. CSL Ch  Recs: Lisbon  CT: Newent  Cong.
Church 1:55.


     81  AMOS   KINGSLEY[5]  (Sarah    Sabin[4],  Mary[3] Billington,
Francis[2], John[1]) twin of Josiah, b. Rehoboth 18 Jan. 1696/7,
d. Becket 23 April 1787 aged 90.[1]
     He  m.  Windham  CT  12  June  1723  RUTH  ADAMS,[2]   b.
Providence, RI  10 April  1702,[3]  dau.  of Henry  and Ruth
(Ellis) Adams.  She d._____ at Becket.[1]
     He lived at Windham CT and moved in 1751 with some of his
children to Becket, where he resided thereafter.[1]

     Children (KINGSLEY) b.  Windham CT; baptized at the First
Church of Windham  and in Scotland parish church that became
the First (Congregational) Church of Scotland CT:[2,4,5]

          i    ISAIAH[6]  b. 11 June 1725
        ~ii    NATHANIEL  bp. 23 April 1727
        iii    JOSEPH  bp. 26 Oct. 1729
         iv    AMOS  b. 3 June 1731; bp. 3 Aug. 1731
          v    SAMUEL (twin)  b. 6 May 1733; bp. 1 July 1733
         vi    JOHN (twin)  b. 6 May 1733; bp. 1 July 1733
        vii    ALICE  bp. 12 Feb. 1738
       viii    RUTH  bp. by Mr. Clap of Scotland Church, n.d.

            ix  ABIAH  bp. as HANNAH 25 April 1742
            x   ELIJAH  bp. 20 Sept. 1744

References:  1. KINGSLEY  GEN  BY  DEANE:  gives as ref. for
            deaths,  VR of  Becket,  p.  94.  2. CSL Barbour
Index:  Windham.  3. RI VR:Providence 2:207.  4. WINDHAM CT
FIRST  CH pp.  13,15,17,20.  5. CSL  Ch Recs: Scotland Cong.
Church.


    82  EZRA  KINGSLEY[5]  (Sarah  Sabin[4],  Mary[3]  Billington,
Francis[2], John[1]) b. Rehoboth 10  Dec. 1698, d. Windham CT  8
April 1759,  aged 60  years,  buried  Palmerstown Cemetery in
what is now Scotland CT.[1]
    He m. (1)  Windham CT  31 Dec. 1719  *ELIZABETH WIGHT,[2]
b. Medfield 17  Oct. 1703,[3]  d. Windham  19 March 1735;[4]
dau.  of  Joshua  and  Elizabeth  (Spowell)  Wight.[4]     Her
father,  Joshua  Wight,  d.  Windham  14  Aug.  1762, but no
probate record for him appears.[2,4]
    Ezra  m. (2) Windham  CT 10 Nov.  1743 MARY FOLLET[T], b.
there 23 March 1711,[2]    d. aft. 1751; dau. of Benjamin and
Patience (Doughty) Follet.[5]    Benjamin Follet, in his will
dated 27  Nov. 1750,  made a  bequest to  dau. Mary, wife of
Ezra Kingsley.[6]
    Ezra Kingsley was  part owner of a grist  mill at Windham
in  1740.  The  last of  his many  deeds was acknowledged 17
Sept. 1755.[7]   There  is  no  probate  record  for him in
Windham District.

    Children  (KINGSLEY) b.  Windham CT,  first four  by wife
Elizabeth, others by Mary:[2,8,9]

        i   EZRA[6]  b. 15 Aug. 1721; d. 1 Nov. 1733
        ii  SALMON  b. 27 Sept. 1723
       iii  ELIZABETH  b. 18 June 1727; bp. 25 June 1727.[8]
        iv  MARY  b. 6 Aug. 1730; bp. 9 Aug. 1730.[8]
        v   EZRA  b. 13 Aug. 1744
        vi  OLIVE  b. 4 Sept. 1746; bp. 26 July 1747.[9]
       vii  LUCRETIA  b. 5 June 1749
      viii  HANNAH  b. 21 Nov. 1751

*Note: This  surname Wight  is often  miscalled "Wright"  or
"White".

References:  1. CSL Hale Cem  Recs, Windham.  2. CSL Barbour
            Index, Windham. 3. VR MEDFIELD p. 104. 4. WIGHT
GEN p.14.  5. ME  NH  GEN  DICT pp.72,200 (Benjamin Follet,
Patience Doughty).  6. Windham  CT Dist. PR  8:457 (Benjamin
Follet).  7. Windham, CT LR H:69, L:25.  8. WINDHAM CT FIRST
CH pp. 13,16.  9. CSL Ch Recs, Scotland Parish.

83  ELDAD  KINGSLEY[5]  (Sarah  Sabin[4],  Mary[3]  Billington,
Francis[2], John[1]) b. Windham CT 8 Jan 1707,  d. Lebanon CT 20
Jan. 1787 aged 80 years.[1]
     He m. Windham  CT 20 June  1733 PRISCILLA BASS,[2,3*]  b.
there  6 June 1715*,  d. 1812 (g.s.  1715-1812), both buried
Scoville and Buckingham  Cem., Lebanon CT.[1]  She  was  dau.
of John and Elizabeth (Neale) Bass. John Bass of Windham, in
his will written 16 April 1752, probated 15 Oct. 1753, named
Priscilla wife of Eldad Kingsley as one of his daus.[4]
     Priscilla  Kingsley  was  admited  to  the  Scotland
Congregational Church  1 Nov.  1741 and  children Oliver,
Eunice  and Lydia  were baptized  there 8  Nov. 1741.[5]  No
probate record for  Eldad or Priscilla appears in Windham CT
District, which included Lebanon in 1787.

     Children  (KINGSLEY)  first  five  b.  Windham, others b.
Lebanon CT:[2,6]

        i   ABNER[6]  b. 27 Jan. 1733/4
       ii   OLIVER  b. 24 Jan. 1734/5
      iii   EUNICE  b. 20 May 1736
       iv   LYDIA  b. 17  May 1739;  d. Lebanon  4 June 1747,
            aged 8 yrs.
        v   ELIJAH  b. 1 April 1742; bp. 18 April 1742
       vi   MARY  b. 6 March 1744
      vii   NATHAN  b. 20 Sept. 1747
     viii   LYDIA  b. 6 June 1753
       ix   TIMOTHY  b. 21 Oct. 1755

References:  1. CSL Hale Cem Recs, Lebanon.  2. CSL Barbour
            Index,  Windham.  3. BASS  GEN  p.  21-2,
32-3,36-7: *states Priscilla b. 6  June 1717.  4. Windham CT
Dist. PR  4:297-299, 385-387 (John Bass).  5. CSL Ch Recs,
Scotland Parish.  6. CSL Barbour Index, Lebanon.


84  SAMUEL  SABIN[5]  (Israel  Sabin[4],  Mary[3]  Billington,
Francis[3], John[1]) b. Rehoboth 21 Jan. 1699/1700; possibly the
Samuel  Sabin  who  was  buried  in  Newman  Congregational
Churchyard 30 June 1756.[1]
     He  m.  Rehoboth,  as  Samuel Sabin, 7 Nov. 1727 HANNAH
HALL,[2]  int.  Rehoboth 2 Sept.  1727 as Hannah Hall to
Samuel "Taber," Jr.,[3] undoubtedly a miscopy of "Saben" for
there  were  no  Tabers  in  Rehoboth  during the eighteenth
century. She was  probably dau. of John and Mary  (Newell)
Hall. No birth  record  appears in Rehoboth for  Hannah, but
the estate  papers of Mr.  John  Hall of Rehoboth, dec'd.
include an  agreement between  Mary Hall,  Easther Hall  and
Hannah Hall, all of Rehoboth, spinster daughters of John
Hall, late of Rehoboth, dec'd. to their brother Edward Hall,

admr. of the estate, dated 3 Oct. 1721. Hannah Hall
acknowledged the agreement at Rehoboth 17 Jan. 1725.[4]
   Apparently this Samuel Sabin, son of Israel, was called
Samuel, Jr. in his marriage intention record and also in the
birth records of his children, because his cousin Samuel,
#66 also called Samuel, Jr. in his 1722 marriage and son's
birth record several years previously, had since died. This
Samuel Sabin's uncle, Samuel Sabin, Sr.,#18, was certainly
living at Rehoboth in 1722 through 1739.
   Samuel evidently went to Maine about 1724 with his
brothers Israel and Jeremiah and was the Samuel Sabin who
served in the militia there from 22 Nov. 1724 to 22 May 1725
during an Indian war.[5] Presumably he returned to Rehoboth
to marry by 1727, but disappeared again between 1727 and
1734. The last certain record is the baptism of his third
child at the Newman Congregational Church (then Rehoboth,
now in RI) in 1739. No land or probate records for him have
been found in Bristol County.

   Children (SABIN) b. Rehoboth, births and baptisms as
children of Samuel, Jr. and Hannah:[6,7]

   i    SARAH[6]  b. 18 July 1734
   ii   JOHN  b. 10 Nov. 1736; bp. 19 Dec. 1736
   iii  SAMUEL  b. 19 Aug. 1739; bp. 7 Oct. 1739

References: 1. REHOBOTH VR BY TRIM, "Ingraham (Newman
            Church sexton) Records," p. 7. 2. REHOBOTH VR
p. 331. 3. REHOBOTH VR p. 458. 4. Bristol Co. PR 5:222,223
(John Hall). 5. MA SOLDIERS 1723-1743 pp. 217-8.
6. REHOBOTH VR p. 738. 7. RI VR: Newman Congregational
Church: 9:521.


   85 JEREMIAH[1] SABIN[5] (Israel Sabin[4], Mary[3] Billington,
Francis[2], John[1]) b. Rehoboth 26 Aug. 1703, d. aft. 1736.[1]
   He m. Berwick, York Co., (ME) 23 Sept. 1724 MARY
ABBOT,[2] dau. of Joseph and Alice (Nason) Abbot of
Berwick.[3] Mary was living at Berwick in 1736 and perhaps
in 1741.[1]
   Jeremiah went to York Co., then MA now ME, about 1724
with his brothers Samuel and Israel, who served there in the
militia. Possibly Jeremiah was the "Joshua" Sabin who also
served as private from 6/14/1725 to 11/28/1725, for no
Joshua Sabin can be identified.[4] "Jer Sabens," signing by
mark, witnessed a deed for land in the town of York 5 Jan.
1725/6.[5] On 2 June 1732 Jeremiah Sabens and wife Mary of
Berwick ME both signing by mark, conveyed to Mary's brother
Thomas Abbot, all right, claim, etc. in the Berwick estate
of "our father Joseph Abbot, deceased."[6]

This Jeremiah Sabin, or his son, may have been the
"Jeremiah Sabean" who signed a Casco Bay ME petition in Nov.
1760; that man was the "Jereh Sabins," grantee of Penobscot
Township, 27 Jan. 1764.[7]  The son Jeremiah was surely the
man who, with his family, "first settled at Argyle, Nova
Scotia in 1762, then moved to the mouth of the Sissiboo
River there."[8,9*]  No death or probate record for Jeremiah
Sabin appears in York County. The church records of Berwick
show that on  8 May 1729 Mary Sabins owned the covenant, and
"their" children were baptized subsequently.

Children (SABIN/SABENS) baptized at Berwick ME:[1]

   i   MARY$^6$ b. ca.  1726; bp.  8 May  1729; she or her
       mother owned the covenant at Berwick  church 22
       Nov. 1741.
   ii  SARAH  b.  ca.  1728;  bp.  8 May 1729; owned the
       covenant at Berwick church 22 Nov. 1741.
   iii Son  bp. 10 May 1730
   iv  JEREMIAH  b. ca. 1732; bp. 3 Sept. 1736,[1**]
   v   SIMON  b. ca. 1734; bp. 3 Sept. 1736
   vi  ESTHER  b. ca. 1736, bp. 3 Sept. 1736

*Note: A.W. Savary, who edited the history shown as Ref. #9,
repeats the error he made in the SAVERY GEN, p. 34,
identifying his ancestor Jeremiah Sabin of Nova Scotia as a
Connecticut born  Jeremiah, who in fact moved to Dutchess
County NY and remained there.  A.W. Savary confessed his
error in SAVERY SUP, p. 15, but never found his Jeremiah
Sabin's correct ancestry in the Rehoboth family.

References:  1. NEHGR 82:89,90,205,211. **The baptism of the
           last three Sabin children is printed as "1730,"
but text shows the year was 1736.  2. NEHGR 55:311.  3. OLD
KITTERY  pp.  270-1.  4. MA  SOLDIERS, 1723-1743, pp 217-8.
5. YORK  DEEDS 11:256.  6. Ibid.  15:212.  7. MA Archives:
card index  to MS collections 117:599, 604; 118:20a.  8. NEW
ENGLANDERS IN N.S., #311. 9. ANNAPOLIS CO N.S. HIST p. 637.


86 JOSIAH  SABIN$^5$  (Israel  Sabin$^4$, Mary$^3$ Billington,
Francis$^2$, John$^1$) b.  Rehoboth 3 June  1705, d. bef.  19 Dec.
1752, perhaps by 1745.[1,2]
   He m.  Rehoboth 18  Nov.  1724 MARY GAY, as appears in
marriage and intentions records.[3].  In the Attleboro birth
record of  son Israel she is called  "Mary Guy."[4]  She has
not yet been identified.
   Although Josiah's marriage and his  children's births and
baptisms are recorded  at Rehoboth and Attleboro,  there are
no land  or probate records  for him in  Bristol County.  An

Israel Sabin was warned out of Rehoboth 1 April 1745, "not
being an inhabitant."[1]    Perhaps this was Josiah's 15-year
old son  Israel, the  only child  of the  family not born in
Rehoboth.
    Sons  Israel  and  Nathaniel  appeared  soon afterward at
Plainfield CT:  Israel married  at Preston  CT 28  Dec. 1748
Avis Bennett,[5]  and on 19 Dec. 1752, Nathaniel Sabin, "son
of Mr. _____ Sabin, late of Rehoboth, dec'd.," appeared at
court in Plainfield CT and  made choice of Mr. David Downing
as  guardian.[2]  Nathaniel  being then  aged 14, the guard-
ianship  probably  indicates  that  the  boy  was  being
apprenticed, but  was not heir  to an estate.    The guardian
David  Downing  was  the  friend  named  in the 1759 will of
Ebenezer  Welch of Plainfield,  Josiah Sabin's cousin. [Fam.
#75, Ebenezer Welch.]
    Where and when  Josiah Sabin and  his wife Mary  died, or
what became of their other children is as yet unknown.

    Children (SABIN) b. Rehoboth, except Israel:[4,6,7*]

      i   URIAH[6]  b. 25 July 1725
     ii   WILLIAM  b. 31 July 1728
    iii   ISRAEL  b. Attleboro 7 Aug. 1730
     iv   MARY  b. 6 Aug. 1733
      v   JOHN  b. 30 Apr. 1736
     vi   NATHANIEL  b. 11 Aug. 1738
    vii   DANIEL  b. 31 July 1741; bp. 1 Nov. 1741
   viii   TIMOTHY  bp. 9 Sep. 1744

References:  1. EARLY REHOBOTH 2:154-5.  2. Plainfield CT PR
            1:165  (Guardianship  of  Nathaniel  Sabin).
3. REHOBOTH  VR p. 331.  4. VR  ATTLEBORO p. 229.  5. CSL Ch
Recs: Griswold (North  Preston) CT Church 1:256. 6. REHOBOTH
VR p.738.   7. RI  VR: Newman  Congregational Church: 9:520.
*All  of  the  children  except  Israel were  baptized in the
Newman (then in Rehoboth) church,  but many of the baptismal
dates do  not agree  with the  Rehoboth vital  records.   The
published  transcript  of  these  particular  church records
contains many discrepancies.


87  MARGARET ₁SABIN[5]  (Israel Sabin[4], Mary[3] Billington,
Francis[2], John[1]) b. Rehoboth 5 Feb. 1706/7, d. prob. Lyme CT
aft. 1748 and bef. 1763.[1]
    She m.  prob. Barrington,  then MA  now RI,  8 Aug. 1737,
recorded Lyme CT;  int. Barrington 15 Jan. 1736/7 ROBERT
OTIS,[2,3]  by tradition b. Ireland ca. 1707,[4]  d. Lyme CT
21 April 1799 "aged about 92."[2]  Robert Otis m. (2) in the
1760s Lydia _____, who d. bef. 1776.  They had a son Robert,
b.  Lyme 10  May 1764,[2]  and  a daughter Sally,[1]  not

_____

Billington descendants. He m. (3) bet. April 1774 (Brockway
estate),[5] and March 1776 (Otis will),[1] Sarah (Fox)
Brockway, widow of Jedediah Brockway of Lyme.[5] She had
eight Brockway children. On 11 Jan. 1796 Robert Otis and
wife Sarah leased, for the term of her natural life, Sarah's
dower in the estate of her former husband, Jedediah
Brockway.[6] Sarah, b. ca. 1718-20, living 5 May 1800, may
have been the widow Sarah Otis who d. 8 April 1819, age
101.[7] Sarah had no Otis children.
     Robert Otis, said to have come to Rhode Island in
1720,[4] moved from Barrington to Lyme CT, where he first
purchased land 1 Jan. 1740.[6] He had many land transactions
in Lyme, the last 11 Jan. 1796.[6] His son Robert Otis, Jr.
first appeared in Lyme land records 14 Jan 1796 when he
bought 5&1/2 acres from Giles Sill; and also witnessed
Robert and Sarah Otis's deed 11 Jan. 1796.[8] The 1790
census of Lyme shows Robert Otis and Robert Otis, Jr. living
side by side.[9]
     The will of Robert Otis of Lyme, dated 2 March 1776, was
proved 26 April 1799, the inventory presented 4 May 1799.
Named in the will were wife Sarah, to have her thirds; sons
Stephen Otis, Richard Otis and dau. Annis "Josseling," each
to have 5 shillings "with what they have received
heretofore;" to dutiful son Robert Otis all land in Lyme; to
youngest dau. Sally Otis all moveables after wife's thirds
have been taken. Samuel Ely, Esq. was to be executor.[1]
David M. Jewett was appointed administrator, with Robert
Otis, son of the deceased, as surety.[1]

     Children (OTIS) born to Robert and Margaret:[2,3,4]

     i    STEPHEN[6] b. Barrington MA now RI, 14 May 1738
     ii   ROBERT b. Lyme CT 18 March 1740; died young,
             without issue before 1764.
     iii  RICHARD b. Lyme 23 June 1745
     iv   ANNAS/ANNIS b. Lyme 25 Sept. 1748; m. Colchester,
             CT in 1770 SAMUEL JOSLING/JOSLIN.[10]

References: 1. New London CT Dist. PR 2:143-146 ; and CSL
          PR File #3868 (Robert Otis). 2. CSL Barbour
Index: Lyme; also LYME CT VR 1:35. 3. RI VR: Barrington:
6:15. 4. *OTIS FAM, pp. 88,127,128; 5. New London CT Dist.
PR, I:340 and File #705(Jedidiah Brockway). 6. Lyme CT LR
7:256; 10:507; 12:375; 13:32-3(Robert Otis); 21:32 (Robert
and Sarah Otis). 7. Hartford Times, 8 June 1819. 8. Lyme CT
LR 20:523(Robert Otis, Jr.). 9. FED CENSUS 1790, Lyme CT.
10. CSL Colchester CT Justice of the Peace Records: Record
Group 3.

*The Otis Genealogy is confused, based largely on tradition, with many errors. Robert Otis's second and third marriages are omitted, and no evidence was found for a daughter Clarinda, as listed with the family.

88  WILLIAM $_1$SABIN[5] (Israel  Sabin[4], Mary[3] Billington, Francis[2], John[1]) b. Rehoboth 14 Oct. 1708, d. aft. 1745.[1]
   He m. (1) Rehoboth 17 May 1733 PHEBE EDDY,[2]  b. Swansea 25 Dec. 1712,[3] d. Rehoboth 21 July 1738; [4]; dau. of Ebenezer and Sarah (Harding) Eddy.[5]
   He was probably the William Sabin who m. (2) at Norwich, CT 24 Dec. 1739 ELIZABETH ATWELL of Norwich.[6]  She has not yet been identified, despite considerable research.
   William Sabin may have lived at both Rehoboth and Norwich CT from the circumstance that his son Nathan, born at Rehoboth, was apparently baptized in Norwich before William settled there after his first wife's death.[1]   On 27 Dec. 1737 William Sabin, wife and children were warned out of Rehoboth, but they remained until after the following July.[7] William Sabin owned no property at Rehoboth. No land or probate records for William have been found at Norwich, but his son Nathan apparently served in Connecticut troops from Norwich during the French and Indian War.[8]

   Children (SABIN), first three by Phebe, others by Elizabeth:[9,6,1]

   i   NATHAN[6] b. Rehoboth 22 Feb. 1733/4; bp. First
       Congregational Church, Norwich CT 11 Jan. 1736
       [1736/7?] as son of William.
   ii  SARAH b. Rehoboth 26 Feb. 1735/6
   iii PHEBE b. Rehoboth 24 Feb. 1737/8; d. there 19 May
       1738
   iv  LUCY  b. Norwich CT 29 May 1743
   v   UNICE bp. Norwich 24 July 1743, perhaps same
       child as Lucy, above?
   vi  ZEBIDIAH bp. Norwich 7 April 1745

References:  1. CSL Ch Recs, Norwich  First Cong.  Ch 2:108,
         120,123.   2. REHOBOTH VR  p. 331.   3. Swansea
Original VR, Bk  B p. 23/51.  4. REHOBOTH VR p.874.  5. EDDY
GEN (1940 ed.) pp. 52-3.   6. CSL Barbour  Index, Norwich.
7. EARLY REHOBOTH 2:146.   8.  CT HIST COLLS 9:181;10:164,
173.  9. REHOBOTH VR p. 738.

   89 $_1$MARY SABIN[5] (Israel Sabin[4], Mary[3] Billington, Francis[2], John[1]) b. Rehoboth 1 June 1711, d. Gill 10 May (or 10 Aug.) 1795, aged 83.[1,2]

She  m.  Norwich  CT  23  Sept.  1731 DANIEL SLATE,[3]  b.
Windham CT  30 March  1708,[4]  d.  Gill 10  Feb. 1789  aged
81;[1,2]  son of William and Elizabeth (Abbe) Slate.[4]
    Probably Mary Sabin went to Norwich CT after her father's
death to live with one of  her uncles, John Ormsby or Joseph
Ormsby  there.  A Mary  Sabens was  admittted  in 1729 to the
First [Congregational]  Church of  Norwich.[5]  She  and her
husband lived at Norwich until 1748 when Daniel Slate bought
land and  they moved  to Middletown CT.  Mary  Slate united
with  the  church  at  Middletown  13  Aug.  1748  from
Norwich.[1,2]
    They remained at Middletown  CT until the 1760s when they
moved to Bernardstown (now Bernardston).[1]  On 18 Aug. 1772
Daniel Slate of  Bernardstown sold to  Daniel Slate, Jr.  50
acres  of  land.  Later Daniel,  Jr. bought three  more
tracts.[6]  No probate record for Daniel Slate, Sr. has been
found.

    Children  (SLATE),  first  eight  recorded at Norwich CT,
five bp. Portland CT Church,  (then East Middletown parish);
last listed in BERNARDSTON HIST: [1,2,3,7]

       i   MARY[6]  b. 7 Sept. 1732
      ii   JOSEPH  b. 12 Feb. 1733/4
     iii   ABIGAIL  b. 15 May 1735
      iv   LUCY  b. 13 March 1737; d. 27 Sept. 1738
       v   DANIEL  b. 17 Dec. 1738
      vi   THOMAS  b. 13 July 1741
     vii   LUCY  b. 17 March 1743
    viii   JONATHAN  b. 27 Jan. 1744/5
      ix   EBENEZER  bp. 8 March 1747, d.y.
       x   ZEBEDIAH  bp. 10 Oct. 1748, d.y.
      xi   ELIZABETH  bp. 2 Sept. 1750
     xii   EBENEZER  bp. 14 June 1752
    xiii   RUTH  bp. 21 April 1754
     xiv   ZEBEDIAH or ZEBULON  b. in 1756

References:  1. BERNARDSTON HIST pp. 492-3.   2. HALE, HOUSE
       FAMS, pp. 106-7; 109-10   3. CSL Barbour Index,
Norwich 1:154-5.  4. NEHGR  111:130-2.  5. CSL  Ch Recs,
Norwich First  Ch 2:208.  6. Franklin Co.  LR 4:143-146.  7.
CSL Ch Recs, Portland Ch on LDS Film #002862.


    90 ELEAZER  SABIN[5]  (Israel  Sabin[4], Mary[3] Billington,
Francis[2], Jonh[1])  b.  Swansea  21  July 1713, d. perhaps by
1746.[1]
    He m.  Jamestown RI 21 Aug.  1737 ABIGAIL OSBORNE,[2]  b.
South  Kingstown RI  25 Feb.  1718/9, d.  perhaps aft. 1746;
dau. of  Nathaniel and  Hannah (_____) Osbon (sic).[3]  She

may have been  the Abigail Sabins who m.  South Kingstown RI
26 Aug. 1746 Samuel Jackways.[1]
    Nothing  more has  been found;  no recorded  children for
Eleazer Sabin appear in Rhode Island.

References:  1. RI  VR:  South  Kingstown:  5:29.  2. RI VR:
            Jamestown: 4:12.  3. RI VR: South Kingstown: 5:50.


    91 $_1$JOHN  WASHBURN$^5$  (Lydia$^4$  Billington, Isaac$^3$, Francis$^2$,
John$^1$) b. Plymouth 19 April 1699, d. there 22 May 1768, aged
69 years.[1]
    He m.  int.  Kingston 28  May  1727 ABIGAIL (PHILLIPS)
JOHNSON,[2]  of  Marshfield, b.  there 29  Oct. 1699,[3]  d.
Plymouth 24 Sept.  1782, a widow;[4]   dau. of Benjamin  and
Sarah  (Thomas)  Phillips,  and widow  of Josiah Johnson of
Scituate, whom  she  m. Marshfield 8 Feb.  1721/2.[5]  Josiah
d. there 18 May 1724, aged 25 yrs.  He and Abigail had a son
Josiah Johnson, b. Marshfield 17 Oct. 1723.[5]
    Widow Abigail  Washburn was  appointed administratrix  of
the  estate of  John Washburn  of Plymouth 9 May 1769.  The
estate was  declared insolvent  14 May  1770, the  inventory
being almost  the only document  in the estate  records.  No
heirs were named.[6]

    Children (WASHBURN) b. Plymouth:[7,8]

       i   JOHN$^6$  b. 8 May 1730
      ii   ABIGAIL  b. 17 Feb. 1731/2
     iii   MARY  b. 21 Nov. 1734; bp. 9 Feb. 1734/6 (sic)
      iv   MERCY/MARCY b. 31 July 1736; bp. 5 Sept. 1736; d.
             4 March 1737/8
       v   SETH  b. 17  April 1738;  bp. 21  May 1738; d. 27
             April 1826.[7]
      vi   PHILIP  b. 5 Sept. 1739; bp. 4 Nov. 1739
     vii   THANKFUL  b. 14 Aug. 1742

References:  1. PLYMOUTH CH  RECS 1:397.  2. VR  KINGSTON p.
            297.  3. MARSHFIELD VR  p. 24.  4. PLYMOUTH  CH
RECS  1:411.   5. MARSHFIELD  VR  pp.  85,  86,  143,  404.
6. Plymouth  Co.  PR  20:213,344  (John  Washburn).   7. MD
14:242.  8. PLYMOUTH CH RECS 1:435.


    92 $_1$ICHABOD WASHBURN$^5$ (Lydia$^4$ Billington, Isaac$^3$, Francis$^2$,
John$^1$) b. Plymouth  7 Feb. 1700/01, d. prob.  Norton bef. 20
Sept. 1769, when his will was exhibited.[1]
    He  m. Marshfield 2 June 1725,[2]  int. Plymouth 13 March
1724/5  BETHIAH  PHILLIPS,[3]   b.  Marshfield 27 Feb.

1704/5;[4]    bp. with siblings at Marshfield Church 15 April
1711,[5]    d. Norton 25  Jan. 1789 in  her 85th yr., wife of
Ichabod  Washburn;[6]  dau.  of Benjamin  and Sarah (Thomas)
Phillips.
     By deed dated 2 March 1746, acknowledged the same day and
recorded  30  Dec.  1747,  Ichabod Washburn, cordwainer, and
wife Bethiah of  Kingston sold for  400 pounds old  tenor to
Wrestling Brewster, their dwelling  house and barn with  one
acre, a wood lot of 14 acres, one-quarter part of a well and
a pew in  the  Women's  Gallery  of  the  meeting house in
Kingston.[7]  They moved to Norton.
     In the will of Ichabod Washburn of Norton,  drawn 24 Jan.
1759,  proved  20  Sept.  1769,  wife  Bethiah, son Malatiah
Washburn and  dau. Bethiah Braman, wife  of Daniel  Braman,
late of Norton,  deceased, were named.  The  real estate was
divided 5 May 1770  between widow Bethiah and  son Malatiah,
but was to  descend to dau. Bethiah Braman  and her heirs if
Malatiah should die without issue.[1]

     Children (WASHBURN) b. Kingston:[8,6]

     i    BETHIAH[6]  b. 24 May 1729
     ii   ICHABOD b. 13 April 1731; d. Norton 14 Nov. 1756,
          unm.
     iii  MALATIAH  b. 29 March 1733
     iv   SARAH  b. 12 Feb. 1736/7; d. Norton 31 May 1750

References:   1. Bristol Co. PR  21:64-66, 378; 22:388 (Icha-
              bod  Washburn).  2. MARSHFIELD VR,  p. 144.  3.
MD 18:149.  4. MARSHFIELD VR, p. 30.  5. MD 31:119 (Baptisms
in Marshfield  Church).  6. VR  NORTON p.  399.  7. Plymouth
Co. LR 39:58 (Ichabod and Bethiah Washburn).  8. VR KINGSTON
pp. 149,151,153,155.


93  1MERCY WASHBURN[5]  (Lydia[4] Billington,  Isaac[3], Francis[2],
John[1])  b. Plymouth 21  April 1702, d.  Kingston 3 May 1796,
aged 94y/3d.[1]
     She  m.  (1)  int.  Plymouth  17  April   1725  ROBERT
CUSHMAN,[2]  b.  Plymouth 2  July 1698,[3]  d. Kingston  13
Sept.  1751  in  his  54th year;  son  of Robert and Persis
(_____) Cushman.[4]  He was  a descendant of Pilgrims  Isaac
Allerton, [6] and John Howland.
     She m.  (2)  Kingston 14  Nov. 1764 JOHN FULLER,[5]  b.
Plymouth 19 Dec. 1698,[6]  d.  Kingston 25 Sept. 1778 in his
80th year;[7]  son of Samuel and  Mercy (Eaton) Fuller and a
descendant of Pilgrims Samuel Fuller, Francis Eaton and John
Billington.[Fam. #58]   He m.  (1)  Plympton 7 Feb. 1722/3
Deborah  Ring, by  whom he  had children  Eleazer, Issachar,

John, Deborah, Susanna, Noah, Ezra, Consider, Eleazer (2nd), and Hannah.[6]  There  were  no  Fuller  children  by  Mercy Washburn.

Robert Cushman, in his will  dated Kingston 2 Sept. 1751, probated 7  Oct. 1751,  appointed his  wife Mercy executrix, and devised his land to eldest son Robert, he to pay brother Isaac and  sisters Lydia,  Jerusha, Rebecca,  Mercy, Hannah, Ruth and Abigail  after the  death of  their mother.[8]  An order  to  distribute  the  real  estate  of Robert Cushman, deceased,  dated 2  May 1760  provided that  Robert Cushman, eldest son, have the whole, reserving his mother's dower and paying their shares to  his brother and sisters, viz.: Lydia Fuller, Jerusha  Cobb, Rebecca Fuller,  Mercy Harlow, Hannah Cobb, Ruth Rickard, Abigail Robbins and Isaac Cushman,[8].

In  a deed dated  3  Nov. 1766 grantors Robert Cushman, Josiah  and Lydia  Fuller, Ebenezer,  Jr. and  Jerusha Cobb, Barnabas and  Rebecca Fuller,  James and  Mercy Harlow, John Cobb  in  right  of  wife  Hannah, deceased, Samuel and Ruth Rickard,  Abigail,  widow  of  Benjamin  Robbins,  and Isaac Cushman, all children  and heirs of Robert  Cushman, late of Kingston, deceased, sold seven acres at Kingston,[9].

Children (CUSHMAN) b. Kingston:[10]

     i    LYDIA[6] b. 29 Sept.  1726; m. JOSIAH FULLER.  [See
          Fam. #55]
    ii    JERUSHA  b. 15 Jan. 1727/8
   iii    REBECCA b. 9 April 1730; m. BARNABAS FULLER. [See
          Fam. #53]
    iv    MERCY  b. 5 June 1731
     v    HANNAH  b. 2 July 1732
    vi    THANKFUL  b. 10 March 1733/4; d. 23 Aug. 1748
   vii    RUTH  b. 22 Dec. 1735
  viii    ABIGAIL  b. 3 April 1737
    ix    ROBERT  b. 27 Oct. 1738
     x    JOB  b. 27 Jan. 1739/40; d. 28 Jan. 1739/40
    xi    ELENAH/ELKANAH  b. 29 Dec. 1740; d. 18 Aug. 1748
   xii    MARTHA  b. 14 Sept. 1742; d. 23 Aug. 1748
  xiii    ISAAC  b. 10 March 1745

References:  1. VR  KINGSTON p.  353.  2.  MD 18:145.  3. MD
            4:111.  4. VR KINGSTON p. 337.   5. VR KINGSTON
p. 204.  6.  MF 1:53,58,60,  64-66.  7. VR  KINGSTON p. 352.
8. Plymouth  Co.  PR  12:387,  15:497  (Robert  Cushman).
9. Plymouth Co.  LR 53:129  (Robert Cushman  et al).  10. VR
KINGSTON pp. 52-56, 335-337.

94 ₁ELISHA WASHBURN⁵ (Lydia⁴ Billington, Isaac³, Francis²,
John¹) b. Plymouth 5 Nov. 1703, d. Kingston 20 July 1734 in
his 30th year.[1]
   He m. Plympton 15 Jan. 1728/9,[2] int. Kingston 26 Oct.
1728 MARTHA PERKINS,[3] b. Beverly 14 Aug. 1707,[4] d.
aft. 12 Feb. 1738/9;[5] dau. of Luke and Martha (Conant)
Perkins. She m. (2) Kingston 11 Jan. 1737 Jonathan Tilson
of Plympton,[6] by whom she had a dau. Eunice Tilson b. 12
Feb. 1738/9.[5]
   Mrs. Martha Washburn was appointed administratrix of the
estate of Elisha Washburn, deceased, 19 Aug. 1734. On 2 May
1735 necessary utensils were set aside for her use.[7] By a
deed dated 7 May 1736 Martha Washburn of Plympton,
administratrix of the estate of Elisha Washburn, dec'd,
having been ordered by the court of Plymouth to sell land to
pay debts, sold for 150 pounds, ten acres to her late
husband's brothers, Ephraim and Barnabas Washburn of
Kingston. In the acknowledgement of this deed on 17 Nov.
1738 "Misᵗ Tilson" is inserted after the name Martha
Washburn.[8]

   Children (WASHBURN) b. Kingston:[9]

      i   LYDIA⁶ b. 12 Dec. 1729
     ii   MARTHA b. 5 May 1732
    iii   ELISHABA b. 13 April 1735; d. 6 Jan. 1747/8.

References: 1. VR KINGSTON p. 388.   2. VR PLYMPTON p. 360.
            3. VR KINGSTON p. 296   4. VR BEVERLY 1:254
5. VR PLYMPTON p. 213.  6. VR KINGSTON p. 298.  7. Plymouth
Co. PR 7:52,63,128 (Elisha Washburn) 8. Plymouth Co. LR
36:160 (Martha Washburn Tilson) 9. VR KINGSTON pp.
150,153,389


95 ₁EPHRAIM WASHBURN⁵ (Lydia⁴ Billington, Isaac³, Francis²,
John¹) b. Plymouth 6 June 1705, d. prob. Kingston bef. 4
Dec. 1775.[1]
   He m. int. Kingston 4 Nov. 1732 EGLOTH STETSON,[2] b.
Plymouth 7 Oct. 1710,[3] d. there 18 Nov. 1792;[4] dau. of
Elisha and Abigail (Brewster) Stetson and a descendant of
Pilgrim William Brewster.
   The inventory of Ephraim Washburn's estate, dated 4 Dec.
1775 was presented 3 Jan. 1776 by the administrator,
Ebenezer Washburn, a nephew. An account of 28 Feb. 1777
showed sums of money paid to Sarah Washburn, Deborah
Washburn, Ezekiel Washburn, the estate of Ephraim Washburn,
Jr., deceased, and others. A later account of 8 April 1777
mentioned "what was set off to the widow."[1]

Children (WASHBURN) b. Kingston:[5,3]

    i    EZEKIEL[6] b. 22 Nov. 1733
   ii    DEBORAH  b. 15 Nov. 1735
  iii    MARCY  b. 23 Sept. 1738
   iv    EPHRAIM  b. 16 March 1741
    v    ALITHEA/ELITHEAH  b. 18 Aug. 1743
   vi    [E]UNICE  b. 20 July 1746
  vii    NEHEMIAH  b. 11 June  1749; d. 13  April 1751, ae
         1y/10m/2d.
 viii    SARAH  b. 22 March 1752

References:  1. Plymouth Co.  PR 24:238,271-4(Ephraim  Wash-
            burn) 2. VR KINGSTON  p. 283.  3. MD 7:178,223.
4. PLYMOUTH CH RECS, 1:420.  5. VR KINGSTON pp. 149,150,153,
154,155,156,390.


    96  BARNABAS [1] WASHBURN[5]  (Lydia[4]  Billington,  Isaac[3],
Francis[2], John[1]) b. Plymouth 12 Feb. 1706/7, d. Kingston 21
March 1770.[1]
    He m. Kingston 14  April 1748 HANNAH SHEAR  or THEARS,[1]
who  has not  been identified.  Kingston town  records call
Hannah "Thears" while church records call  her "Shear."  She
was  b.  ca.  1720,  d.  Kingston  19  May  1787  aged 67, a
widow.[1]
    The  will of  Barnabas Washburn,  dated Kingston 20 March
1770, probated 6 Aug.  1770, provided wife Hannah the use  of
his estate for her life, thence to his two sons Barnabas and
Elkanah.  Barnabas's brother-in-law John Adams was appointed
executor.[2]

    Children (WASHBURN) b. Kingston:[3]

    i    BARNABAS[6] b. 1 April 1749
   ii    ELKANAH  b. 3 Jan. 1750/1
  iii    ELISABETH  b. 1 Aug. 1754; d. 1 Jan. 1770.

References:  1. VR KINGSTON  pp. 288,388, 389.   2. Plymouth
            Co.  PR   20:396  (Barnabas  Washburn).   3. VR
KINGSTON pp. 149,150,389.


    97  JABEZ  WASHBURN[5] (Lydia[4]  Billington, Isaac[3], Francis[2],
John[1]) b. Plymouth 10 April 1708, d. Kingston 31 March 1794,
aged 86 years.[1]
    He  m.  (1)  Kingston  2  Dec. 1731 JUDITH FAUNCE,[2]  b.
Plymouth 1 Jan.  1710/1,[3]  d. Kingston 3  March 1752, aged
41y/2m/2d; dau.  of John  and Lydia  (Cooke) Faunce.[4]  She

was a descendant of Pilgrims Francis Cooke and Stephen
Hopkins.

He m. (2) Marshfield, rec. Kingston, 5 Dec. 1754 DEBORAH
THOMAS,[2] b. Marshfield 28 April 1718 (sic), bp.
Marshfield 12 May 1717 (sic),[5] d. Kingston 8 Oct. 1802 in
her 85th year; dau. of Israel and Bethiah (Sherman)
Thomas.[6]

Jabez Washburn was deacon of the church at Kingston for
over forty years. In his will dated 4 Nov. 1791, presented
7 July 1794, Jabez Washburn of Kingston named wife Deborah,
to have one-third of the moveables; and directed that the
estate then be divided into five parts, one fifth to each of
three living children: son Judah Washburn and daus. Rebecca
Washburn and Susannah Washburn; one-fifth to the children of
son Jabez, deceased; and one-fifth to granddaughter Molly
Holmes, part of which had been given at her marriage. Son
Judah Washburn was appointed executor.[7] (Granddaughter
Molly, wife of Sylvester Holmes, was dau. of deceased son
John Washburn.)

Children (WASHBURN) b. Kingston, seven by Judith, last
two by Deborah:[8]

    i    JABEZ[6] b. 22 April 1733; d. 16 Feb. 1775 ae 41.
    ii   ELISHA b. 17 March 1734/5; d.s.p. 29 June 1754,
         ae 20.
    iii  SUSANNA b. 7 May 1737; d. 26 April 1756 ae 19,
         unm.
    iv   JOHN b. 18 July 1739; d. __June 1763, ae 23, at
         sea
    v    MOLLY b. 15 May 1742; d. 14 June 1754 ae 12.
    vi   REBECCA b. 14 April 1744; d. unm. 23/24 July 1827
         ae 84/85
    vii  JUDAH (son), b. 10 July 1746; d. 8 May 1824 ae
         78.
    viii THOMAS b. 30 Sept. 1755; d. 11 March 1759 ae
         3y/5m.
    ix   SUSANNAH b. 3 July 1762; d. unm. 28 Feb. 1824 ae
         62.

References: 1. VR KINGSTON p. 389. 2. VR KINGSTON p.
297. 3. MD 5:100. 4. VR KINGSTON p. 390.
5. MD 7:134; 31:122. 6. VR KINGSTON p. 388. 7. Plymouth
Co. PR 35:120-122(Jabez Washburn). 8. VR KINGSTON pp.
150,151, 152,154,155,156,391.


98 EBENEZER WASHBURN[5] (Lydia[4] Billington, Isaac[3],
Francis[2], John[1]) b. Plymouth 18 Aug. 1709, d. Kingston 13
Sept. 1738, aged 29y/26d.[1]

He m. int. Kingston 21 Oct. 1732 LYDIA FAUNCE,[2]  b.
Plymouth 10 June 1714,[3]  d. 3 April 1784 in 70th yr., bur.
Thompson Street Cemetery, Halifax;[4]  dau. of John and
Lydia (Cooke) Faunce. She was a descendant of Pilgrims
Francis Cooke and Stephen Hopkins.  She m. (2)  Kingston 1
Aug. 1765, as his third wife, Thomas Waterman of Plympton,[5]  b. there __ Oct. 1707,[6]  d. Plympton 22 Aug.
1789,[7] son of Robert and Mary (Cushman) Waterman.
    Lydia Washburn was granted letters of administration on
the estate of Ebenezer Washburn of Kingston 3 Oct. 1738.
The division was made 20 March 1756 to the heirs, with the
eldest son Ebenezer receiving half, and Simeon and his
sister Lydia Davis, wife of Nicholas Davis, each receiving
one-fourth share.[8]

    Children (WASHBURN) b. Kingston:[9]

      i   LYDIA[6] b. 1 Oct. 1733;  m. NICHOLAS DAVIS. [See
          Fam. #55]
     ii   EBENEZER  b. 14 Sept. 1735
    iii   SIMEON  b. 20 Jan. 1737/8

References:  1. VR KINGSTON p. 388.  2. VR KINGSTON p. 296.
          3. MD 5:100.  4. MD  14:11.  5. VR KINGSTON  p.
298.  6. MD  3:164.  7. VR PLYMPTON p. 529.  8. Plymouth Co.
PR  7:431; 14:102-3(Ebenezer  Washburn). 9. VR  KINGSTON pp.
150, 153, 155.


    99  THANKFUL[1] WASHBURN[5]  (Lydia[4]  Billington,  Isaac[3],
Francis[2], John[1]) b. Plymouth 24 Feb. 1714/15, d. Kingston 15
Jan. 1805, aged 88y/10m/8d.[1]
    She m. int. Kingston 1 March 1739/40 JOHN ADAMS,[2]  b.
Plymouth 14 June 1714,[3]  d. Kingston 15 April 1806, aged
91y/9m/21d;[4]  son of Francis and Mary (Busk) Adams.
    Clothier and dyer, he was active politically, serving as
deputy sheriff 1784-1800. The family Bible of son Francis
has been published.[5,6]  No probate record for John or
Thankful Adams appears in Plymouth County probate index.

    Children (ADAMS) b. Kingston:[7]

      i   JOSEPH[6] b. 2 Oct. 1740
     ii   FRANCIS  b. 14 Dec. 1741
    iii   JOHN  b. 12 March 1742/3
     iv   EBENEZER  b. 17 Nov. 1744
      v   JEMIMA  b. 6 Oct. 1746
     vi   MELZAR  b. 3 July 1750
    vii   SARAH  b. 7 Jan. 1752

```
     viii  MERCY   b. 7 July 1753
       ix  LYDIA   b. 25 Feb. 1755
        x  SUSANNA b. 7 July 1759
```

References:  1. VR KINGSTON p. 313.   2. VR KINGSTON p. 299.
             3. MD 2:227.  4. VR KINGSTON p. 312.  5. ADAMS
GEN (1861).  6. NEHGR 124: 147-8.   7. VR KINGSTON pp.
12,13,14,15.


100 1SAMUEL WARREN[5] (Eleanor[4] Billington, Isaac[3], Francis[2],
John[1]) b. Middleboro 9 Aug. 1707, d. aft. 28 Nov. 1770.[1]
     He m. Middleboro 13 June 1734 REBECCA DUNHAM,[2] b.
Plymouth 2 Feb. 1706,[3] d. aft. 26 April 1769;[4] dau of
Eleazer, Jr. and Meriam (Phillips) Dunham.[5]
     Samuel Warren and son Jabez were mentioned 28 Nov. 1770
in the diary of Baptist minister Isaac Backus, of Titicut
parish, Middleboro, when the Warrens were moving to Oakham,
Worcester County, but were delayed by a storm.[1]
     Samuel and Rebekah Warren of Middleborough received a
bond from their son Jabez for the whole of Samuel's
homestead farm in Middleborough, the deed executed and
acknowledged 26 April 1769, rec. 10 April 1770.[4] On 9
July 1770 "Jabez Warren of Middleborough" bought 81 acres
with mansion house and buildings at Oakham, Worcester Co.
Jabez and wife Zilpah Warren of Oakham sold this same land
29 March 1773, and moved away, perhaps father Samuel still
with them.[6]   Neither of two Samuel Warrens whose estates
were filed in Worcester Co. in 1775 and 1778 appear to be
this Samuel.

     Children (WARREN) perhaps incomplete, prob. b. Middle-
boro:[4,7,8]

```
      i  BETTY[6] bp. Middleboro 4 Oct. 1741
     ii  JABEZ   b. _____
    iii  ?SAMUEL b. _____ unproven.[8]
     iv  Child of Samuel Warren d. Middleboro 18 Sept.
         1754.[9]
```

References:  1. BACKUS DIARY p. 786.  2. MD 13:251.  3. MD
             5:53.   4. Plymouth Co. LR 55:118 (Samuel and
Rebekah Warren).  5. (PLYMOUTH) ANC LANDMARKS, Appendix p.
317.  6. Worcester Co. LR 67:37; 71:102 (Jabez Warren)
7. Middleboro 1st Cong. Ch Recs, typescript, p. 36.
8. NEHGR 55:169.  9. Middleboro VR, deaths, addendum, p. 11.

101  CORNELIUS $_1$ WARREN$^5$  (Eleanor$^4$  Billington,  Isaac$^3$,
Francis$^2$, John$^1$) b. Middleboro 12 June 1709, d. ca. 1750,
certainly before 15 April 1752 when his widow remarried.[1]
    He m. Plymouth 18 Jan. 1732/3 MERCY WARD,[2]  b. Plymouth
8 March 1708/9,[3]  d. aft. 20 Oct. 1770; dau. of Nathan and
Elizabeth (Pope) Ward.[4]  She m. (2) Plymouth 15 April 1752
James Howard, widower of  Sarah Billington. [See Fam. #37].
James Howard d. Plymouth 12 April 1763.[1,5]
    Cornelius Warren and his wife were warned out of Plymouth
15 Feb. 1732/3; and he, his wife and family were warned from
Plymouth again 7 June 1737.[6]  Cornelius Warren was  given
land  in  Middleboro  by  his  father  Samuel  Warren 1 June
1739.[7]  No  probate  record  for Cornelius  Warren  has been
found.

    Children  (WARREN)  three  baptized  Middleboro,  fourth
unproven:[8,4]

        i    JOSEPH$^6$  bp. 1 Sept. 1734
       ii    ELEANOR  bp. 1 Aug. 1736
      iii    BENJAMIN  bp. 9 Dec. 1738
       iv    ?CORNELIUS  b. _____,[4].

References:  1. MD 18:141  2. MD 14:74  3. MD 12:11 4. NEHGR
             55:169.  5. PLYMOUTH CH RECS 1:430. 6. PLYMOUTH
CO CT RECS 2:179   7. Plymouth Co. LR 32:229 (Samuel Warren)
8. Middleboro 1st Cong. Ch Recs, typescript p. 34.


102 $_1$JAMES  WARREN$^5$ (Eleanor$^4$  Billington, Isaac$^3$, Francis$^2$,
John$^1$) b. Middleboro 24 Feb. 1710/11, d. 1790 at Westport MA
or Tiverton RI*.[1]
    He m. int. Freetown 4 Sept. 1735 MARY TERRY,[2]  prob. b.
Freetown  ca.  1715,  d.  aft.  28 June 1768 (father's
will);[1,3]  dau.  of Benjamin and Joanna (Spur) Terry.  She
was a descendant of Pilgrim Thomas Rogers.
    On 4 Dec. 1788 James Warren  of Westport  sold to  sons
Cornelius of Westport and Gamaliel of Tiverton, RI 16  acres
in Westport;  James acknowledged the deed  at Newport, RI 26
Dec. 1788.[4]

    Children  (WARREN)  first and last  b. Freetown, others at
Middleboro:[1,2,5]

        i    SAMUEL$^6$  b. 29 Sept. 1737
       ii    MARY  b. 6 Sept. 1739
      iii    CORNELIUS  b. 29 July 1741
       iv    GAMALIEL  bp. 8 Jan. 1744
        v    JAMES  b. 13 Nov. 1745

*Note: WARREN GEN, p. 23 shows JAMES d. at what is now Fall
River in 1790: his tombstone (created in 1800s) reads
"settled in Tiverton, now Fall River and died there about
1790, was buried on his farm and removed from thence by his
great-grandson, Theodore Warren who erected this stone in
his memory." Mary (Terry) Warren is "said to have died at
Nine Partners, New York."

References: 1. MF 2:286.     2. Freetown VR  pp. 27,80.
            3. NEHGR 55:170.  4. Bristol Co. LR 67:382
(James Warren).  5. MD 15:122.


103 [1]NATHAN WARREN[5] (Eleanor[4] Billington, Isaac[3], Francis[2],
John[1]) b. Middleboro 5 March 1712/3; d. Middleboro 15 Feb.
1784 in 71st yr, bur. Nemasket Cemetery.[1]
    He m. prob. by 1745 RACHEL _____, b. ca. 1719; d.
Middleboro 15 Aug. 1788 aged 69 yrs., a widow.[2,3,]
    Elder Isaac Backus, minister of the Baptist church in
Titicut Parish, Middleboro, preached at Nathan Warren's
house in 1754 and 1756, as well as conducting funeral ser-
vices for four of their children who died in a diphtheria
epidemic in 1755.[4]
    On 24 March 1781 (deed ack. same, rec. 28 March 1783)
Nathan Warren of Middleboro, blacksmith, with wife Rachel
releasing dower, sold for 200 pounds to his son Nathan, Jr.,
38 acres of land at Middleboro received from his father
Samuel Warren, 10 acres bought from his brother Benjamin
Warren, and other land. Nathan Warren, Sr., having lost his
sight, signed by mark. Witnesses were Silvanus Warren and
Zenas Warren, [Fam. #105, ii & vii.] The same day Nathan
Warren, Jr. mortgaged the same property to Silvanus Warren
of Middleboro, gentleman, as surety, Silvanus becoming
bondsman for Nathan, Jr. who agreed to take care of Nathan
Warren, Sr. and his wife for the rest of their lives.[5]

    Children (WARREN) prob. b. Middleboro; poss. incom-
plete:[2,4,5,6,]

        i  Child[6] b.____; d. 10, bur. 11 Nov. 1755; funeral
           preached by Elder Isaac Backus,[6]
       ii  Child b. ____; d. 13, bur. 14 Nov. 1755, "I
           preacht again at the funeral of another of
           Nathan Warrens Children: and found 2 more
           dangerously sick, all with the throat dis-
           temper which has been a most terrible disease
           to the Children of this Countery...,"[6]
       iv  Child b.____; d. 15 Nov. 1755; "dangerously sick
           14 Nov. 1755."

    v   Child  b.____; d. 18 Nov.  1755; "sick on 14 Nov.
        1755."
    vi  NATHAN  b.  ca.  1757-8  (computed  from  age  at
        death).[3]
    vii ?RACHEL, who m. 9 Dec. 1784 Zenas Tinkham. [2, no
        proof]


References:  1. MD 15:105.   2. WARREN GEN  p. 24  says "The
            surname  of his wife Rachel has not been found,
though  it is thought by some of her descendants to have been
Doty." A son Silvanus ascribed to this family is believed to
be the  son of  Benjamin Warren,  Fam. #105.   3. MIDDLEBORO
DEATHS  p.  219.  4. BACKUS  DIARY  pp.  323, 391, 392, 419.
5. Bowman File: Plymouth Co.  LR 62:21,  two deeds: (Nathan
and Rachel Warren), (Nathan Warren, Jr.).  6. Middleboro VR,
deaths, addendum, p. 11.


104 ₁JOANNA WARREN⁵ (Eleanor⁴ Billington, Isaac³, Francis²,
John¹) b. Middleboro 25  March 1717, d.  aft. 2 April 1764,
when she signed a family deed in Middleboro.[1]
    She m.  Plympton 15  Oct.  1735 WILLIAM BARLOW,[2]  b.
Sandwich 14  April 1713,[3] d.  perhaps  in Vermont, aft. 20
Sept.  1781;  son  of  John  and  Elizabeth (Dillingham)
Barlow.[4]
    On 2 April  1764 William  Barlow, cordwainer, and Joanna
his wife,  William Barlow, Jr.,  Eliakim  Barlow, blacksmith,
and  Patience Barlow,  spinster,  all  of  Middleborough,
conveyed 30  acres there  to Abiel  Leach, Jr.[1,5]   Twelve
days  later,  14 April 1764,  William Barlow of Middleborough
purchased from  Samuel Child, Jr., the west half of lot #108
in the ninth  range in Woodstock CT.[1,6]   The family moved
then to Woodstock; but  on 20 Aug. 1772, William  Barlow and
son  William, Jr. both sold  their Woodstock land,[1,6]  and
by 1773 had settled in Peru (then called Bromley) Bennington
Co. VT.[1,7]
    The  last  known  record  for  William Barlow, Sr. demon-
strates  the confusion  in Vermont  at that  time, with land
claimed  by both  New  York  and  New Hampshire:  In a deed
calling  him "of Brumbly in the county of Charlotte NY," now
Bennington Co. VT, he  sold 300 acres  "on the west part of
the  400  acres  I  live on,"  25 May 1778.  This deed was
acknowledged by William  Barlow in Rutland  Co. VT 20  Sept.
1781.[1,8]

    Children (BARLOW) b. Middleboro:[9,10,11]

    i   WILLIAM⁶ b. 12 July 1738
    ii  ELIAKIM  b. 17 March 1739/40  [See Fam. #117]

```
   iii  PATIENCE  b. 3 Aug. 1742
    iv  ELEANOR  b. 20 Oct. 1745
     v  JOHN  b. 1 Dec. 1747
    vi  JOANNA  b. 8 March 1749
   vii  SAMUEL  b. 8 June 1750
  viii  WARREN  b. 29 June 1752
    ix  MICAH  b. 5 June 1756
     x  SARAH  b. 25 May 1758
```

References:  1. TAG 35:68-70.  2. VR PLYMPTON p.418.  3. MD
             30:103.  4. TORREY'S MARRIAGES p. 42.  5. Ply-
mouth Co.  LR 49:119.  6. Woodstock CT  LR 3:421; 4:264,270
(William  Barlow).  7. VT GAZETTEER.  8. Bennington Co.  VT
LR  1:298  (William  Barlow).  9. MD  4:70; 22:149.  10. MQ
43:114; 11. MIDDLEBOROUGH VR 1:24,77,132-3.


105  BENJAMIN[1] WARREN[5]  (Eleanor[4]  Billington,  Isaac[3],
Francis[2],John[1]) b. Middleboro 30 July 1720, d. there 11 Jan.
1802, aged 81.[1,2,3]
     He m. Middleboro 31 Dec. 1741 JEDIDAH TUPPER,[4] b.
Sandwich 21 Aug. 1725,[5]  d. Middleboro 20 Oct. 1807 in
83rd yr.;[1,2,3]  dau. of Ichabod and Mary (_____) Tupper.
     Benjamin  and Jedidah Warren  joined  the  church at
Middleboro 7 March 1741/2, [1].  "Under date of 9 Feb. 1782,
Benjamin conveyed to his  son Sylvanus all his  homestead in
Middleborough, bordering on lands of  his brother Nathan; to
which his  wife Jedidah resigned her right of dower."[6]  No
probate  record  has  been  found  in  Plymouth  County  for
Benjamin Warren.

     Children  (WARREN)  b.  Middleboro,  baptisms First Cong-
regational Church of  Middleboro as children of Benjamin and
Jedidah Tupper Warren:[7,8]

     i  MEHITABLE[6]  b. 15 Sept. 1743
    ii  SILVANUS b. 9  March 1746; m. (1) int. Middleboro
          5 Feb., m. __ Oct. 1774 HULDAH PEIRCE  BOOTH;
          m. (2) int. Middleboro 24  June 1781 SARAH
          WASHBURN.[9]
   iii  JEDIDAH b. 20 Feb. 1748
    iv  ICHABOD  b. 13 May 1750
     v  LUCY bp. 18 Nov. 1753; d.y.
    vi  SILAS  b. 18 Feb. 1756
   vii  ZENAS  b. 22 March 1758
  viii  ANDREW  b. 14 Nov. 1760
    ix  LUCY bp. 29 May 1763
     x  HANNAH  (twin) bp. 26 May 1765

xi   SUSANNAH (twin) bp. 26 May 1765
xii  EUNICE bp. 21 May 1769

References:  1. MIDDLEBORO  FIRST  CH  p. 91.  2. MIDDLEBORO
            DEATHS  p.   219.   3. MD   15:104,105.   4. MD
15:219.   5. NEHGR 99:62.   6. WARREN GEN  pp. 24-5, with errors.  7. MD 22:151.  8. Middleboro 1st Cong. Ch Recs, typescript, pp. 44,46,47.  9. MIDDLEBOROUGH VR 2:76,80-1,100.


106 ₁SARAH  WARREN⁵ (Eleanor⁴  Billington, Isaac³, Francis²,
John¹) b. Middleboro 9 Feb. 1721/2, d. prob. Middleboro bet.
27 April 1779 and 17 Sept. 1783.[1]
     She m. Middleboro  24  June  1740 WILLIAM   REED/READ,
Jr.,[2]   b. Middleboro 18 July 1715,[3]  d.  Middleboro 7
April 1776;[4]  son of William and Elizabeth (_____) Reed.
     Administration  on  the  estate  of  William Reed of Mid-
dleborough was  granted to  son William  Reed, 2nd on 6 May
1776.  Dower was  set off  to the  widow Sarah 3 Sept. 1777.
The estate,  deemed "unsuitable for division" was settled on
son  William,  he  paying his  siblings equal  sums for their
shares in  1777, 1779  and 1780.   Receipts were  shown from
Benjamin  Reed,  Elizabeth  Reed,  Elijah  Reed, Robert Hoar
(husband  of  Sarah),  Abraham Peirce and  wife Priscilla, all
of Middleborough.[5]
     Sarah Reed  made her  will 27  April 1779  (not recorded)
bequeathing  all  household  goods  and  moveable effects to
daughter Elizabeth Reed;  "as for my  other children I  have
before  the  date  hereof  given  each one  their parts,"
witnessed by Benjamin Reed  and Abiah Reed.  A  citation was
issued 17 Sept. 1783 for  a 6 Oct. court hearing  concerning
the  will  to:  Benjamin  Reed,  Sarah Hoars, wife of Robt.
Hoars, heirs of Priscilla Pearce, wife of Abraham Pearce and
all  other  heirs  at  law  of  the  estate  of  Sarah Reed,
deceased.[1]

     Children (REED) b. Middleboro:[6]

     i    PRISCILLA⁶ b. 8 Dec. 1742
    ii    WILLIAM  b. 24 Jan. 1744
   iii    BENJAMIN  b. 29 Jan. 1746
    iv    SARAH  b. 15 Jan. 1748
     v    ELISABETH  b. 4 May 1750
    vi    ISRAEL  b. 17 March 1752; nothing more known
   vii    ELIJAH b.  _____; birth  not  recorded, but he
          receipted for his share  of his father's estate
          11 Oct.  1780, indicating  he  was  then  of
          age.[5] Perhaps the  second recorded Elisabeth
          (to follow) was actually Elijah:

                viii  ELISABETH b. 9 Sept. 1759
                  ix  ABNER  b. 12 Aug. 1764; nothing more known

References:  1. Plymouth  Co.  PR  File #16,704,  (Unrecorded
             will  of  Sarah  Reed  and  citation).   2. MD
15:219.   3. MD  6:180.   4. Middleboro VR, deaths, p. 75.
5. Plymouth  Co.  PR  23:108;  24:351-4;  29:51-2;  (William
Reede).  6. MD 26:24,25.


107 $_1$JOSIAH  WARREN$^5$ (Eleanor$^4$ Billington, Isaac$^3$, Francis$^2$,
John$^1$) b. Middleboro 9 May 1724, d.  prob. Middleboro bef. 4
June 1760.[1]
    He  m.  Middleboro  5  April  1747 JOANNA SPOONER,[2]  b.
Middleboro 15  Aug 1729,[3]  d. aft.  4 April 1763;[1]  dau.
of Benjamin and Joanna (Tobey) Spooner.[4]
    Letters of administration were granted to Micah Bryant on
the  estate of  Josiah Warren,  late of  Middleborough, husbandman,  4  June  1760.   The  inventory, presented 14 July
1760,  showed  a  small  amount  of personal  property, but no
real estate.  After an allowance for necessaries was made to
the  widow 4 April  1763, the estate  was adjudged insolvent
and proceedings discontinued.[1]

    Possible child, but no proof, (WARREN):[5]

        i  JOSIAH$^6$  b._____

References:  1. Plymouth Co.  PR 15:515;  16:398,452 (Josiah
             Warren) 2. MD 16:109.  3. MD 7:243.  4. SPOONER
DESC  1:63-4.   5. Bowman  File  for  Warren:   shows Josiah
Warren, who m. Middleboro 29 March 1770  Susannah Makepiece,
(MD 30:12), a **possible** child.


108 $_1$JEMIMA  WOOD$^5$  (Mary$^4$  Billington,  Isaac$^3$, Francis$^2$,
John$^1$) b. Middleboro 21 July 1712, d. Sandwich bet.  5 March
and 10 May 1782.[1]
    She  m. Sandwich 15  May 1739 as  his second wife, GIDEON
ELLIS,[2]  possibly b.  5 Feb. 1700/1 (assuming  an  error of
10  years in Rochester vital  record;[2] d. Sandwich bef. 10
Dec.  1760;[3]  **perhaps**  son  of  Freeman and Mary (_____)
Ellis.[2]   He  m.  (1) Plymouth 11 Feb.  1719/20 Anna
Clarke,[4]  by  whom  he  had ten  children: Abigail, Gideon,
Thomas,  Eleanor,  Elijah,  Ebenezer,  Susannah, Anna, Elisha,
and Anna (2nd).[5,6]
    Gideon Ellis of Sandwich died intestate bef. 10 Dec. 1760
when the inventory of his estate was taken.  In the division

of the estate the widow Jemima receipted 23 March 1763 for
the shares due the four youngest surviving children: Abiel,
Ephraim, Samuel and Reuben Ellis. The distribution of
Gideon's estate mentions eleven children.[4]
    Jemima Ellis of Sandwich, widow, in her will dated 5
March 1782, probated 10 May 1782, named sons Abiel, Elnathan
and Reuben, mentioned her rights in the estate of her son
Samuel deceased, and son Ephraim's daughter.[1]

    Children (ELLIS) by wife Jemima, recorded Sandwich:[5,3]

```
     i   ELNATHAN[6]  b. 5 Jan. 1739/40
    ii   SETH  b. 23 May 1742; d. 21 Feb. 1760
   iii   ABIEL  b. 6 Oct. 1744
    iv   JOHN  b. 2 March 1745/6; d.y.
     v   EPHRAIM  bp. 10 Sept. 1749
    vi   GIDEON  bp. 19 May 1751; d.y.
   vii   SAMUEL  b. 22 Sept. 1753
  viii   REUBEN  b. 25 Aug. 1755
```

References: 1. Barnstable Co. PR 14:101 (Jemima Ellis)
            2. NEHGR 120:113-117, (1966); also 119:268-270
(1965). [This Ellis genealogy errs in giving Jemima Wood's
mother as Patience, who was her stepmother.] 3. Barnstable
Co. PR 12:143,275;(Gideon Ellis). 4. MD 14:39    5. MD
30:101  6. MD 13:111


109 ₁JEDIDAH WOOD[5] (Mary[4] Billington, Isaac[3], Francis[2],
John[1]) b. Middleboro 27 March 1715, d. there 9 March 1788
aged 73 years.[1,2]
    She m. Middleboro 25 March 1735 MOSES EDDY,[3] b.
Plympton 24 Aug. 1709,[4] d. Middleboro 1 Dec. 1794 in 85th
year;[1,2] son of Jabez and Mary (Rickard) Eddy. He m. (2)
Bridgewater 30 Dec. 1788 widow Kezia (_____) Keith,[5] b.
Feb. 1723/4, d. Middleboro 1 Oct. 1804, "aged 80 last
Feb."[1,2]
    Moses and Jedidah Eddy, with dau. Mary/Molly, were
pillars of Elder Isaac Backus's First Baptist Church,
Titicut Parish, Middleboro.[2] The will of Moses Eddy,
dated Middleboro 30 May 1794, probated 5 Jan. 1795, gave
wife Kezia her dower and the property she brought with her;
made bequests to Abigail, Huldah, Jedidah and Cynthia
Washburn, daughters of Jonathan Washburn "who now lives with
me." "Friend" Jonathan Washburn was to inherit the
remainder of the estate and to be executor.[6] Moses had
sold his farm to Jonathan Washburn 9 Jan. 1775, but the deed
was not recorded until 9 Dec. 1794, after Moses's death.[7]
[Jonathan Washburn was a nephew of Moses Eddy's first wife
Jedidah Wood, and son of Jonathan and Judah (Wood) Washburn,

#113. Jonathan's wife Hannah Conant, daughter of Nathan and Hannah (Lazell) Conant, was a step-granddaughter of Mary (Wood) Conant, #111.]

Child (EDDY) prob. b. Middleboro:

    i  MARY[6] b. ca. 1737; perhaps the "Mary Wood," (sic-error for Eddy?) dau. of Jedidah, bp. Middleboro Church 7 Aug. 1737;[8] d. unm. Middleboro 30 Aug. 1764 in her 28th year.[1,2]

References: 1. MIDDLEBORO DEATHS p. 61 2. BACKUS DIARY pp. 127, 249, 1222, 1502, etc. 3. GEN ADVERTISER 1:112 4. EDDY GEN, p. 62, which errs in stating that Moses and Jedidah (Wood) Eddy had no children, although none survived them. 5. VR BRIDGEWATER 2:388 6. Plymouth Co. PR 35:199 (Moses Eddy) 7. Plymouth Co. LR 77:65 (Moses Eddy to Jonathan Washburn) 8. Middleboro 1st Cong.Ch Recs., p. 33.


110 1EPHRAIM WOOD[5] (Mary[4] Billington, Isaac[3], Francis[2], John[1]) b. Middleboro 8 May 1716, d. there 8 Nov. 1783 in his 68th year.[1,2]
    He m. (1) Middleboro 5 Aug. 1743 HANNAH PARLOW,[3] b. Middleboro 16 Aug. 1723,[4] d. there 23 March 1768,[2] bur. Middleboro (n.d.);[1] dau. of Thomas and Hannah (King) Parlow.
    Ephraim m. (2) Middleboro 3 Jan. 1773, int. Bridgewater 12 Dec. 1772 SARAH FRENCH of Bridgewater,[2,5] whose identity has not been learned. She was living in 1783.[6]
    Ephraim Wood was a Baptist, member of Elder Isaac Backus's church in Titicut Parish, Middleboro, from 1762 until his death.[2] Ephraim Wood of Middleborough, in his will dated 6 Nov. 1783, probated 1 Dec. 1783, named wife Sarah; sons Elnathan and Reuben; unmarried daus. Jerusha and Rebecca Wood and dau. Jedidah, wife of Francis Billington. Son Elnathan was appointed executor.[6]

Children (WOOD) b. Middleboro, all by Hannah:[7,1,6]

    i    JERUSHA[6] b. 7 June 1744
    ii   ELNATHAN b. 22 Aug. 1745
   iii  MARY b. 14 May 1747; d. 10 April 1761 in 14th yr.
    iv  HANNAH b. 14 Feb. 1749, d.y., poss. 5 Dec. 1761,[9]
    v   EPHRAIM b. 7 April 1751, d.s.p. 18, bur. 21 Feb. 1774.[2,9]
    vi  ELKANAH b. 19 July 1752, d. 12 April 1761 in 9th yr.
   vii  REBECCA b. 25 Sep. 1755

  viii  JEMIMA  b.  13  Dec.  1756,  d.  18  May 1761, ae
        4y/5m/5d.
    ix  JEDIDAH  b.  2  July 1759;  m.  FRANCIS BILLINGTON,
        [Fam. #114].
     x  REUBEN  b.  ca.  1761;  d.s.p. 31 Oct.  1790 in his
        29th  year;  [1,2,8,]  mentioned  in  father's
        will.[6]

References:  1. MIDDLEBORO  DEATHS pp.  234, 241.  2. BACKUS
            DIARY pp.  627,  898,  1130,1299.  3. Middleboro
VR,  marriages.      4. MD    12:231.    5. VR    BRIDGEWATER.
6. Plymouth  Co.  PR  13:34  (Ephraim  Wood).    7. MD 23:45.
8. Middleboro VR, deaths, p. 89.


111  MARY WOOD[5] (Mary[4] Billington, Isaac[3], Francis[2], John[1]),
b. Middleboro 5 Oct. 1719, d. Bridgewater 19 Aug. 1802, aged
83 years.[1]
    She m.  Bridgewater 29  Oct. 1745  THOMAS CONANT,[1]    b.
Bridgewater 27 Feb. 1704/5,[1]  d. there 14 June 1786 in his
82nd  year;[1]    son  of  Nathaniel and Margaret (Laughton)
Conant.  He m. (1) in 1730 Martha Ames,[2]  b. Bridgewater 7
March  1704,[3]  d. there 10  (____) 1745 (sic);[1]  dau. of
William and Mary Ames, by  whom he had seven children.    Two
of  these,  Rebecca  and Bethiah,  apparently died young, not
being mentioned in their father's will.
    Thomas Conant, in his will dated Bridgewater 18 May 1774,
probated 2 July 1787,  named wife Mary, sons Nathan  and Abner, daus. Sarah wife of  John Hefford, Mary wife of Zebulon
Bryant,  Zilphah  wife  of  Samuel  Keith,  Jr. and Jedidah,
Abigail and Keturah (no surnames given).   Mentioned was Seth
Lathrop who married his dau. Martha, now dead with no issue.
Son Ezra was named executor, to have half the home stable by
the  South meeting house,  plus other property  given him by
deed.[4]  Children  Nathan,  Sarah, Mary,  Zilphah and Martha
were by the first wife, not Billington descendants.

    Children (CONANT) b. Bridgewater, to Mary:[5]

      i  ABNER[6]  b.  11 Oct. 1746; d.s.p. aft. 1774.
     ii  ZENAS b.  ca.  1748;  prob.  child who d. 11 May
         1759.
    iii  EZRA  b. 22 July 1750
     iv  JEDIDAH  b. 22 Feb. 1752
      v  ABIGAIL  b. 3 Jan. 1754
     vi  KETURAH  b. 13 Dec. 1756

References:   1. VR   BRIDGEWATER 1:79; 2:416,451.   2. BRIDGE-
             WATER   BY  MITCHELL,  p.  140.    3. MD  6:8.
4. Plymouth Co. PR 30:157-159(Thomas Conant).  5. VR BRIDGE-
WATER 1:75,76,77,80.

112  LYDIA WOOD[5] (Mary[4] Billington, Isaac[3], Francis[2], John[1])
b. Middleboro 1 July 1722, d. there 28 Jan. 1761 in 39th
year.[1]
    She m. Halifax 4 June 1741 JOHN TOMSON,[2]  b. Middleboro
11 June 1717,[3]  d. there 22 June 1766, aged 49;[1]  son of
Shubael and Susanna (Parlow) Tomson. He was a descendant of
Pilgrims Peter Brown  and Francis Cooke.  John Tomson m. (2)
Plympton 10 Aug. 1762 Sarah  (Bryant) Soule,[4]  b. Plympton
31 Oct. 1731,[4]  d. Halifax 20 Aug. 1805;[5] dau. of George
and Sarah (Ripley)  Bryant. She m. (1)  Zachariah Soule and
m.  (3) at Halifax  in 1771, Reuben  Tomson.[6]  John Tomson
had  one daughter  by wife  Sarah:  Mary  Tomson, b. 27 Dec.
1763.[7]
    John Tomson of  Middleborough, yeoman, in his  will dated
12 May  1766, presented 4  Aug. 1766, named  wife Sarah; son
Shubael  to have  "land of  my father  Shubael;" sons Isaac,
John and  Ezra; daus.  Susanna Thomas,  Lidia Tomson,  Sarah
Tomson, Fear Tomson, Priscilla Tomson and youngest dau. Mary
Tomson.[8]

    Children (TOMSON) b. Middleboro to Lydia Wood:[9]

        i    SHUBAEL[6]  b. 11 March 1741/2
        ii   SUSANNA  b. 1 Nov. 1743
        iii  ISAAC  b. 1 Feb. 1745/6
        iv   JOHN  b. 6 May 1748
        v    EZRA  b. 4 July 1750
        vi   LYDIA  b. 21 June 1752
        vii  SARAH  b. 6 Oct. 1754
        viii UZZA b. 10 Dec. 1756; d. 11 June 1758, ae 18m/1d.
        ix   FEAR  b. 6 Nov. 1757
        x    PRISCILLA  b. 11 April 1760

References:  1. MD  15:219.   2. HALIFAX  VR  p.  33.  3. MD
          3:86.   4. VR PLYMPTON  pp. 49,410.  5. HALIFAX
VR  p. 94.  6. MF  3:163.  7. MD 23:71.  8. Plymouth Co. PR
19:382.(John Tomson)  9. MD 15:220,221; 20:35; 23:43.


113  JUDAH   (JUDITH)  WOOD[5]  (Mary[4] Billington, Isaac[3],
Francis[2], John[1])  b. Middleboro 11 April 1728, d. Middleboro
at Titicut 20 Nov. 1811, aged 83.[1]
    Judah m. Middleboro 23 May 1751 JONATHAN WASHBURN, Jr. of
Bridgewater,[2]  b. ca.  1728, d.  Middleboro at  Titicut 6
April 1792,  aged 63;[1]  son of  Benjamin and  Bethiah
(Kingman) Washburn.[3]  He was  a  descendant of Pilgrim
Francis Cooke.
    They lived  at Middleboro and  were from 1754  members of
the  Baptist  church  of  Elder  Isaac  Backus  in  Titicut
Parish.[4]  No  records  of  their  children's  births, nor

probate records for Jonathan or Judah Washburn appear.
Mitchell's **Bridgewater** states: "Jonathan [Washburn] of
Middleboro, (son of Benjamin) m. Judith, dau. of Elnathan
Wood, and had Jonathan, Benjamin, Isaac, Salmon and perhaps
others. Isaac went to Taunton--Benjamin has a son Jonathan
in South Bridgewater."[5] Five sons of this family and
their marriages are detailed in a typescript genealogy by
Ella F. O'Gorman at the D A R Library.[3] The author calls
Zenas "Linus," but gives him a wife who actually married
Zenas, according to the vital record. The four older sons
in both accounts agree, and presumably Mitchell obtained
family records from a living child of one of the sons.

Son Jonathan Washburn was the principal heir in the 1794
will of Moses Eddy, whose first wife was Jedidah Wood, #109,
Jonathan's aunt.[6] No other connection between Moses Eddy
and the young Jonathan can be made except that of uncle and
nephew-by-marriage. On 4 April 1792 the elder Jonathan
Washburn conveyed to "my son Salmon Washburn" half of
certain lands at Middleborough purchased in 1758 and 1767;
and one-fourth of a tract purchased in 1791.[7] In Oct.
1793 Zenas Washburn of Burlington, Chittenden Co. VT quit
claimed to his brother Salmon Washburn of Middleborough his
right or share of lands that belonged to "our honoured
father, Jonathan Washburn, late of Middleborough, deceased,"
bounded partly by Benjamin Washburn.[8]

Children (WASHBURN) probably b. Middleboro, perhaps
incomplete:

    i   BENJAMIN[6] b. ca. 1752; (calculated from age at
        death) [1]
    ii  JONATHAN b. ca. 1753; (from age at death) [1]
    iii ISAAC b. 1 Feb. 1755;[9,10]
    iv  SALMON b. ca. 1761
    v   ZENAS b. ca. 1763-5

References: 1. MIDDLEBORO DEATHS pp. 221-2. 2. MD 18:84.
3. Washburn MS. 4. BACKUS DIARY p. 264: The
editor states Jonathan's wife was "Hannah," who was son
Jonathan Jr.'s wife. 5. BRIDGEWATER BY MITCHELL p. 349.
6. Plymouth Co. PR 35:199 (Moses Eddy) 7. Plymouth Co. LR
87:176(Jonathan Washburn to Salmon Washburn). 8. Plymouth
Co. LR 118:86-87(Zenas Washburn to Salmon Washburn).
9. TAUNTON BY EMERY pp. 33,34. 10. Rev. Pension #W1677
(Isaac Washburn).

114 NATHANIEL[5] BILLINGTON (Isaac[4-3], Francis[2], John[1]) b.
Middleboro 7 Feb. 1732/3, d. Goshen aft. 1800 and bef.
1806.[1,2]

He  m.  (1)  Middleboro  14  Jan.  1754  MARY  DONHAM,  who
apparently  d.  without  issue  before  1756.[3]  Mary's  identity
has  not  been  established.
    He  m.  (2)  Middleboro  5  Aug.  1756  his  cousin  ELEANOR
WARREN,[4]  bp.  Middleboro  1  Aug.  1736,[5]  d.  aft.  1789  and
apparently  bef.  1806;[6]  dau.  of  Cornelius  Warren  and  his
wife  Mercy  Ward,  Family  #101.  Eleanor  Warren  was  a
descendant of  Pilgrim  Richard  Warren,  as  well  as  of John
Billington.
    Nathaniel  Billington  served  in  the  Revolution  from
Middleboro.  In  a  deed  dated  14  Sept.  1789,  acknowledged  15
Sept.  1789  in  Hampshire  Co.,  Nathaniel  Billington  of
Middleborough,  with wife  Eleanor  releasing  dower,  sold  10
acres  and  a  barn  at  Middleborough  to  Robert  Cushman.[6]  They
moved  to  Hampshire  County,  where  he  appears  in  the  1790
census  at  Ashfield  near  son  Francis.  Nathaniel  is  the  only
Billington  in  the  1800  census  of  Hampshire  County.  His  son
Francis[6] died  by  1799,  leaving  children  Hannah,  Nathaniel
and  Francis  Billington,  who  shared  in  their  grandfather's
estate.[1,2]
    A  Hampshire  County  deed  dated  16  Oct.  1806  lists  the
heirs  selling  property of  Nathaniel  Billington,  deceased,
with  the  following  grantors:  Isaac  Billington  of  Wayne,
Kennebec  Co.  [ME];  Elenor  wife  of  Abel  Olds  of  Swanton,  Sena
(Asenath)  wife  of  Josiah  Orcutt  of  High-Gate,  all  of
Franklin  Co.  VT;  and Nancy  Billington  of  Goshen,  Hampshire
Co.,  spinster,  all  children  and  heirs  of  Nathaniel  Billington  of  Goshen,  deceased;  also  Barnabas  Taylor  of  Buckland
for  his  wife  Hannah  Taylor,  and  on  behalf  of  her  brothers
Nathaniel  and  Francis  Billington,  minors  of  Middleborough,
all  three  grandchildren  of  said  Nathaniel.[2]

    Children  (BILLINGTON)  b.  Middleboro,  all  by  wife
Eleanor:[7,8]

    i    ISAAC[6]  b.  10  Dec.  1758;  bp.  6  May  1764;  m.  RE-
         BECCA WEST
    ii   [worn]CIS  (FRANCIS)  b.  15  Jan.  1761;  bp.  with
         brother  Isaac  6  May  1764;  m.  JEDIDAH WOOD,  [Fam
         #110].
    iii  *[worn]ANIEL  (?Nathaniel)  b.  7  Feb.  1[worn]
         (1763?);  prob.  died  young.  No  baptism  for  him.
    iv   LUCY  b.  27  Nov.  1765;  bp.  18  May  1766;  d.
         Middleboro  12  April  1785  ae  19  yrs.[8]
    v    ELEANOR  bp.  15  May  1768;  m.  ABEL  OLDS
    vi   MARY  b.  perhaps  1770;  bp.  1  July  1771;  evidently
         d.y.
    vii  NANCY  bp.  14  Sept.  1771;  spinster  of  Goshen  in
         1806.  She was  prob.  the  Nancy  Billington  who
         d.  Middleboro  27  Aug.  1849  "aged  82"  in  the
         almshouse.[9]

viii  ASENATH/SENA  bp. 25 Oct. 1772; m. JOSIAH ORCUTT
  ix  OLIVE  bp. 11 June 1780; apparently d.y.

*The partly illegible birth entry for "[worn]ANIEL" follows
the name of brother Francis,[7] but although Francis and
Isaac were baptized together in 1764, there is no baptismal
record for Nathaniel; nor does he appear as an heir in the
family deed cited. The adult Nathaniel Billington of Maine,
presumed to be this son of Nathaniel, probably was a son of
Ichabod Billington, #116.

References; 1. FED CENSUS 1790 and 1800. 2. Hampshire Co.
LR 32:311 (Heirs of Nathaniel Billington).
3. MD 19:46. 4. MD 24:57. 5. NEHGR 55:169. 6. Plymouth
Co. LR 68:259 (Nathaniel and Eleanor Billington). 7. MD
22:149 (Isaac); MD 23:46 ([worn]cis & [worn]aniel); MD 23:71
(Lucy). 8. Middleboro 1st Cong. Ch Recs pp. 46,47,48,49
(Isaac, Francis, Lucy, Eleanor, Mary, Nancy, Asenath, and
Olive Billington). 9. MIDDLEBORO DEATHS p. 20.


115 SETH$^5$ BILLINGTON (Isaac$^{4-3}$, Francis$^2$, John$^1$) b.
Middleboro 11 May 1735, d. Pelham bef. 21 Oct. 1783.[1]
    He m. (1) Middleboro 30 Dec. 1756 DEBORAH SMITH,[2] b.
Middleboro 24 Dec. 1736,[3] d. Middleboro 22 July 1762 in
her 26th yr.;[4] dau. of John and Deborah (Barden) Smith.
    He m. (2) Middleboro 15 Jan. 1765 *Mrs. BETTY WASHBURN,
both of Middleboro.[5] She d. aft. the 1800 census, when
she was living at Rutland VT, next to her son Frederick.[6]
    Seth Billington lived at Middleboro and then moved to
Pelham. The will of Seth Billington, dated Pelham 13 July
1782, probated 21 Oct. 1783, gave wife Betty many items plus
"what she brought with her;" devised to son John all real
estate except the west part of the home lot and 1/4 of a
sawmill; to son Frederick, under 21, the remaining real
estate and other property; to dau. Lidey [Weston] a heifer,
she having received her share. The witnesses were Eliakim
Barlow, Mary Barlow and Ebenezer Gray.[1]

    Children (BILLINGTON) b. Middleboro, first two by Deb-
orah, third by Betty:[7,8]

    i  LYDIA$^6$ b. 22 Jan. 1758
   ii  JOHN b. 24 Nov. 1760
  iii  FREDERICK b. 3 June 1769

*She may have been the Betty Dellis/Dilley who m. Bridge-
water [VR p.391] 11 May 1749 Reuben Washburne. They had two
sons b. Middleboro: Seth b. 1751 and Isaiah b. 1754. Betty
was the widow of Reuben Washburn by 30 June 1757 when she

was admitted to full communion in the Baptist Church of
Elder Isaac Backus at Middleboro. [BACKUS DIARY pp.
36-7,61,344, 454,465,641,788]

References: 1. Hampshire Co. PR Box 14, No. 47 (Seth
                 Billington).    2. MD    24:58.    3. MD  8:248.
4. MIDDLEBORO DEATHS p.  20.   5. MD 24:57.  6. FED CENSUS
1800.  7. MD 22:147,149.  8. MD 26:26.

116 ICHABOD[5] BILLINGTON (Isaac[4-3], Francis[2], John[1]) b.
Middleboro 23 May 1737, d. prob. Kennebec Co. [ME] between
1810 when he appears in that census, and 26 Sept. 1815, when
Ichabod, Jr. had dropped the suffix from his name.[1,2]
     He m. Middleboro 26 Oct. 1758 BETTY PECK of Bridge-
water,[3] whose identity is as yet unknown. She was living
7 April 1774 when she signed a deed with her husband.[4]
     Ichabod Billington, tanner, was a member of the Baptist
church of Isaac Backus, Titicut Parish, Middleboro from 1764
until after 1774.[5] Deeds show Ichabod was a resident of
Middleboro in 1768, of Plymouth by 3 June 1771 when he and
his wife Betty sold land,[4] and on 2 Sept. 1778 when he
acknowledged a Plymouth deed.[4] But 14 June 1779 Ichabod
was of Winthrop, Lincoln Co., then MA now ME, when he bought
lot #172 near Amoriscoggin Pond in that county. This land
became part of Kennebec Co. [ME], in 1799.[6]
     Ichabod Billington had several land transactions in Maine
and Plymouth Co. through 1809, suggesting, but not proving,
some family relationships. No probate record has been found
in Kennebec or Somerset Counties ME for him or his wife.
Only two of his children's births were recorded (in
Middleboro).[7] Maine town vital records show several
Billington marriages, with birth dates of parents as well as
their children. The Billington adults can be accounted for
in no other way than as children of Ichabod. Perhaps proof
may eventually be found.

     Children (BILLINGTON) recorded Middleboro:[7]

     i   HANNAH[6] b. 1 Sept. 1760; nothing more known. Can
         this name have been an error for Nathaniel,
         #iii below?
     ii  BETTY b. 24 May 1762; no further record.

     Probable but unproven children (BILLINGTON), b. prob.
Middleboro or Plymouth. These Billington adults of
appropriate ages were closely associated in Maine town, land
and census records with Ichabod Billington:

iii  NATHANIEL b. perhaps ca. ?1759, thus the eldest;
     m. (1) by 1784 ABIGAIL HANDY, b. Sandwich 18
     Sept. 1757;[8]  m. (2) ca. 1791-2 PHEBE (DOTY)
     CARY, b. Liverpool, England 6 Oct. 1762.[9]
     Seven children b. Wayne ME.[8,9,10]  [See also
     Family #114.]
 iv  ICHABOD, Jr. b. ca. 1764; was prob. "my
     apprentice Ichabod Billington" to whom Stephen
     Davis, Jr. of Barnstable made a bequest of 3
     pounds in his will dated 26 June 1777, probated
     21 Dec. 1777.[11]; m. by 1791 ELIZABETH HANDY,
     b. Sandwich 18 Sept. 1764;[8]  two children b.
     Wayne ME.[9]
  v  JOB b. 29 Sept. 1770; m. China ME 17 Sept. 1797
     HANNAH BURRELL, dau. of Abraham and Hannah
     (Cushing) Burrell, b. Harlem [now China] ME 19
     Sept. 1778;[12]  seven children recorded at
     Albion, Kennebec Co. ME.[13]  The 1800 census
     of Harlem, Kennebec Co. ME, shows Job moved
     there in 1798 from elsewhere in Maine.[14]
 vi  *MARY b. 19 Oct. 1772;[9]  m. by 1789 ABISHA
     STURTEVANT; ten children.[9]  On 21 July 1809
     Abisha Sturtevant of Wayne [ME], carpenter,
     bought from Ichabod Billington of Wayne,
     tanner, title to 20 acres in Plymouth.[15]
vii  *REBECCA b. 10 March 1775;[9]  m. CONSTANT
     DEXTER; three children.[9]  Constant Dexter of
     Wayne, Kennebec Co., yeoman, bought from Icha-
     bod Billington of same, yeoman, 50 acres of lot
     #172 at Wayne on 21 Feb. 1805.[16]
viii LYDIA b. 1776 (from age at death), or 31 May 1778
     per Monmouth ME VR,[17]  as Lydia Allen without
     maiden surname, wife of JOSEPH ALLEN. Lydia is
     said to be a Billington by descendants.

References:  1. FED CENSUS 1810 & 1820.  2. Kennebec Co. ME
LR 30:321,322 (Ichabod and Elizabeth Bill-
ington).  3. MD 24:131.  4. Plymouth Co. LR 56:86; 90:211;
102:18; (Ichabod and Betty Billington).  5. BACKUS DIARY pp.
541,573,625,899.  6. Kennebec Co. ME LR 13:112 (Ichabod
Billington).  7. MD 22:150; 23:46.  8. NEHGR 126:55-57.
9. Wayne, Kennebec Co. ME VR, microfilm: Birth dates of
*Mary and *Rebecca Billington are listed with family group
vital records of their husbands and children. 10. WAYNE ME
HIST passim.  11. Barnstable Co. PR 20:360 (Stephen Davis,
Jr.).  12. China, Kennebec Co. ME VR, microfilm.  13. Al-
bion, Kennebec Co. ME VR, microfilm.  14. FED CENSUS 1800,
Harlem, Kennebec Co. ME p. 1224.  15. Plymouth Co. LR
128:274,275 (Ichabod Billington to Abisha Sturtevant).
16. Kennebec Co. ME LR 12:398 (Ichabod Billington to Constant Dexter).  17. Monmouth, Kennebec Co. ME VR, microfilm.

117 MARY[5] BILLINGTON (Isaac[4-3], Francis[2], John[1]) bp. Middleboro 3 Oct. 1739, d. prob. Brookfield aft. 9 March 1810.[1]
    She m. Middleboro 3 Dec. 1761 ELIAKIM BARLOW[6],[2] b. Middleboro 17 March 1739/40,[3] d. Brookfield between 1 Feb. and 4 March 1806;[4] son of William and Joanna (Warren[5]) Barlow, Family #104. He was a descendant of Pilgrims John Billington and Richard Warren.
    Eliakim Barlow served in the Revolutionary War and lived at Pelham, where he was in the 1790 census. Afterward he moved to Brookfield. The will of Eliakim Barlow, dated Brookfield 1 Feb. 1806, probated 4 March 1806, named wife Mary and daughter Mary Tinkham, a widow, living at home; sons Isaac and William and daus. Deborah wife of Josiah McKee and Joanna Wilson.[4] On 8 March 1810, acknowledged the next day, widows Mary Barlow and Mary Tinkham sold land in Brookfield from the estate of Eliakim Barlow.[1]

    Children (BARLOW) prob. b. Pelham:[4]

        i   DEBORAH[6] b. ca. 1762
       ii   MARY/POLLY b. ca. 1766
      iii   ISAAC b. ca. 1768
       iv   JOANNA b. ca. 1772
        v   WILLIAM b. ca. 1778

References: 1. Worcester Co. LR 175:483 (Mary Barlow and Mary Tinkham). 2. MD 24:133. 3. MQ 43:114; also MIDDLEBOROUGH VR p.77. 4. Worcester Co. PR, Case #3432 (Eliakim Barlow).


118 TIMOTHY MARTIN[5] (John Martin[4], Mercy[3] Billington, Francis[2], John[1]) b. Rehoboth 14 June 1716, d. bef. 25 Aug. 1755.[1]
    He m. Attleboro 9 April 1741 MARY FULLER of Rehoboth, "dau. of John,"[2] b. Attleboro 22 April 1717,[3] d. aft. 1758;[1] dau. of John and Elizabeth (_____) Fuller. Mary was Timothy's stepsister. She m.(2) Attleboro 12 Nov. 1755 John Fuller,[2] unidentified, perhaps her cousin.
    Administration on the estate of Timothy Martin of Attleborough was granted to his widow Mary Martin 25 Aug. 1755, but an account of his estate dated 2 April 1757 calls the widow "Mary Fuller late Mary Martin;" and on 3 April 1758 John Fuller of Attleborough and wife Mary Fuller were appointed guardians of Abel, Sarah and Timothy Martin, children of Timothy Martin, dec'd.[1] Timothy's father John Martin, in his will of 31 March 1758, made bequests of small amounts to grandchildren Timothy, Sarah and Abel Martin.[4]

Children (MARTIN) b. Attleboro:[5]

>     i    TIMOTHY[6]  b. 22 Aug. 1743
>    ii    SARAH  b. 19 July 1745
>   iii    ABEL  b. 3 May 1750; bp. 5 Aug. 1750;[6]

References:   1. Bristol   Co  PR   14:537;   15:308-9,317-8;
           126:18,24-5; (Timothy Martin).   2. VR ATTLEBORO
p. 434.   3. VR ATTLEBORO p. 132.   4. Bristol Co. PR 16:432
(John Martin).   5. VR  ATTLEBORO pp. 174,175.   6. Attleboro
2nd Ch p. 9.


119  ROBERT  MARTIN[5]    (John  Martin[4],  Mercy[3]  Billington,
Francis[2]. John[1]) b. Rehoboth 2 July 1718, d. aft. 1771.[1]
    He m.  Attleboro 30 April 1741  ELIZABETH WELLMAN,[2]  b.
Attleboro  22 Oct.  172_,[3]  or  b. Montague 22 Oct. 1725;
[4]  dau. of Joseph  and Charity (Hall) Wellman. She d. aft.
1754.
    Several deeds  in 1760,  1765 and  1770 show  that Robert
Martin, cooper, lived  at Attleboro near the  Rehoboth line,
owning  land in both  towns.  His land  adjoined that of his
brother Amos  Martin.  On 12  June 1770 Robert  sold a house
and  small  lot  in  Attleborough  to his son Job Martin.[5]
Robert was on the 1771 Tax list at Attleboro.[1]
    No probate record has been  found for Robert Martin.  His
sons John, Job  and Daniel served  in the Revolutionary  War
from Attleboro.[6]

Children (MARTIN) b. Attleboro except where noted:[7,8]

>     i    MOLLY[6]  bp. 14 Nov. 1742
>    ii    JOHN  b. 30 Oct. 17__;[7]   (1745);[4]
>   iii    JOB  b. 29 Dec. 1747
>    iv    DANIEL b. Rehoboth 24 March 1754; bp. Attleboro 7
>          April 1754

References:   1. MA TAX LIST, 1771 p.552.   2. VR ATTLEBORO p.
           491.   3. VR ATTLEBORO  p. 281.   4. WELLMAN GEN,
pp.101-2.   5. Bristol   Co.  LR  44:445,446; 53:95,96(Robert
Martin).  6. MSSR, 10:280,281,287, 288,289.   7. VR ATTLEBORO
pp.174,175.   8. REHOBOTH VR p. 672.


120  AMOS  MARTIN[5]   (John   Martin[4],  Mercy[3] Billington,
Francis[2], John[1])  b.  Rehoboth  28  April  1722, living in
Attleboro in 1771.[1]
    He  m.  (1)  int.  Rehoboth  29  Sept.  1750 ANNA DAGGETT
(incorrectly called "Hannah" of Attleboro),[2]  b. Attleboro

18 July 1728,[3]   d. bef. 19  March 1757, and  prob. bef. 3
Oct. 1756; dau. of  Capt.  Mayhew  and  Joanna  (Biven or
?Blevin) Daggett.  An  agreement among  the heirs of Mayhew
Daggett of  Attleborough, acknowledged  23 June  1752, shows
the division of his estate and was  signed, among others, by
dau. Anna and her husband Amos Martin.[4]
    He m. (2) 27 April 1757,[6]   int. Attleboro 19 March 1757
ESTHER CHAFFEE,[5]    b. Attleboro 10 March  172(3?), dau. of
Daniel and Alice (Millard) Chaffee.  Esther d. bef. 21 March
1763 when  Daniel Chaffee willed her share  of his estate to
his grandson, Joel Martin.[5,6]
    Amos Martin of  Attleborough,  yeoman,  and wife Esther
deeded 14  acres partly  in  Attleborough  and  partly  in
Rehoboth to Jonathan Sheperson 14 Oct. 1758; Amos Martin of
Attleborough,  joyner, sold  2 & 3/4 acres  to [his brother]
Robert Martin  of Attleborough, cooper, 20 March 1765.  Amos
Martin is on  the 1771 tax list  at Attleboro,[7,1] but no
probate record has been found for him.
    Sons  Comfort,  Amos, Jr.,  and  Joel  Martin  were
Revolutionary War soldiers from Attleboro and Norton.[8]

    Children  (MARTIN)  first  two  b.  to  Anna,  third  by
Esther:[9,10,11]

    i   COMFORT[6] b. Rehoboth 23 Dec. 1751; bp. Attleboro
        3 Oct. 1756 as son of Amos.
   ii   AMOS  b. Rehoboth 15 Sept. 1754; bp. 3 Oct. 1756.
  iii   JOEL  b.  Attleboro 17 July 1761; bp. 14 May 1762
        as son of Amos; d. unm. bef. 20 Nov. 1780 when
        his cousin Abner Chaffee sold his share of Joel
        Martin's  estate,  originally  inherited  from
        their grandfather Chaffee.[6]

References:  1. MA  TAX LIST,  1771 p.  552.  2. REHOBOTH VR
           p.474.  3. DOGGETT FAM pp. 100,101 states Capt.
Mayhew  Daggett's daughter was Anna  Marten wife of "Carrol"
Marten,  an  error.   4.  Bristol  Co.  PR  13:185-7 (Mayhew
Daggett).   5. VR ATTLEBORO p. 69  (birth date incomplete);
int. p.  490.  6. CHAFFEE GEN, pp. 35,36,67,68.  7. Bristol
Co. LR 43:386 (Amos and Esther Martin); 53:96 (Amos Martin).
8. MSSR 10:273,274,279,280,287,288.  9. REHOBOTH VR p. 672.
10. VR ATTLEBORO pp. 174,175.  11. Attleboro 2nd Ch p. 9.


121  JOTHAM  CARPENTER[5] (Desire  Martin[4], Mercy[3] Billington,
Francis[2], John[1]) b. Rehoboth 1 Aug. 1708, d.  Cumberland RI
10 May 1777 in his 69th year.[1]
    He m. (1) Rehoboth 11 May 1728 MEHITABLE THOMPSON,[2]  b.
Rehoboth  17 May 1701,[2]  d. there 10 Feb. 1746/7;[2]  dau.

of John and Elizabeth (_____) Thompson. In the final
division of the estate of John Tompson of Rehoboth, dated 5
April 1749, "heirs of dau. Mehittable who was wife of Jotham
Carpenter" are mentioned among others.[3]

He m. (2) Swansea (recorded Rehoboth) 17 March 1747/8
FREELOVE (HAILE) KINGSLEY,[4] b. Swansea 3 April 1712,[5]
d. Cumberland RI 30 Jan. 1803;[6] dau. John and Hannah
(Tillinghast) Haile and widow of Oliver Kingsley, whom she
m. (1) Swansea 31 Dec. 1729.[5] She had four children by
first husband (Kingsley): Pardon b. 1730, Lydia b. 1733,
Peleg b. 1735 and Ann b. 1736, not Billington
descendants.[5]

Jotham Carpenter lived at Rehoboth and Swansea; moved
from Rehoboth to Cumberland RI after 1761. Jotham
Carpenter, in his will dated Cumberland 17 June 1776,
probated 2 June 1777, provided wife Freelove her thirds and
other property; devised to his two sons Jotham and Oliver,
his real property in Cumberland; bequeathed money to six
daus.: Dorcas Bullock, Sibball wife of Henry Ingalls,
Mehetabel wife of Nathan Mason, Elizabeth wife of Nathaniel
Carpenter now in Gilford, Freelove Whipple and Desire Lang,
widow, who was to have domicile rights as long as she
remained the widow of William Lang. His wife and son Jotham
were appointed executors.[1]

Freelove Carpenter, widow, executed her will at
Cumberland RI 12 Oct. 1801, probated 28 Feb. 1803. She gave
furniture and clothing to daughters Freelove [Carpenter]
Whipple and Desire [Carpenter] [Lang] Ballou; named
daughters Lydia [Kingsley] [Thurber] Blake and Anna
[Kingsley] Bliss; devised the residuary estate to sons
Oliver and Jotham Carpenter, they to be executors.[6]

Children (CARPENTER) all b. Rehoboth, except where noted;
first seven children by Mehitable, others by Freelove:[7,8]

    i    OLIVER[6] b. 1 March 1729; d.y.
   ii    DORCAS b. 16 May 1731
  iii    *ISAACK b. Swansea 8 Jan. 1734/5; doubtless d.y.;
         not in father's will or any other document to
         show he survived infancy.
   iv    *NATHAN b. Swansea 18 Feb. 1736/7; d.y.; not in
         father's will.
    v    SYBIL b. 26 Feb. 1739/40
   vi    MEHITABEL b. 28 July 1742
  vii    ELIZABETH b. 20 Dec. 1746
 viii    FREELOVE b. 27 April 1749
   ix    JOTHAM b. 28 Nov. 1750
    x    OLIVER b. 15 Nov. 1753
   xi    DESIRE b. 26 Oct. 1755

*Contrary to the account in CARPENTER (REHOBOTH) GEN pp. 238, 398-9, there is no indication that the sons "Isaiah" (Isaack in birth record) and Nathan lived to maturity. The adults described as these sons of Jotham Carpenter do not belong to this family. The adult "son" Nathan is a composite of two other men named Nathan Carpenter, one of Connecticut and one of Rhode Island; and son Isaack, as "Isaiah," is mistakenly identified as an adult Isaiah Carpenter of Vermont.

References: 1. Cumberland RI PR 5:276-8 (Jotham Carpenter); abstract also in RIGR 2:179. 2. REHOBOTH VR pp. 80,751,810 (Death record in error shows Mehitable wife of "Jonathan" Carpenter, Jr.). 3. Bristol Co. PR 12:36-8, (John Tompson). 4. REHOBOTH VR p.220. 5. Swansea Original VR, Bk. B pp. 23/51,94/206,120,93,121,15. 6. Cumberland RI PR 8:62-3 (Freelove Carpenter); also RIGR 3:174. 7. REHOBOTH VR p. 575. 8. Swansea Original VR, Book B, pp. 76,52/112: (Isaack and Nathan born to Jotham and "Mehetabl" Carpenter).


122 HANNAH CARPENTER[5] (Desire Martin[4], Mercy[3] Billington, Francis[2], John[1]) b. Rehoboth 6 June 1712, d. prob. Tiverton RI aft. 21 July 1773 when she signed a deed with husband David Round, and bef. 24 Dec. 1776 when he signed alone.[1]
     She m. Rehoboth 6 Oct. 1730 DAVID ROUND,[2] b. Swansea 28 Jan. 1706,[3] d. Tiverton RI 30 June 1797 in his 91st year;[4] son of John and Abigail (_____) Round.
     Elder David Round was a Baptist minister at Rehoboth and at Tiverton RI, where he moved by 1757. In that year he and wife Hannah, of Tiverton, sold their Rehoboth land to brother-in-law Hezekiah Hix.[5] By deed dated 21 July 1773 David and Hannah Round sold Tiverton land to son David, Jr. the last land record in which Hannah's name appears.[1] On 20 April 1790 David Round of Tiverton, for love and affection, conveyed his homestead farm to son John Round, a son whose birth is not recorded at Rehoboth.[6]
     Another Tiverton Baptist minister, Elder Peleg Burroughs, refers often in his journal to Elder David Round. He noted during the first week of May 1785 that he (Burroughs) "wrote a will for David Round," but there is no probate record in Tiverton. David perhaps had disposed of his property by 1797. His friend Elder Peleg Burroughs preached the funeral sermon 1 July 1797.[7]

     Children (ROUND) all except John recorded Rehoboth:[8,9]

     i   JERUSHA[6] b. 6 Dec. 1731
     ii  DAVID b. 5 Feb. 1733/4

         iii  HEZEKIAH  b. 21 July 1739
          iv  HANNAH  b. 11 Feb. 1741/2
           v  AMOS  b. 17 Sept. 1744
          vi  NATHAN  b. 25 Dec. 1746
         vii  JOHN  b. perhaps ca. 1747/8
        viii  MARY  b. 9 June 1749

References:  1. Tiverton  RI  LE  3:64  (David  and  Hannah
    Round); 3:486 (David Round).  2. REHOBOTH VR p.
80.  3. Swansea  Original  VR,  Bk  B  p.  14/26.  4. NEHGR
105:213.  5. Bristol Co.  LR  45:206  (David  and  Hannah
Round).  6.  Tiverton RI LE  3:657 (David Round  to son John
Round). 7. BURROUGHS'S JOURNAL  pp. 188,356.  8. REHOBOTH VR
p. 733.  9. ROUND FAM pp. 46-52.


123  RENEW  CARPENTER[5]  (Desire  Martin[4], Mercy[3] Billington,
Francis[2], John[1]), b. Rehoboth 6 June 1714, d. there  9 Feb.
1787, buried Stevens Corner Cemetery.[1]
    She m. Rehoboth 26 April 1733 JABEZ ROUND,[2]  b. Swansea
28 Sept. 1708,[3] d. Rehoboth 14 March 1790;[1]  son of John
and Abigail (_____) Round.
    Jabez  and  Renew  Round  were  Baptists.  They lived at
Swansea after marriage, but moved to Rehoboth between 10 May
and  7 Nov.  1737.[4] Jabez  Round  of  Rehoboth,  in his will
executed 31 May 1785, probated 1 May 1790; named wife Renew;
sons  Isaac, Jabez,  Oliver and Simeon; daughters Isabel wife
of  Reuben  Daggett,  widow  Rebecca  Graham,  Rhoda  Round
(unmarried),  Sybbel  wife  of John  Smith and Esther  wife of
Samuel Easterbrook.  Executors were  sons Jabez  Round, Jr.
and Simeon Round.[5,6]

    Children  (ROUND) first  two b.  Swansea, others b. Reho-
both; all recorded Rehoboth:[4,7]

          i  ISAAC[6] b. 23 Jan. 1733/4
         ii  JABEZ  b. 8 Jan. 1735/6;  VR error has 1745/6.[4]
        iii  ISABEL  b. 23 Oct. 1737
         iv  ABIGAIL  b. __ Jan. 1740; d.y.
          v  ISAIAH  b. 30 Jan. 1741; d.y.
         vi  REBECCA  b. 21 March 1742
        vii  SIBBELL  b. 10 Sept. 1744
       viii  OLIVER  b. 1 April 1747
         ix  RHODA  b. 26 Jan. 1750
          x  ESTHER  b. 8 Oct. 1752
         xi  SIMEON  b. 4 Feb. 1755

References:  1. Stevens Corner Cem Recs.  2. REHOBOTH VR  p.
        324.  3. Swansea Original  VR, Bk. B p. 32/66.
4. MQ  51:196.  5. Bristol  Co.  PR 30:424  (Jabez  Round).
6. ROUND FAM, pp. 52-57. 7. REHOBOTH VR pp. 733-734.

124  DESIRE  CARPENTER[5] (Desire  Martin[4], Mercy[3] Billington,
Francis[2], John[1])  b. Rehoboth 3  June 1716, d.  there 28 May
1800.[1]
     She  m.  int.  Rehoboth  15  April  1738  HEZEKIAH HIX or
HICKS,[2]  b. prob. Rehoboth ca.  1715,[3]  d. there 5 Feb.
1788 aged 73 years;[1]  son of James and Mary (Wells) Hix.
     Hezekiah and Desire  Hix were Baptists.  Hezekiah  Hix of
Rehoboth wrote  his will 1  Dec. 1780, which  was probated 1
April 1788, naming beloved wife Desire,  to be executrix and
residuary legatee; with bequests to eldest son Hezekiah Hix,
youngest  sons Gideon,  Jotham, Abel  and Nathan  Hix; daus.
Hannah Hail, Mary Knap  and Desire Burt.[4]  As  adults, all
of the sons changed the spelling of their surname from "Hix"
to "Hicks."

     Children (HIX/HICKS)  first seven  recorded at  Rehoboth;
birth dates of others from gravestone inscriptions:[5,1,6]

     i    HANNAH[6]  b. 17 May 1740; m. JAMES HAILE
     ii   JAMES  b. 21 April 1742; d.s.p. 12 Feb. 1760
     iii  HEZEKIAH  b. 10 Aug. 1744
     iv   MARY  b. 17 March 1746/7; m. AARON KNAP
     v    DESIRE  b. 27 Dec. 1750; m. ABEL BURT
     vi   GIDEON  (twin), b. 26 May 1752
     vii  JOTHAM  (twin), b. 26 May 1752
     viii ABEL  b. in 1755
     ix   NATHAN  b. 20 April 1762

References:  1. Stevens  Corner  Cem;  also  REHOBOTH  GRAVE
             STONES pp. 225,254, 261,262.  2. REHOBOTH VR p.
460.   3. Bristol  Co.   PR  7:23,  543; 8:23-4,57-8,181 and
Docket  (James  Hix).  4.  Bristol  Co. PR 29:462 (Hezekiah
Hix).  5. REHOBOTH  VR  p.  635.  6.  HICKS(HIX)  FAMS pp.
29,30.


125  ESTHER  CARPENTER[5] (Desire  Martin[4], Mercy[3] Billington,
Francis[2], John[1]) b. prob. Rehoboth ca. 1718, d. Warren RI 28
Oct. 1794, aged 76 yrs.[1]
     She  m.  (1)  Swansea  4  Jan.  1735  [1735/6]  NATHAN
BARDEEN,[2]  b. ca.  1709, d.  Swansea 17  Nov. 1736 in his
28th year.[3]  His identity has not been learned.
     Esther  m.  (2)  Swansea  4  Jan. 1737 [1737/8] NATHANIEL
BOWEN,[2]  b. there 1 Jan. 1703/4,[4]  d. Warren RI 24  Dec.
1794, aged 91  yrs.;[1] son of  Thomas and Thankful  (Mason)
Bowen of Swansea.
     Nathaniel Bowen  lived on inherited  land in the  part of
Swansea that became Warren RI in 1746.  There are no probate
records for Nathan Bardeen, Nathaniel Bowen or  Esther Bowen
in  Bristol  County  or  Warren RI.   There  are,  however,

numerous land transfers in Warren records from Nathaniel Bowen, with wife Esther sometimes signing, to his stepson Nathan Barden; to sons Thomas, John, James and William Bowen; to daus. Avis McMillion and Anna Bowen; and to grandson Peleg Bowen, son of son Peleg.[5] A detailed account has been published.[6]

Child by first husband (BARDEEN/BARDEN):[7]

   i  NATHAN[6]  b. Swansea 23 Feb. 1736/7

Children by second husband (BOWEN), first two b. Swansea, others at Warren RI:[7,8]

    ii   PELEG  b. 26 Jan. 1738/9
   iii   THOMAS  b. 21 Dec. 1743
    iv   ANNE  b. 11 April 1749, d.y.
     v   JOHN  b. 14 May 1751
    vi   REUBEN  b. 24 Nov. 1753; prob. d.y.
   vii   JAMES  b. 11 May 1755
  viii   MARY  b. 12 Nov. 1757
    ix   AVIS  b. 12 Dec. 1758
     x   WILLIAM  b. 25 Sept. 1760
    xi   ANNE  b. 2 June 1766

References: 1. MASON GEN p. 32.   2. Swansea Original VR, Bk. B, p. 93/205. 3. Swansea Original VR Bk. B, p. 143/262.   4. Swansea Original VR Bk. A, p. 38.   5. Warren, RI LE 2:37,136,460,491,564; 3:3,5,8,25,26,88,92,93,94, 100,117,183 (Barden and Bowen family deeds).  6. MQ 48:67-72 (May 1982).   7. Swansea Original Bk B, pp. 52/112, 121, 69/157.  8. RI VR: Warren: 6:48.

126  HEZEKIAH CARPENTER[5] (Desire Martin[4], Mercy[3] Billington, Francis[2], John[1]) b. Rehoboth 6 Jan. 1724/5, d. prob. Hopkinton RI bet. 2 May 1803 and 4 April 1808.[1]
   He m. (1) Swansea 16 Aug. 1745 PHEBE BOWEN, b. Swansea 7 Feb. 1727, d. bef. 1778; dau. of Stephen and Phebe (Slade) Bowen.[2]
   He m. (2*) Hopkinton RI 20 May 1778 PRUDENCE JOHNSON,[3,4] who has not been identified. She d. aft. 3 June 1810 when she signed a receipt in her husband's estate.[1]
   Hezekiah lived at Johnston RI before 1760 and at Hopkinton RI by 1775. Hezekiah Carpenter of Hopkinton, in his will dated 2 May 1803 and proved 4 April 1808, gave one-fourth the improvement of his estate to "my last wife Prudence;" $666.66 to eldest son Daniel, half the amount or $333.33 each to dau. Elizabeth Russel, to deceased dau.

Sarah Eagleton's five heirs, to daus. Lydia Fenner, Hannah
Burdick and Esther Crandall.    Son John Carpenter inherited
the remainder of the estate and was named executor.[1]
    Receipts were shown from widow Prudence Carpenter of
Hopkinton, dated 1810; and others from: Daniel Carpenter and
wife Thankful of Cayuga Co. NY; Hannah and John Burdick of
Milton, Cayuga Co. NY; Elizabeth and David Russel of Sci-
pio, Cayuga Co. NY; Lydia and John Fenner, and Esther
Crandall, all of Hopkinton. The five heirs of deceased dau.
Sarah Eagleton, from receipts shown in clerk's copy dated
Nov. 1803 (sic-1808?) were: Wilkerson Eggleston (sic) and
Sarah Robinson, wife of Thomas Robinson, all of Hopkinton;
Jabesh Eagleston (sic) and Reuben Lake, of Hadley, Saratoga
Co. NY; and Samuel Rogers of Greenwich NY. Thomas Robinson,
Reuben Lake and Samuel Rogers were apparently husbands of
Eagleton/Eggleston granddaughters of Hezekiah Carpenter.[1]

    Children (CARPENTER), first five presumably by Phebe,
last two by Prudence, no birth records found:[1,4]

      i   ELIZABETH[6]  b. ca. 1746
     ii   DANIEL  b.___
    iii   SARAH  b.___; d. bef. 1803
     iv   LYDIA  b.___
      v   HANNAH  b. ca. 1755
     vi   JOHN  b. ca. 1779
    vii   ESTHER  b. ca. 1780

*Note: An additional marriage "to Joanna Aldrich, 1 July
1769" is ascribed to this Hezekiah Carpenter in Ref. #4, but
in fact, Joanna married a different Hezekiah Carpenter of
Connecticut. [See WOODSTOCK CT BY BOWEN 3:171.]

References: 1. Hopkinton RI PR 4:138-9,183,195 (Hezekiah
            Carpenter). 2. Swansea Original VR, Bk B p.
57/129. 3. RI VR, Hopkinton 5:10. 4. CARPENTER (REHOBOTH)
GEN, pp. 124, 239. This gives birthdates of the two youngest
children, which fit their marriage dates.

OTHER BILLINGTONS

Genealogical researchers should be aware that the surname Billington is not rare in England, and that immigrants of the name, with no discernible relationship to Pilgrim John, have arrived in America almost continuously since 1620. Descendants of John Billington of the Mayflower, with the Billington surname, are actually a very small group. A few of many unconnected Billingtons are here mentioned as a guide. This is by no means a complete list.

A Thomas Billington who appeared at court in Salem in 1647 and died at Taunton in 1662, a John Billington at Boston who was arraigned in Sufflolk County Court in 1673, and a Benjamin Billington who gave testimony, in the same court in 1702, all had no apparent connection to each other or to the family of the Mayflower passenger.[Robert S. Wakefield, "Some Descendants of Francis[2] Billington," TG 3:243].

Many later Billingtons in Tennessee, as well as in New Jersey, Pennsylvania and New York, apparently descend from James Billington, living at Newark NJ by 1742. No connection to the Plymouth family has been found, as James himself was probably the immigrant. James Billington, schoolmaster of Newark, married at the Acquackanonk (Dutch) Church 1 May 1742 "Anna America," (perhaps surname Garner). Anna Billington, widow of James, "of Barbadoes Neck" (near Newark) m. (2) at Second River Dutch Church, 22 Jan. 1764 James Rolson "born in Old England."[NJ Archives 22:614]. A later marriage (her third) shows that 1 Aug. 1767 John Roskrow, from Cornwell in England, married Aany Garner, widow of James Roleson of Barbadoes Neck, [NJ Archives 12:346]. James and Anna America (?Garner) Billington seem to have been the parents of at least five sons.

The 1850 federal census of Andover MA shows a family headed by a John Billington aged 27, born in England.

John Billings of Maine, written "Billing" or "Billings" from the earliest of his records in 1635, was never a "Billington" as stated in several secondary accounts. There is nothing to show Billings was ever in any way connected to Billington.[ME NH GEN DICT, pp, 92-3].

The Society of Mayflower Descendants does not have records pertaining to these "other Billingtons."

## ABBREVIATIONS

| | | | |
|---|---|---|---|
| ae | aged | n.d. | no date |
| b. | born | n.f.r. | no further |
| bef. | before | | record found |
| bet. | between | n.p. | no place |
| bp. | baptised | N./No. | north |
| bur. | buried | NS | Nova Scotia |
| ca. | about | N.S. | new style (date) |
| Cem./cem. | cemetery | O.S. | old style (date) |
| ch. | children | p./pp. | page(s) |
| Ch. | church | pos./poss. | possibly |
| Co. | county | PR | probate records |
| Col. | colony | prob. | probably |
| Comm. | committee | pub. | published |
| d. | died | rec. | record(s) |
| dau(s). | daughter(s) | rem. | removed |
| decd. | deceased | repr. | reprinted |
| Dist. | district | res. | resided |
| d.s.p. | died without issue | S./So. | south |
| d.y. | died young | sic | copy correct |
| E. | east | Soc. | society |
| ed. | edition/editor | TR | town record(s) |
| g.s. | gravestone | unm. | unmarried |
| gdn. | guardian | unpub. | unpublished |
| granddau. | granddaughter | vol(s). | volume(s) |
| LR | land records | VR | vital records |
| m. | married | W. | west |
| m. int. | marriage inten- | wid. | widow |
| | tions | -y-m-d | years, months, |
| MS(S) | manuscripts | | days |
| NB | New Brunswick | | |

When no state is indicated after a city or town, the reader
should assume Massachusetts. The following two letter pos-
tal abbreviations are used for states:

| | | | |
|---|---|---|---|
| CT | Connecticut | NJ | New Jersey |
| MA | Massachusetts | NY | New York |
| ME | Maine | RI | Rhode Island |
| NH | New Hampshire | VT | Vermont |

# REFERENCES

## Key To Abbreviated Titles

The following is an alphabetical list of abbreviated titles used in the references in this volume. When the abbreviated title is in capital letters the reference is in print -- a book or periodical. When the abbreviated title is not in capital letters, it represents unpublished material -- hand-written or typed. With respect to printed vital records, the abbreviated titles VR MANSFIELD, DUXBURY etc. indicate alphabetized vital records; the abbreviated titles MARSH-FIELD VR, TRURO VR etc. followed by page numbers, indicate vital records published non-alphabetically. Other abbreviations used in the references and in the genealogies themselves, as well as in this Key to Abbreviated Titles, appear on the opposite page. All places are assumed to be Massachusetts unless otherwise indicated.

NOTE: Readers should not assume that the books listed below have been accepted as references by the Mayflower Society. Some are cited merely to call attention to their errors, or to show that they have been consulted by the authors.


ADAMS GEN (1861)
Adams, George; "Genealogy of the Adams Family of Kingston, Mass;" Boston, 1861.

AMERICAN LOYALIST CLAIMS
Coldham, Peter Wilson; "American Loyalist Claims;" Washington DC, 1980.

ANNAPOLIS CO N.S. HIST
Calnek, W. A.; "History of the County of Annapolis N.S.;" Toronto, 1897; repr. 1972.

Attleboro 2nd Ch
Carter, Marion W.P.; Membership and Vital Records of the Second Congregational Church of Attleboro, MA; mimeograph; Washington DC, 1924.

BACKUS DIARY
McLoughlin, William G., ed.; "The Diary of Isaac Backus;" 3 vols., Providence RI, 1979.

BASS GEN
Bass, Charissa Taylor, completed by Walton, Emma Lee; "Descendants of Deacon Samuel and Ann Bass;" Freeport IL, 1940.

BENT FAM
Bent, Allen H.; "Bent Family in America," Boston, 1900.

BERNARDSTON HIST
Kellogg, Lucy Cutler; "History of Bernardston, [Mass.]"
Greenfield MA, 1902.

BOSTON NEWS OBITS
"Index of Obituaries in Boston Newspapers 1704-1800." 3
vols., Boston, 1968.

BOSTON VR
"Reports of the Record Commissioners," Vols. 9 and 24;
births, marriages and deaths, 1630-1699 and births
1700-1800; Boston 1883 and 1893. Vols. 28 and 30: marriages
1700-1751 and 1751-1809; Boston, 1898 and 1902; reprint
Baltimore MD, 4 vols. in 2, 1977 and 1978.

Bowman File
Bowman, George Ernest; Manuscript genealogy of (some) May-
flower Families, comp. 1896-1941; 232 microfiche; filmed by
Massachusetts Society of Mayflower Descendants, 1983.

BRADFORD'S HIST (1952)
Bradford, William; "Of Plimouth Plantation, 1620-1647;"
edited by Samuel E. Morison; New York, 1952.

BRAINTREE RECS
Bates, Samuel A.; Records of the Town of Braintree
1640-1793; Randolph MA, 1886.

BRIDGEWATER BY MITCHELL
Mitchell, Nahum; "History of the Early Settlement of Bridgewater, Mass. including an Extensive Family Register;" Boston
1840; repr. Bridgewater, 1897; repr. Baltimore MD, 1970.

BRISTOL CO MA PR ABSTRACTS
Rounds, H.L. Peter; "Abstracts of Bristol County, Massachusetts Probate Records, 1687-1762," 2 vols., Baltimore MD,
1987, 1988.

BUMPUS FAM
Bumpus, Carle Franklin; "Bompass, Bumpas, Bump, Bumpus and
Allied Families, 1621-1981;" Baltimore MD, 1985.

BURROUGHS'S JOURNAL
Sherman, Ruth Wilder, ed.; "Peleg Burroughs's Journal,
1778-1798;" Rhode Island Gen. Soc., 1981.

CARPENTER (REHOBOTH) GEN
Carpenter, Amos B.; "A Genealogical History of the Rehoboth
Branch of the Carpenter Family in America;" Amherst MA, 1898

CHAFFEE GEN
Chaffee, William H.; "Chaffee Genealogy," New York, 1909.

COLE FAM
Cole, Ernest Byron; "The Descendants of James Cole of
Plymouth," New York, 1908.

CSL Barbour Index
Bound volumes of alphabetized vital records to about 1850,
from all CT towns, as copied by Lucius B. Barbour. Also a
statewide alphabetical card index of these records,
interfiled with similar entries from private sources, at CT
State Library; filmed by L.D.S. Gen. Society.

CSL Ch Rec
Bound volumes of alphabetized vital records from over 600 CT
churches and a single alphabetical card index for all; at CT
State Library.

CTHS COLL
Connecticut Historical Society Collections, Vol.1, 1860,
Hartford.

CT MARR
Bailey, Frederick W.; "Early Connecticut Marriages as Found
on Ancient Church Records Prior to 1800;" 7 vols.; New Haven
CT, 1896-1906; reprint, 1 vol.; Baltimore MD, 1968, 1982.

CT NUTMEGGER
"The Connecticut Nutmegger," Quarterly of The Connecticut
Society of Genealogists, Vol. 1, 1968, Glastonbury CT.

DEDHAM VR
Hill, Don G., ed.; "The Record of Births, Marriages and
Deaths, and Intentions of Marriage, in the Town of Dedham;"
2 vols., Dedham MA, 1886.

DOGGETT FAM
Doggett, Samuel B.; "A History of the Doggett Family;"
Boston, 1894.

Dutchess County [NY] Tax Lists
Buck, Clifford M.; "Dutchess County [NY] Tax Lists,
1740-1779;" includes South or Southern Precinct, which
became Putnam County in 1812. unpublished MS, ca. 1982.

DUXBURY RECS
Etheridge, George; "Copy of the Old Records of the Town of
Duxbury, Mass. from 1642 to 1770." Plymouth, 1893.

EARLY NB PROB RECS
Hale, R. Wallace; "Early New Brunswick (Canada) Probate
Records, 1785-1835;" Heritage Books, Bowie MD 1989.

EARLY REHOBOTH
Bowen, Richard L.; "Early Rehoboth;" 4 vols.; Rehoboth MA,
1945-50.

EASTON HIST
Chaffin, William L.; "History of the Town of Easton, Mass.;"
Cambridge MA, 1886; reprint 1975.

EDDY GEN
Eddy, Ruth S.D.; "The Eddy Family in America, a Genealogy;"
Boston, 1930; 1941 edition.

ESSEX QUARTERLY COURTS
Dow, George F. & Thresher, Mary G.; "Records and Files of
the Quarterly Courts of Essex County, Mass., 1636-86." 9
vols.; Salem, 1911-74.

FAMS OF OLD FAIRFIELD
Jacobus, Donald L.; "History and Genealogy of the Families
of Old Fairfield;" Fairfield CT, 1932.

FED CENSUS 1790
"Heads of Families at the First Census, 1790;" 12 vols.;
Washington DC, 1907-09; reprint Baltimore MD, 1952-66.

FED CENSUS 1800
"Heads of Families at the Second Census, 1800;" originals at
US National Archives; also on microfilm and in printed books

FED CENSUS 1810
"Heads of Families at the Third Census, 1810;" originals at
US National Archives, also on microfilm; most states in
print.

FED CENSUS 1820
"Heads of Families at the Fourth Census, 1820;" originals at
US National Archives, also on microfilm; most states in
print.

GEN ADVERTISER
Greenlaw, Lucy H.; "The Genealogical Advertiser," a
Quarterly Magazine of Family History; vols. 1-4; 1898-1901;
reprint Baltimore MD, 1974.

GENEALOGIST'S MAGAZINE
The Genealogist's Magazine, Journal of the Society of
Genealogists, London, England, Vol. 1, 1911.

HALE, HOUSE FAMS
Jacobus, Donald L.  and Waterman, Edgar F.; "Hale, House and
Related Families," Hartford CT, 1952.

HALIFAX VR
Bowman, George  E.; Vital records of the  Town of Halifax MA
to the end of the year 1849; Boston, 1905.

HARVARD GRADS
Sibley, John L.; "Biographical Sketches of Graduates of
Harvard University in Cambridge, Mass.;" Cambridge, vol. 1,
1873.

HICKS (HIX) FAM
Hodge, Harriet W.; "Hicks (Hix) Families  of Rehoboth  and
Swansea, Mass.;"  Winnetka IL, 1976.

HINGHAM HIST
"History of  the Town of Hingham, Mass.;"  3 vols.; Hingham,
1893; reprint Somersworth NH, 1982.

HUNTINGTON FAM
Huntington, E.B.; "A  Genealogical Memoir of  the Huntington
Family..., Descendants of  Simon and  Margaret Huntington;"
Stamford CT, 1863.

IGI Recs
International Genealogical Index: alphabetical lists of
births, baptisms and marriages from public and private
records world wide, arranged by country, state  or province,
counties, etc.; on microfiche  at the L.D.S. Genealogical
Society Library and branches.

KING PHILIP'S WAR
Bodge, George M.; "Soldiers in King Philip's War;" 2nd & 3rd
ed., 1906; reprint Baltimore MD, 1967, 1976.

KINGSLEY GEN BY DEANE
Deane, Edna  Hartshorn; "Amos  Kingsley, 1768-1847,  A
Biography and Genealogy," Utica NY, 1960.

Little Neck Cem
Kent, Mrs. Frank P.; Smith, Mrs. Otho; Kent, Jessie R.;
"Little Neck Cemetery Inscriptions:" cemetery originally in
Rehoboth, MA, now in  Riverside (East Providence) RI;
typescript comp. by D A R 1944.

LOYALISTS OF MA
Jones, E. Alfred; "The  Loyalists of Massachusetts, Their
Memorials, Petitions and  Claims;" London, 1930; repr.
Baltimore, 1969

MA Archives
Archives of the Commonwealth of Massachusetts, Boston.

MA PIONEERS
Pope, Charles H.; "The Pioneers of Massachusetts;" Boston,
1900; reprint Baltimore MD, 1965, 1981.

MA SOLDIERS 1723-1743
Stachiw, Myron O., ed.; "Massachusetts Officers and Soldiers
1723-1743, Dummer's War to the War of Jenkins' Ear," pub. by
Soc. of Colonial Wars in MA and NEHG Soc., Boston, 1979.

MA TAX LIST 1771
Pruitt, Bettye Hobbs, ed.; "The Massachusetts Tax Valuation
List of 1771;" Boston, 1978.

MANWARING
Manwaring, Charles W.; "A Digest of the Early Connecticut
Probate Records;" 3 vols. Hartford CT, 1902-6

MARSHFIELD BY RICHARDS
Richards, Lysander S.; "History of Marshfield, Mass. with
Genealogy;" 2 vols. Plymouth, 1901-5.

MARSHFIELD VR
Sherman, Robert M. & Ruth W.; "Vital Records of Marshfield,
Mass. to the year 1850;" Warwick RI, 1969.

MARTIN FAM
Martin, Henry J., "Notices: Genealogical and Historical of
the Martin Family of New England;" Boston, 1880. [Some
errors in this account.]

MASON GEN
Mason, Alverdo H.; "Genealogy of the Sampson Mason Family;"
East Braintree MA, 1902.

MAYFLOWER INDEX
pub. by General Society of Mayflower Descendants, Plymouth,
1960.

MD
"The Mayflower Descendant"; a quarterly magazine of Pilgrim
history and genealogy; Vol. 1, 1899; published by the Massachusetts Society of Mayflower Descendants.

ME NH GEN DICT
Noyes, Sybil; Libby, C.T.; Davis, Walter G.; "Genealogical
Dictionary of Maine and New Hampshire;" 1928-35; reprint
Baltimore MD, 1972, 1983.

MF1
van Antwerp, Lee D.; Radasch, Arthur H. & Katharine W.;
Sherman, Robert M. & Ruth W.; "Mayflower Families Through
Five Generations;" Descendants of the Pilgrims who landed at
Plymouth, Mass. December 1620; Vol. 1 families: Francis
Eaton, Samuel Fuller and William White; Plymouth MA, 1975.

MF2
Sherman, Robert M.; Vincent, Verle D.; Wakefield, Robert S.;
Finlay, Lydia R.D.; Westgate, Alice W.A.; "Mayflower
Families Through Five Generations;" Descendants of the
Pilgrims who landed at Plymouth, Mass. December 1620. Vol. 2
families: James Chilton, Richard More and Thomas Rogers;
Plymouth MA, 1978.

MF3
Soule, Col. John E.; Terry, Dr. Milton E.; Harding, Anne B.,
ed.; "Mayflower Families Through Five Generations;"
Descendants of the Pilgrims who landed at Plymouth, Mass.
December 1620. Vol. 3 family: George Soule; Plymouth, 1980.

MF4
MacGunnigle, Bruce Campbell; "Mayflower Families Through
Five Generations;" Descendants of the Pilgrims who landed at
Plymouth, Mass. December 1620. Vol. 4 family: Edward Fuller;
Plymouth, 1990.

Middleboro 1st Cong Ch Recs
Weston, Chester E., comp.; Baptismal Records of the First
Congregational Church of Middleborough, 1710-1820; type-
script, n.d.

MIDDLEBORO DEATHS
Wood, Alfred; "Record of Deaths, Middleboro, Mass.;" Boston,
1947.

MIDDLEBORO FIRST CH
"Book of the First Church of Christ in Middleborough;"
Boston, 1852

MIDDLEBORO PROPRIETORS' RECS
Middleboro Proprietors' Records, 1858

Middleboro VR
Weston, Chester E.; Typed alphabetized and bound volumes of
births (1667-1853), marriages (1669-1853), intentions
(1744-1859) and deaths (1667-1854) in the Town Clerk's
office, Middleboro, MA.

MIDDLEBOROUGH VR
Merrick, Barbara L. and Williams, Alicia, eds., "Middleborough Vital Records;" 2 vols.; Boston, 1986.

MOURT'S RELATION
Heath, Dwight E., ed.; Bradford, William and Morton, George;
"Mourt's Relation," retitled "A Journal of the Pilgrims at
Plymouth;" N.Y., 1963.

MQ
"The Mayflower Quarterly;" Vol. 1, 1935; published Plymouth,
MA by the General Society of Mayflower Descendants.

MSSR
"Massachusetts Soldiers and Sailors of the Revolutionary
War;" 17 vols.; Boston, 1896-1908.

NB LOYALISTS
Dubeau, Sharon; "New Brunswick (Canada) Loyalists;"
Agincourt, Ontario, 1983.

NB VITAL STATISTICS FROM NEWSPAPERS
Vital Statistics Committee, New Brunswick Genealogical
Society; "New Brunswick (Canada) Vital Statistics from
Newspapers, 1784-1815;" Vol. I, Fredricton NB, 1982.

NEHGR
"New England Historical and Genealogical Register;" Vol. 1,
1847; published at Boston by the New England Historic
Genealogical Society.

NEW ENGLAND HIST
Winthrop, John, Esq., "The History of New England from 1630
to 1649;" ed. by James Savage; Boston, 1854.

NEW ENGLANDERS IN N.S.
Crowell, Fred E.; "New Englanders in Nova Scotia;" (film)
NEHGS, Boston, 1979.

Norwich CT Fifth Ch Recs
"Records of the Fifth Church of Norwich, [CT], 1739-1824;"
typescript, D A R Library, Washington DC. The Fifth Church
was in the section of Norwich that became Bozrah in 1786.

NORWICH CT BY CAULKINS
Caulkins, Frances Manwaring; "History of Norwich, Conn;"
Hartford CT, 1866.

NYGBR
"The New York Genealogical and Biographical Record;" Vol. 1,
1870; published by the Society.

OLD KITTERY
Stackpole, Everett S.; "Old Kittery and Her Families;"
Lewiston ME, 1903.

OTIS FAM
Otis, William A.; "A Genealogical and Historical Memoir of
the Otis Family in America;" Chicago IL, 1924.

OTTERY ST. MARY CH
Tapley-Soper, H., ed.; "The Ottery St. Mary Church Register,
1601-1837;" Devon and Cornwall Record Society, Exeter,
England, 1908-1929.

PILGRIM READER
Willison, George F.; "The Pilgrim Reader;" Quotes from
William Bradford's writing as copied or paraphrased in:
Prince, Thomas; "Chronological History of New England in the
Form of Annals;" 1736.

(PLYMOUTH) ANC LANDMARKS
Davis, William T.; "Ancient Landmarks of Plymouth;" 2nd ed.
1899; repr. Pt. 2 titled "Genealogical Register of Plymouth
Families"; Baltimore MD

(PLYMOUTH) BURIAL HILL BY DREW
Drew, Benjamin, comp.; "Burial Hill, Plymouth;" Plymouth MA,
1894.

(PLYMOUTH) BURIAL HILL BY KINGMAN
Kingman, Bradford. "Epitaphs from Burial Hill, Plymouth,
Massachusetts, from 1657 to 1892, With Biographical and
Historical Notes;" Brookline, MA 1892; reprint Baltimore MD
1977.

PLYMOUTH CH RECS
"Plymouth Church Records, 1620-1859;" 2 vols.; New York,
1920-23; reprint Baltimore MD, 1975.

Plymouth Colony LR
Also known as Old Colony Deeds. 6 vols. MSS at Plymouth Co.
Register of Deeds. Vol. 1 appeared in print as Vol. 12 of
"Plymouth Colony Recs"; Vol. 2 and Vol. 3, as far as page 52
are printed in MD. All are on L.D.S. microfilm.

Plymouth Colony PR
Also known as Old Colony Wills; 4 vols. MSS at Plymouth Co.
Register of Deeds. Vol. 1, Vol. 2 and Vol. 3 as far as part
1, page 153 are printed in MD. All are on L.D.S. microfilm.

PLYMOUTH COLONY RECS
Shurtleff, Nathaniel B. & Pulsifer, David; "Records of the
Colony of New Plymouth in New England;" 12 vols.; Boston,
1855-61; reprint 12 vols. in 6; New York, 1968.

PLYMOUTH CO CT RECS
Konig, David T., ed.; "Plymouth County Court Records
1686-1859;" 16 vols.; Wilmington DE, 1978.

PLYMOUTH TOWN HIST
Davis, William T.; "History of the Town of Plymouth;"
Philadelphia, 1885

PLYMOUTH TOWN RECS
"Records of the Town of Plymouth;" Plymouth, 1869, 1892,
1903.

PLYMPTON BY WRIGHT
Wright, Eugene A.; "History of Plympton, Mass. 1640-1945;"
ed. by Bricknell, Charles H.; Plympton, 1973.

PRATT, PHINEHAS DESC
Pratt, Eleazer F.; "Phinehas Pratt and Some of His
Descendants;" Boston, 1897.

PRESTON CH
"First Congregational Church of Preston, CT, 1698-1898;"
Preston, CT, 1900.

PROVIDENCE EARLY RECS
"The Early Records of the Town of Providence;" 21 vols.,
printed under authority of the City council, Providence RI,
1892-1915.

REHOBOTH GRAVE STONES
Trim, Robert Shelton; "Rehoboth Grave Stone Records;"
Rehoboth MA, 1980.

REHOBOTH VR
Arnold, James N.; "Vital Records of Rehoboth, 1642-1896.
Marriages, Intentions, Births, Deaths;" Providence RI 1897.

REHOBOTH VR BY TRIM
Trim, Robert S.; "Unrecorded Vital Records of Rehoboth;"
Rehoboth MA, 1980.

Rev Pension
Selected records from Revolutionary War Pension application
files at the National Archives, Washington, DC; also
available on microfilm at the regional Federal Archives and
Records Centers.

RI CENSUS 1774
Bartlett, John R.; "Census of the Inhabitants of the  Colony
of  Rhode Island and  Providence Plantations, 1774;" reprint
Baltimore, 1969.

RI CENSUS 1782
NEHGR vols. 127,128,129.

RI COL RECS
Bartlett, John Russell, ed.; "Records of the Colony of Rhode
Island and Providence Plantations;" 10 vols.; Providence RI,
1856-1865.

RI GEN DICT
Austin,  John O.;  "The  Genealogical  Dictionary  of Rhode
Island,  comprising three  generations of  settlers who came
before 1690;"  Albany NY, 1887; reprint Baltimore, 1969.

RI GR
Beaman, Alden G.,ed.; "Rhode Island Genealogical  Register;"
Vol. 1, 1978.

RIHS COLL
"Rhode  Island Historical  Society Collections;"  Vol. 1-34,
irregular 1827-1902, quarterly 1918-41, Providence.

RI LE
"Rhode Island Land Evidences;" Vol. 1, 1648-1696  Abstracts;
Providence RI, 1921; reprint Baltimore, 1970.

RI MILITARY CENSUS 1777
Chamberlain,  Mildred M.,  ed.,   "The  Rhode  Island  1777
Military Census;" Baltimore, 1985.

RI ROOTS
"Rhode  Island  Roots;"  Quarterly  of  the  Rhode  Island
Genealogical Society;  Vol. 1, 1975

RI VR
Arnold,  James  N.;  "Vital  Records  of  Rhode Island,1636-
1850;"  21 vols.; Providence RI, 1891-1912.

ROLL OF OFFICERS IN MEDICAL SERVICE
Johnston,  Col. William;  "Roll of  Commissioned Officers in
the  Medical  Service,  20  June  1767  to  23  June  1898;"
Aberdeen, (Scotland) 1917.

ROUND FAM
Rounds, H.L.  Peter; "The John  Round Family of  Swansea and
Rehoboth, Massachusetts;" Baltimore, 1983.

SALEM BY PERLEY
Perley, Sidney; "History of Salem, Massachusetts, 1626-1716;" 3 vols.; Salem, 1924-28.

SAVAGE
Savage, James. "A Genealogical Dictionary of the First Settlers of New England Showing Three Generations of Those who came Before May 1692.." 4 vols.; Boston, 1860-62; reprint Baltimore MD, 1965 & 1981.

SAVERY GEN
Savary, A.W.; "A Genealogical and Biographical Record of the Savery Family (Savory and Savary) and of the Severy Family....," Boston, 1893.

SAVERY SUP
Savary, A.W.; "Savery Genealogy Supplement;" Boston, 1905.

SOUTH KINGSTOWN RI MARRIAGES
Miller, William D.; "Dr. Joseph Torrey and his Record Book of Marriages;" in R.I. Historical Society Collections 18:102 ff., 1925; also "South Kingstown Marriages," repr.

SOUTH KINGSTOWN RI TOWN COUNCIL RECS
Stutz, Jean C., "South Kingstown, Rhode Island Town Council Records, 1771-1795;" pub. by Pettaquamscutt Historical Society, Kingston, RI, 1988.

SPOONER DESC
Spooner, Thomas; "Records of William Spooner of Plymouth, Mass., and His Descendants;" Vol. 1; Cincinnati OH, 1883.

Stevens Corner Cem
Stevens Corner Cemetery Records, Rehoboth MA; typescript on LDS Film #581,921

STEVENS-MILLER ANC
Holman, Mary L., "Ancestry of Colonel John Harrington Stevens and His Wife, Frances Helen Miller;" Concord NH, 1948.

SWANSEA VR BK A
Mason, Alverdo H.; "Records of the Town of Swansea; Book A;" Braintree MA, 1900.

Swansea VR, Original Recs
Original Vital Records of Swansea MA, LDS Microfilm #903,395

SWETT GENEALOGY
Stackpole, Everett S.; "Swett Genealogy;" Lewiston, ME, n.d.

TAG
"The American Genealogist;" Vol. 1, 1922; published at Warwick RI since 1983.

TAUNTON BY EMERY
Emery, S.H.; "History of Taunton, Mass.;" Syracuse NY, 1893.

TG
Thompson, Neil D., editor; "The Genealogist;" Assoc. for the Promotion of Scholarship in Genealogy, Ltd.; Vol. 1, New York, 1980.

TORREY'S MARRIAGES
Torrey, Clarence A.; "New England Marriages Prior to 1700;" Baltimore, 1985.

VR MA
Vital records for about 200 towns in Massachusetts have been printed in alphabetized versions. Attleborough 1934, Beverly 1906-7, Bridgewater 1926, Chelmsford 1914, Kingston 1911, Medfield 1903, Norton 1906, Pembroke 1911, Plympton 1923, Taunton 1929, Wenham 1904.

VT GAZETTEER
Hemenway, Abby M., ed.; "Vermont Quarterly Gazetteer;" Ludlow VT, 1868___.

WARREN GEN
Roebling, Mrs. Washington A.; "Richard Warren of the Mayflower and Some of His Descendants;" Boston, 1901.

Washburn MS
O'Gorman, Ella Foy; "Ancestry of Clara Emoline Washburn Farwell;" 1933, typescript D A R Library, Washington DC.

WAYNE ME HIST
Walton, George W.; "History of Wayne, [Maine];" Augusta ME, 1898.

WELLMAN GEN
Wellman, Joshua Wyman; "Descendants of Thomas Wellman of Lynn, Mass.;" Boston, 1918.

WIGHT GEN
Wight, William Ward; "The Wights, A Record of Thomas Wight of Dedham and Medfield and Descendants, 1635-1890;" Milwaukee WI, 1890.

WINDHAM CT FIRST CH
"Records of the [First] Congregational Church in Windham,
Conn., 1700-1851;" pub. by Connecticut Historical Society
and Society of Mayflower Descendants in the State of
Connecticut; Hartford, 1943.

WINSLOW PAPERS
Raymond, William O., ed.; "Winslow Papers AD 1776-1826;"
pub. under auspices of the New Brunswick Historical Society,
St. John, NB, 1901; reprint Boston, 1972.

WOODSTOCK CT BY BOWEN
Bowen, Clarence W.; "History of Woodstock, Conn.;" 8 vols.;
Norwood MA, 1935.

YORK DEEDS
"York [county ME] Deeds, 1642-1737;" 18 vols. in 19;
Portland ME, 1887-1910.

## INDEX OF NAMES

With a few exceptions, each name in the text and foot-notes is indexed. The exceptions are: authors or titles of reference books, and heads of military units under whom a descendant or spouse served.

Each married woman is indexed under her maiden name, and also under each married name, giving her maiden name in parenthesis. For example, Christian PENN, who married twice, appears also as Christian (Penn) EATON and Christian (Penn)(Eaton) BILLINGTON. A married woman of unknown maiden name is shown as Jane (-----) BILLINGTON.

When variant spellings of a surname occur, they are alphabetized under the more popular spelling, followed by one or more of the alternate spellings.

BRAMAN (continued)
  Bethiah 117
  Daniel 117
  Joseph 78
BRENTON
  Abigail 9
BREWSTER
  Abigail 119
  William 119
  Wrestling 117
BRIGGS
  John 75
BRINDLE
  Deborah 12
BRINDLEY
  Francis 12
BRINLEY
  Katherine (-----) 12
BROCKWAY
  Jedediah 113
  Sarah (Fox) 113
BROOK(E),BROOKS
  Anne (-----)(Derrick) 8
  Elizabeth (Winslow) 8
  John 7,8,9
  Robert 8
BROUGHTON
  Amos 104
  Elizabeth 104
  Elizabeth (Woodruff) 104
  Hannah 105
  Hannah (Allis) 105
  John 58,104,105
  Mary 104
  Phebe 104
  Tabitha 58,104
  Tabitha (Kingsley) 104
BROWN
  Ann (Bullock) 66
  Ann/Anna 47,66
  Jabez 66
  James 67
  Jane (-----) 66
  Nathaniel 67
  Oliver 66
  Peter 89,133
  Rebecca 66
  Sarah 67
  Sarah (-----) 66
  Sarah (Jenckes) 67
  William 22

BRYANT
  George 133
  James 89
  Joanna 92
  Lydia 91
  Mary 49,50,132
  Micah 129
  Patience (Raymond) 89
  Sarah 133
  Sarah (Ripley) 133
  Zebulon 132
BULLOCK
  Abigail 37,69,70
  Abigail (Kinnecutt) 69
  Ann/Anna 48,66,68,70
  Anna (Child)(Cole) 68
  Comfort 68
  Dorcas 142
  Elizabeth 37,38,47,48,67,68,69,70
  Elizabeth (Barnes) 47
  Elizabeth (Billington) 37
  Elizabeth (Ingraham) 37
  Esther 48
  Hopestill 37
  Israel 38,47,48,67
  Jabez 68,69
  Jerusha 68,69
  Jerusha (Smith) 68
  John 38,47,48,66,67,68,69
  Joseph 69,70
  Josiah 67
  Lillis 72
  Marcy 38
  Mary 37,47,48,68
  Mehitable 37
  Patience (Bosworth) 68
  Prudence 47,48,67
  Richard 37,38,47,48,69,70
  Samuel 37
  Sarah 67
  Sarah (Brown) 67
  William 70
  Zerviah 48
BUMP/BUMPUS/BUMPAS
  Abigail (Rose/Rouse) 81
  Bethia 53,84
  Edward 52
  Esther (-----)(Warner 82
  Hannah (-----) 52
  Jemima 53,81
  Joseph 43,61
  Josiah 52,53,83

CHAFFEE (continued)
 Alice (Millard) 141
 Daniel 141
 Esther 141
CHAMBERS
 Susannah 73
 Susannah (Lemote) 74
 William 74
CHERRY
 Margaret 86
CHILD
 Abigail (Eddy) 68
 Anna 68
 John 68
 Samuel 126
CHILTON
 James 88,89,91
CHIPMAN
 Ward 26
CHURCH
 Martha 9,10
CHURCHILL
 Abigail 49,50
 Ebenezer 73
 Eleazer 49
 Maria (Rider) 87
 Mary (Bryant) 49,50
 Thomas 73
CLAPP
 Ebenezer 20
 Sarah 20
 Sarah (Winslow) 20
CLARKE
 Anna 129
CLEMENTS
 Hannah (Eaton) 85
 John 85
CLOPPER
 Garret 16,26
 Henry George 16
 Penelope 16
COBB
 Ebenezer 118
 Hannah 118
 James 86
 Jerusha 118
 John 118
 Martha 86
 Ruth 86
CODDINGTON
 Abigail 93
 Bethia 94

CODDINGTON (continued)
 Bethia (Bassett) 93
 Elizabeth (Jones) 93
 William 93,94
COIT
 Joseph 100
 Mary (Spaulding) 100
COLBRON
 Hen: 4
COLE
 Anna (Child) 68
 David 68
 Deborah (Edwards) 87
 Joanna 15
 Martha 50
 Samuel 87
CONANT
 Abigail 132
 Abner 132
 Bethiah 132
 Ezra 132
 Hannah 131
 Hannah (Lazell) 131
 Jedidah 132
 Keturah 132
 Margaret (Laughton) 132
 Martha 119,132
 Martha (Ames) 132
 Mary 63,132
 Mary (Wood) 131,132
 Nathan 131,132
 Nathaniel 132
 Rebecca 132
 Sarah 132
 Thomas 132
 Zenas 132
 Zilphah 132
COOKE
 Francis 87,89,121,122,133
 John 39
 Lydia 120,122
COOPER
 Mary (Sabin) 43
 Nathaniel 43
CORWIN/CURWIN
 Abigail 8
 Eliza 8
 Elizabeth (Herbert)(White) 8
 Elizabeth (Winslow)(Brooks) 8
 Elizabeth/Elyzabeth 7,8
 George 7,8,9,12
 Hannah 8

CORWIN/CURWIN (continued)
  John 8
  Jonathan 8
  Penelope 9,11
  Susanna 8,9,12
COTTON
  Josiah 24
  Nathaniel 10
  Priscilla (Watson) 24
COVELL/COVEL
  Mary 98,99
  Stephen 99
CRADDOCK
  George 12
  Mary 12
CRANDALL
  Esther 147
CRANE
  Abiah 94
CRARY
  Christobel 83
CROMWELL
  Oliver 4
CROSSMAN
  Eleazer 41
  Elizabeth 41
  John 41
  Joseph 41
  Martha 41
  Martha (Billington)(Eaton) 41
  Mary 41
  Mercy 41
  Nathaniel 41
  Robert 41
  Samuel 41
  Sarah 41
  Sarah (Kingsbury) 41
  Susanna 41
  Thomas 41
CROUCHER
  John 78
  Sarah (Billington) 78
CURTIS
  John 45
CURWEN
  Samuel 22
CUSHING
  Hannah 138
CUSHMAN
  Abigail 118
  Elenah/Elkanah 118
  Hannah 118

CUSHMAN (continued)
  Ichabod 63
  Isaac 118
  Jerusha 118
  Job 118
  Lydia 88,118
  Martha 118
  Mary 122
  Mercy 118
  Mercy (Washburn) 90,117
  Patience (Holmes) 63
  Persis (-----) 117
  Rebecca 86,118
  Robert 33,90,117,118,135
  Ruth 118
  Thankful 118
CUTLER
  Joanna 90
DAGGETT
  Anna 140
  Hannah 140
  Isabel 144
  Joanna (Biven/?Blevin) 141
  Mayhew 141
  Reuben 144
DAVIS
  Ellen (Watson) 23
  John 23
  Lois (Fuller) 88
  Lydia 122
  Nicholas 88,122
  Stephen 138
DELANO
  Bethia 86
  Huldah 25
  Sarah 86
DELLIS/DILLEY
  Betty 136
DERRICK
  Anne (-----) 8
DEXTER
  Constant 138
  Rebecca (Billington) 138
DIBBLE/DIBELL
  Abigail 103
  Benjamin 103
  Lydia 103
  Mary 103
  Mary (Benjamin) 103
DILLENE
  Mary 43

DILLINGHAM
  Elizabeth 126
DINGLEY
  Jacob 91
  Ruth (Winslow)(Shaw) 20
  Ruth S. 20
  Susanna 90
  Susanna (Fuller) 91
  Thomas 20
DIXSON
  John 101
DONHAM/DUNHAM
  Eleazer 123
  Lemuel 63
  Mary 63,135
  Mary (Tilson) 63
  Meriam (Phillips) 123
  Nathaniel 63
  Rebecca 123
DOTEN
  Deborah (-----) 87
  Hannah 87
  Jacob 87
  Solomon 87
DOTY
  Edward 14,20,21
  Joanna (Bryant) 92
  Phebe 138
  Sarah 14
DOUGHTY
  Patience 108
DOUGLAS
  (-----) 80
  Elizabeth 80
  Elizabeth (Bent) 80
DOWNING
  Abigail 90
  David 103,112
DYER/DYRE
  Hannah 15,16
  Hannah (Howland) 15
  William 15
EAGLESTON
  Jabesh 147
EAGLETON
  Sarah 147
EASTERBROOK
  Esther 144
  Samuel 144
EATON
  Barnabas 53,54,85
  Benjamin 36

EATON (continued)
  Bethia (Delano) 86
  Bethia(h) 42,55
  Christian (Penn) 36
  Elizabeth 53,54,84,85,86
  Elizabeth (-----) 41
  Elizabeth (Clemens) 85
  Elizabeth (Fuller) 53
  Francis 36,41,102,117
  Hannah 85
  Keziah 53,85,86
  Lot 85,86
  Margaret (Cherry) 86
  Martha 41
  Martha (Billington) 41
  Martha (Cobb) 86
  Mary 85
  Mehitabel 86
  Mehitabel (Alden) 85
  Mercy 42,53,54,117
  Merebah/Meribah 85,86
  Nathan 85,86
  Patience (Tinkham) 85
  Rachel 36
  Ruth (Leonard) 86
  Samuel 41,53,85
  Sarah 41,52,85
  Sarah (-----) 36
  Sarah (Delano) 86
  Seth 85,86
  Wealthy 85,86
  Ziba 85,86
EDDY
  Abigail 68
  Anne 69
  Ebenezer 114
  Hasadiah 88
  Jabez 130
  Jedidah 63,131
  Jedidah (Wood) 130
  Job 63
  Keziah (-----)(Keith) 130
  Mary (Rickard) 130
  Mary/Molly 130,131
  Moses 130,134
  Phebe 114
  Sarah (Harding) 114
EDWARDS
  Deborah 87
  John 87
  Sarah (Woodin) 87

EGGLESTON
  Hezekiah 17
  Wilkerson 147
ELLIS
  Abiel 130
  Abigail 129
  Anna 129
  Anna (Clarke) 129
  Ebenezer 129
  Eleanor 129
  Elijah 129
  Elisha 129
  Elnathan 130
  Ephraim 130
  Freeman 129
  Gideon 129,130
  Jemima 63,130
  Jemima (Wood) 129
  John 130
  Mary (-----) 129
  Reuben 130
  Ruth 107
  Samuel 130
  Seth 130
  Susannah 129
  Thomas 129
ELY
  Samuel 113
FALLOWELL
  Katheren (Finney) 45
FARRELL/FURRELL/FAZZEL
  Patrick 48,70,71
  Rachel 71
  Rachel (Beere/Beers) 49,70,71
FAUNCE
  James 91
  Joanna (Fuller) 91
  John 120,122
  Judith 120
  Lydia 122
  Lydia (Cooke) 120,122
FENNER
  John 147
  Lydia 147
FFLOYDE
  Richard 4
FINNEY
  Anna 44
  Katheren 45
  Robert 45
FISHER
  Elizabeth 94

FOLLET(T)
  Benjamin 108
  Mary 108
  Patience (Doughty) 108
FOSTER
  Mercy 21
FOWLES
  ----- 22
FOX
  Sarah 113
FRASER
  James 26
FRAZIER
  Alexander 68
  Elizabeth 68
  John 68
  Mary (Bullock) 68
  Mercy (Lumber) 68
  Merebah 68
  Phenix 68
FREKE
  Mary 11
FRENCH
  Elizabeth 94
  Mehetable 99,100
  Nathaniel 100
  Sarah 131
  Sarah (Spaulding) 100
FROST
  Margaret 75
  Nicholas 75,76
FULLER
  Abigail (Harlow) 86
  Amos 86
  Ann 7
  Ann(a) (Tinkham) 89
  Archippus 87
  Barnabas 86,118
  Benjamin 54,88
  Consider 90,91,118
  Deborah 87,90,118
  Deborah (-----)(Doten) 87
  Deborah (Edwards)(Cole) 87
  Deborah (Ring) 90,117
  Ebenezer 54,88
  Edward 7
  Eleazer 90,91,117,118
  Elizabeth 53,54,64,86,89
  Elizabeth (-----) 64,139
  Elizabeth (Nichols)(Bowen) 53
  Elizabeth (Weston) 91
  Elkanah 92,93

LAWRENCE (continued)
  James 98,99
  John 98,99
  Joseph 56,98,99,103
  Marcy 98
  Mary 99
  Mercy/Marcy (-----) 98
  Samuel 98,99
LAZELL
  Hannah 131
LEACH
  Abiel 126
  Elizabeth 25
LEE
  Fanny 23
  Lucy 24
LEMOTE/LEMATE/LEMONT
  Abigail 74
  Catherine (Nicholson) 74
  George 73,74
  Joseph 74
  Marcy 74
  Mary 74
  Matthew 73,74
  Mercy/Marcy (Billington) 73
  Susannah 74
  Thankfull (Whittemore) 74
LEONARD
  Charity 85
  Elizabeth (Eaton) 86
  Elkanah 76
  George 26
  Perez 86
  Ruth 86
LINCOLN
  Elizabeth 18
  Elizabeth (Robinson) 94
  Nathaniel 94
  Rachel 94
LITTLE
  Bethia 13
  Isaac 13
  Mary 13
  Mary (Otis) 13
LONGLAND
  Francis 31,35
LOUD
  Wm. Solomon 17
LUMBER
  Mercy 68
LUTHER
  Johanna 105

LUTHER (continued)
  Lydia (Kinnecutt) 105
  Theophilus 105
LYDE
  Ann 12
  Byfield 12
  Deborah 12
  Deborah (Byfield) 12
  Edward 9,12
  Katherine (-----)(Brinley) 12
  Mary 12
  Mary (Wheelwright) 12
  Susanna (Corwin) 12
  Susannah 9
LYFORD
  John 32
MACOMBER
  Joseph 85
  Thankful 84
  Thankful (Canedy) 85
MacQUITHEY/MacWITHY
  Sarah 103
MACY
  Dorkaj 44
MARCY
  Charlotte 21
MARSTON
  Benjamin 10,14,15,22
  Elizabeth 14,15,23
  Elizabeth (Winslow) 10,14
  Eunice 24
  John 14,15
  Lucia 14
  Lucy 15,24
  Mehitable (Gibbs) 14
  Patience 14,15,23
  Patience (Rogers) 14
  Penelope 15
  Sarah 14,15
  Sarah (Swett) 22
  Winslow 14,15
MARTIN
  Abel 64,139,140
  Abigail (Read) 46
  Amos 64,65,140,141
  Anna 141
  Anna (Daggett) 140
  Christopher 3
  Comfort 141
  Daniel 140
  Desire 46,65
  Elizabeth (-----)(Fuller) 64

MARTIN (continued)
  Elizabeth (Salter) 46
  Elizabeth (Wellman) 140
  Esther (Chaffee) 141
  Francis 46
  Gideon 64,65
  Grace 55,59
  Job 140
  Joel 141
  John 42,46,64,65,139,140
  Mary 139
  Mary (Fuller) 139
  Mercy 38,42,46
  Mercy (Billington) 46
  Molly 140
  Richard 46
  Robert 46,64,65,140,141
  Sarah 64,139,140
  Sarah (Willmarth) 64
  Timothy 64,65,139,140
MASON
  Mehitable 142
  Nathan 142
  Thankful 145
MAXWELL
  Abigail 73
  Abigail (Lemote) 74
  John 74
MAY
  Charity 45
  Dorcas (Billington) 44
  Dorcas/Dorkes 38,42,44,45,46
  Edward 44,45
  Hannah 45
  Hannah (King) 44,45
  Israel 45
MAYHEW
  Thomas 74
MC KEE
  Deborah 139
  Josiah 139
MC MILLION
  Avis 146
MERRIFIELD/MARYFIELD
  Content 76
  Content (Billington) 75
  Francis 75,76
  Margaret 76
  Margaret (Frost) 75
  William 75,76
MILLARD
  Alice 141

MILLER
  Edward Winslow 16,26
  Hannah (Dyer) 16
  Mary 16
  Mary (Winslow) 26
MORTON
  Eleazer 76
  Joanna 88,91
  Nathaniel 76
MOWRY
  Mehitable 58
MURDOCK
  Andrew 86
  Meribah (Eaton) 86
NASON
  Alice 110
NEALE
  Elizabeth 106,109
Negro
  Jene 102
NEGUS
  Hannah 22
NEWCOMEN
  John 33
NEWELL
  Mary 109
NEWTON
  Francis 31
  Robert 31
NICHOLS
  Elizabeth 53
NICHOLSON
  Catherine 74
NILES
  Elizabeth (Watson) 23
  Nathaniel 23
  Penelope 51
OLDHAM
  John 32
OLDS
  Abel 135
  Eleanor (Billington) 135
  Elenor 135
OLIVER
  Hopestill 10
  Magdalene 3,6
ORCUTT
  Asenath/Sena (Billington) 136
  Josiah 135,136
  Sena (Asenath) 135
ORMSBY
  Grace 55,95

RIDER
  Hannah 88
  Lois 88
  Maria 87
RING
  Deborah 90,117
  Eleazer 90
  Mary (Shaw) 90
RIPLEY
  Sarah 133
ROBBINS
  Abigail 118
  Benjamin 118
  Ebenezer 88
  Eunice (Fuller) 88
  Rebecca 91
ROBINSON/ROBSON
  Ebenezer 97,102
  Elizabeth 94
  Experience 55,98
  Experience (Sabin) 97
  Grace 97
  Hannah (Wheaton) 97
  Jeremiah 97
  John 97
  Joseph 57
  Martha (Sabin) 59
  Martha (Welch) 57
  Naoma 97
  Peter 59
  Sarah 97,147
  Thomas 147
ROGERS
  Patience 14
  Samuel 147
  Thomas 24,124
ROLESON/ROLSON
  Anna America(Garner)(Billington) 148
  James 148
ROSE/ROUSE
  Abigail 81
  Edward 81
  James 80
  John 80
  Rebecca (Bumpus) 81
  Sarah (Billington) 80
ROSKROW
  John 148
ROUND
  Abigail 144
  Abigail (-----) 143,144
  Amos 144

ROUND (continued)
  David 65,143
  Esther 144
  Hannah 65,143,144
  Hannah (Carpenter) 143
  Hezekiah 144
  Isaac 144
  Isabel 144
  Isaiah 144
  Jabez 65,144
  Jerusha 143
  John 143,144
  Mary 144
  Nathan 144
  Oliver 144
  Rebecca 144
  Renew 65,144
  Renew (Carpenter) 144
  Rhoda 144
  Sibbell 144
  Simeon 144
RUSSEL(L)
  David 147
  Elizabeth 146,147
  James 8
  Jane 22
  Marcy 22
  Mercy (Foster) 21
  Nancy 22
  Sarah 21
  Sarah (Sever) 22
  Thomas 21,22
SABIN(S)/SABENS/SABEAN
  Abigail 116
  Abigail (Osborne) 115
  Ann 95
  Avis (Bennett) 112
  Daniel 112
  Ebenezer 56
  Eldad 95
  Eleazer 59,115,116
  Elijah 96
  Elizabeth 59
  Elizabeth (Atwell) 114
  Elizabeth (Williams) 59
  Esther 111
  Experience 43,56,97
  Grace 55,56,96
  Grace (Ormsby) 55,95
  Hannah 110
  Hannah (Hall) 109
  Isaac 56,95,96